UNBECOMING A PRIEST

Unbecoming a Priest

A Memoir

~>

Anthony Bartlett
Foreword by Gena St. David

CASCADE *Books* · Eugene, Oregon

UNBECOMING A PRIEST
A Memoir

Copyright © 2023 Anthony Bartlett. All rights reserved. Except for brief quotations in critical publications or reviews, no part of this book may be reproduced in any manner without prior written permission from the publisher. Write: Permissions, Wipf and Stock Publishers, 199 W. 8th Ave., Suite 3, Eugene, OR 97401.

Cascade Books
An Imprint of Wipf and Stock Publishers
199 W. 8th Ave., Suite 3
Eugene, OR 97401

www.wipfandstock.com

PAPERBACK ISBN: 978-1-6667-5481-0
HARDCOVER ISBN: 978-1-6667-5482-7
EBOOK ISBN: 978-1-6667-5483-4

Cataloguing-in-Publication data:

Names: Bartlett, Anthony W., author. | St. David, Gena, foreword.
Title: Unbecoming a priest : a memoir / Anthony Bartlett ; forword by Gena St. David.
Description: Eugene, OR : Cascade Books, 2023.
Identifiers: ISBN 978-1-6667-5481-0 (paperback) | ISBN 978-1-6667-5482-7 (hardcover) | ISBN 978-1-6667-5483-4 (ebook)
Subjects: LCSH: Bartlett, Anthony W. | Catholic Church—Clergy—Biography.
Classification: BX4705.B38335 A3 2023 (print) | BX4705.B38335 A3 (ebook)

Cover image shows sixth-century emperor Justinian I flanked by soldiers and Bishop Maximianus, with his clergy, in basilica of San Vitale, Ravenna, Italy, visited by author in 1977.

*To Linda, without whom not a single word of this story
would make sense. She is its heart and final logic,
a faithful daughter of the one true logos. She ever holds
my heart and life in her hands.*

He who chooses the beginning of the road chooses the place it leads to. It is the means that determines the end.

—HARRY EMERSON FOSDICK

If history moves forward, knowledge of it travels backwards, so that in writing of our own recent past we are continually meeting ourselves coming the other way.

—TERRY EAGLETON

Initially, Jesus preached neither himself nor the church, but the kingdom of God. The kingdom of God is the realization of a fundamental utopia of the human heart, the total transfiguration of this world, free from all that alienates human beings, free from pain, sin, divisions, and death.

—LEONARDO BOFF

When God made time, he made plenty of it.

—IRISH PROVERB

Contents

Foreword *by Gena St. David* ix
Preface xiii

one	TRAINS	1
two	ANGEL TALES	9
three	BISHOPS, NEWTS, AND CAVES	16
four	CHILDHOOD WARS	22
five	VISIONS AND SAINTS	37
six	HEAD BOY AT A CONVENT	47
seven	TEENAGE THEOLOGIAN	54
eight	LUCRETIUS	69
nine	DEAD NUNS	81
ten	HIMMELFAHRT	93
eleven	TIN AND OTHER METALS	103
twelve	ROME: RUIN AND REVELATION	117
thirteen	BUCKDEN *ADOLESCENS*	142
fourteen	EIGHT MILES HIGH FALLING FAST	163
fifteen	EVER UPRIVER	171
sixteen	HAYES UNBOUND	186
seventeen	SPELLO	199
eighteen	REENTRY FOR THE FIRST TIME	213
	Concluding Anarchistic Postscript	225

Foreword

I encountered Anthony Bartlett's words for the first time one Sunday when they were quoted in a sermon at my home church of Vox Veniae in Austin, Texas. My friend Weylin Lee was preaching and he quoted an unknown-to-me-at-the-time author, and my ears pricked up. The surprisingly nonviolent image of God in Bartlett's description of Jesus was captivating. Later on, I reached out to Weylin: "Who was the author?" After some online sleuthing, I found an avenue for messaging Tony and asked for a meeting.

For Tony's part, I think he took my call because he was curious why a social scientist from Austin was so intent on speaking with him. We are, in many ways, unlikely conversation partners. Tony is an exquisitely trained theologian; he's collaborated with some of the most influential thinkers of our time. He once served as a priest to Mother Teresa and her sisters. Tony has traveled the globe, from stately mansions to crumbling shacks—from alleyways of London, to barrios of Bogotá, to hermitages of the Italian countryside—in his quest to experience the fullness of human life hinted at in the gospel of Christ.

For my part, I'm a therapist and researcher who rarely leaves Texas, and I've been immersed in neuroscience for two decades. I have had the privilege of collaborating with some of the most well-known clinicians of our time during my career. And yet, my first love was Scripture and theology. When I was twelve, I had a profound experience with the felt presence of God through the Gospels and the ancient creeds by candlelight in my room, while the rest of my family slept. The beneficial impact on my bodily sense of safety and trust in those early encounters with God stayed with me. So by the time I met Tony, I too had been on a journey, exploring everything I could in evangelical tradition, in contemplative prayer, and in listening to the Scriptures through the earpiece of brain science, in my quest to understand the nonviolent image of God hinted at in the story of Jesus.

Tony became a generous teacher. We met online for sessions, and he pointed me in the direction of authors I should read; I started meeting nearly weekly with Tony, his wife Linda, and their community through online studies and conversation groups. I visited their home in Syracuse, New York, a gorgeous two-story house nestled in the shade of maple, ash, and white spruce—a site that doubles as the Bethany Center for Nonviolent Theology and Spirituality. In those days, I was emerging from an intense and unexpected season of grief, and meeting the Bartletts was a timely gift. I came initially for the theology, but I stayed for the gentle invitation to "know and be known."

I soon realized the Bartletts have fostered communities like the Bethany Center in every place they've ever lived. They welcomed me into its most recent iteration, a community I came to know in its seasoned years. For over two decades, the folks connected with the Bethany Center—previously Wood Hath Hope—have practiced living their theology together, and allowing their understanding of divine nonviolence to shape their relationships. There is a noteworthy trust, honesty, and resilience I observe among them. I'm still identifying the key variables that make their nonviolent practice so distinct, but as a therapist I recognize it is rare. The best explanation I can offer is that relating to a nonviolent image of God soothes their nerves, so they embody nonviolence in a way that defies the bodily bell curve.

A micro-example comes to mind: one afternoon there was a tense moment between two group members (I may have been one of them). I felt nervous after, but Tony and Linda were pillars of unanxious compassion. I expressed regret and eagerness to repair the rupture. Tony's message to me later was illustrative: "Gena, nothing to worry about. You were maybe a little direct, but that's part of who you are and now who we are as a group. It was evident that your questions were coming from a place of truth and love. In other words, we are all educating each other, so we become what we're meant to be in the Lord. God's Peace."

Tony's vitamin shot of reassurance produced within my own body the patience for a slower, more genuine reconciliation process with the group member who has since become a valued friend. And the nonviolent image of God reflected in Tony and Linda's teachings and interactions, and in Tony's other, narrative-flipping manuscripts such as his most recent, *Signs of Change* (Cascade, 2022), has deepened my own sense of trust in God. When I pray, read the Scriptures, and reflect on the story of Christ, I feel myself being soothed on the inside, and nonviolence is starting to blossom on the outside.

Throughout my time with the Bartletts and the Bethany community, I've been observing Tony closely. To say "observing" sounds a bit clinical, but my training makes me cautious and curious. When I discovered that Tony shared a personal acquaintance with another theologian, James Alison—whom I trusted already for his moral and relational integrity—I reached out to James and put the question to him bluntly: "Who are these Bartletts *really*?" James encouraged me that Tony and Linda are as humble and transparent as they appear.

In the evangelical world where I come from, there is no shortage of charismatic leaders. And they too are on a quest. They too feel touched by God. They too are inspiring teachers. Tony and Linda are all of these things, and also there is something different about them. They are leaders who wash the feet of others, elevate the stories of others, and bless the sacredness of others.

One morning in particular stands out in memory; we sat in a room at Tony and Linda's home in Syracuse, and Tony was "on a roll" speaking about his understanding of Scripture and the cross. His telling of the Christ story is persuasive and he holds listeners spellbound. Yet, at the slightest indicator that another person has something to say—no matter who it is—Tony pauses and his face lights up, so delighted is he to welcome another's voice. And the voices he welcomes are diverse; the Bethany Center embodies a vast range of ages, genders, orientations, races, backgrounds, and countries of origin.

Having observed all of this for some time, I felt as if I knew Tony even before reading his story. And yet reading his story had a profound impact on me. When a person tells an honest story about themselves, we feel it. We recognize the author is practicing what Brené Brown has taught us: be awkward, brave, and kind. And the self-portrait Tony offers here is endearing for this reason. We are given a raw, courageous, and gentle description of what it's like to live in his body, in every sense. The first body is of a man—birthed to a mother in a particular time, place, and story. The second is a corporate body—the church, entrusted with ancient wisdom and the vulnerability of the poor. And somewhere within and between those bodies is God.

When a story rings true about a person, it serves as a photo negative: God becomes visible around the edges of what is "not God." But how tempted are we to tell a more flattering story? How enticing it is to think God will be better highlighted by our triumphs than our frailties? And even when therapy or relational security frees us from vanity, how worried are we that an unvarnished account of our innards will tarnish the image of God? And if that sounds absurd, just wait; some new reason for applying a little polish will pop up. An honest personal narrative is compelling because it is rare, and because it is proof the author has contended with a myriad of obstacles to truthfulness. In rearview, Tony's story unfolds as the authentic trajectory of a "wounded healer," and he extends to us the transformative touch of a withered hand, restored.

And yet in many places, the church today is more wounded than healed. The human church, held together by tendons and sinews stretched across continents and centuries, struggles to tell an honest personal narrative about itself. May the church—the body of Christ, broken for you—take a page from Tony's book and learn to give a truthful account of its shadows, that God's image may be made visible in the figure-ground reversal. The Jesus who shows up in Tony's story is visibly human, pushing forward the transformation not just of the church but of all embodied humanity.

Listening to a friend speak candidly about themselves, we are gifted with a chance to learn something about ourselves. Our life experiences differ, but our bodies are astonishingly similar; our desires bear a hereditary resemblance, and our brains and spirits seek nourishment from a common source. And if Bartlett's story is irresistible it is because cloaked in its particularities is the naked suggestion that God might be drawing each of us too into the same fiery passion and skin-warm tenderness, as we shed our fears and tell our truth. We join God, elbow deep in the rich compost of memories we would prefer to discard; we are indebted to Bartlett for showing us how this is done.

—Gena St. David

Preface

WHAT AN EPIC THING it is to write an autobiography! Even a relatively small one like this. On the one hand, there's the strange and terrible fact of a life itself, and its constant gestation over three score and ten years, and more. Step by step, piece by piece, but in every moment, the human soul is keeping track, garnering its story, constructing its narrative within itself as it goes. Get into conversation with any average patron at a bar and they'll give you an immediate snapshot of the current story going inside them, and whether you want it or not.

Then there's something quite separate. There's writing it all down on the page, telling the story in the cool and clear of the written word. Why is that so different? One reason is because your bar story, and all its various cousins in daily life, is not quite a true history. The random snapshot of conversation is only chaotically connected with what this person's soul might have said yesterday, let alone ten years ago, twenty years ago. There really is no requirement of coherence.

But that's not all. For a writer, an overall coherence and logical framework are a minimum. But if soul-wise you are still at the level of the average "me" conversation, it still will not work. You are too enmeshed in the story, caught up in it. The "I" or the self is far too cloying, the words too thick with adolescent wallowing, unappeased anger, self-pity, or righteous entitlement, for the story to live and breathe freely and for its own sake. What you are writing is much more journaling, personal protest, or self-care, rather than real story.

To write a genuine autobiography, everything must be handed over somehow, let go of, so it may stand and speak only for itself. Only then can it truly be a story, something that lives and breathes on its own. Something that belongs ultimately more to the reader than the writer. As the author you have to come to this point of spiritual surrender. But how do you make that happen?

You wouldn't know from reading these chapters, but I have attempted this memoir perhaps a dozen times. I was never satisfied. It was only when I tried to write it in the third person that it began to come right. Subsequently I switched back to first person, but somehow an element of distance and letting go had been achieved, and it remained. The "I" had become a third-person narration. With that there came a sense of peace, of not wanting to prove anything, of not making an argument, of letting the words, in fact, speak for themselves. Of just telling the story.

I also came to understand that movement, time, and pacing are essential. Pace stops you wallowing. If there is anger, the effect of time and movement will defuse it; lightning may strike, but the storm passes and the air clears. And if there is entitlement, the humbling of timebound flesh will deal with that. A classic narrator like Augustine does not need pace because all the while he is talking to God; he achieves a sense of time as a mirror of eternity, and every word is a breathless now. If there is pace in Augustine's writing, it is majestic, like the turning of the heavenly spheres themselves. Thomas Merton projects some of this, but he has a much more modern pace too, responding to the frequent chaotic movement of his youth and early manhood. That is one of the reasons why his autobiography is so immensely popular. My work here is almost entirely caught up in time and movement, in the driven postwar beats of the twentieth and twenty-first centuries. Yet, at the same moment, paradoxically, it contains a refracted, nuclear-accident version of Augustine's eternity. It is time, in fact, blasted from the beginning by eternity, and then, after that, its gradual, progressive decontamination. That is why my story heads in an opposite direction from Merton. The Trappist monk was looking for the order and truth of God in an insane world. I was looking for the existence of a world in the aftermath of an apocalypse. It is very important for the reader to recognize and assimilate this crucial shift, especially if they come from any conventional kind of church background.

When it comes to it, therefore, it is not just the passing of time but time's contemporary crisis that is the core of my story and at the source of its letting go. Indeed, the urgencies of time are the true literary guarantor of the modern voice and something we look for instinctively. My life, as so many others, is pitched between Hiroshima and the facts of global warming and parallel political chaos, between a time of two and a half billion people on the earth and one of nearly eight billion. This is the context in which any contemporary biography, priest or otherwise, must get written, and it changes the voice inevitably to the urgent pressure of human time. Thus, my story's belonging to our contemporary rhythms of crisis is what forms its narrative daily bread, sounds the beat of its heart, and pushes the current of its blood.

The figure of God will necessarily appear itself in crisis because of this overall condition, but the figure of Jesus is at home in crisis and pulls the meaning of God along with it.

It is the time-filled figure of Jesus that then emerges in the story, not as metaphysical guarantee, but as transformative companion in crisis. This is perhaps the final element of its letting go. To let the crisis both proclaimed and healed so marvelously by the Gospels speak for itself—this is the final guarantor of my story's identity. Where Augustine has his conversation with the eternal God, I have the story-overturning companion on the road to Emmaus.

Mine is the eponymous story of becoming a priest and then "unbecoming" one. I use this term in an unusual intransitive sense, as an un/becoming, because it neatly suggests the whole experience as just that: the progressive undoing of a status even and exactly as it's assumed. (The other possible, "unworthy" meaning is self-evident in the story.) What then of this dynamic un/becoming? I cannot resolve its contradiction. It hangs there, especially as the story nears its end, as a strange insoluble riddle. Was it always meant to be, so that there is something theologically true in the whole pathway? Or was my journey the only possible road from an actual falsehood? A sad and disruptive human necessity. The riddle then is perhaps the final and crucial part of the story, handed over to time and the reader to resolve.

For the rest there are the usual acknowledgments. Individuals named are not coincidental. They are historical and belong intimately to the narrative. At the same time memory is famously partial, and the light by which others will remember incidents may often, and inevitably, be different from mine. It's even possible to be factually wrong. Memory conflates and selects. But I have used journals and diaries, and I believe if anything is incorrect it is relatively superficial. The important thing is the integrity of the overall story, and this, I affirm, is incontestable.

In writing the story I have tried to be faithful to the emotions and responses of the various versions of myself over the years, without wantonly offending more contemporary proprieties and sensibilities. It is always a balancing act of faithful reporting about who I was at a particular moment in time, while not carrying over into the text clumsy repetitions of abandoned behaviors and immature and outmoded attitudes.

In some instances, I have changed the names of individuals, especially in episodes from the religious life, and this is done in order to remove as much as possible any sense of animus. "I never could stand that righteous prig, Tom!" If you change "Tom" to an alias "Larry" it's actually hard to write that phrase with any sense of conviction. But even with names changed it will not be difficult for others who were there to know of whom I am talking. Thus, the historical record is essentially preserved and at stake. Real people create real relationships, healthy or otherwise, and if those relationships stretch over time they create an enduring context for the self, to thrive or to weaken, to develop or to drown. It is this reality that cannot be smudged over but must be given its full weight as history.

The story largely takes place before I took on the serious writing of theology. I am still learning this craft, and I am sure I always will be, but a key component in what I have developed is the emergent (for us) nonviolence of biblical revelation. This means that human beings only lately, only now really, are coming to understand the inherent nonviolence of the biblical God. What, in fact, could be revealed that we didn't already know, unless it were an unfathomable nonviolence of the Creator God? An event of unmerited grace is clearly an event of nonviolence, but if we balance this with a parallel, unexplained and equally gratuitous withholding of grace, then we plunge the initial event in an abyss of violence. This is the conundrum of a lot of traditional theology, one that I have approached, instead, in terms of the evolving nonviolence of the Bible and the deep and transformative firsthand meaning it communicates. In other words, I urge a positive historical change in human meaning rather than try to resolve an abstract theological problem from an eternal perspective.

This approach fits my own story and its evolving account, rather than taking any preordained perspective. So, I have to trust that just as I believe an evolutionary narrative concretely reveals a God of infinite grace and nonviolence, in the same way the present memoir reflects a mysterious but palpable divine compassion and, indeed, a true historical human becoming in my own life.

Syracuse, New York, August 2022

one

TRAINS

The train rolled out of the station and there was no turning back.

Even now I feel that sick, scared moment. I was seventeen and heading for novitiate, the preparatory year for religious vows: obedience (no independence), poverty (no possessions), chastity (no sex). Outside the window, along the journey, the fields are white and harvested. Summer is nearly over, while my own springtime has not even begun.

The world is slipping from my grasp, but in that strange contradictory way that is the signature of the whole crazy story I have to tell, I am also taking hold of it in the only way I can.

I say this now, on reflection, but back then I was as dumb as any teenager can be.

I was scared, but also excited, and glad. Glad to be joining a religious order, to be dedicating my life. I was brave and bold, and dumb.

Everything else around me is screaming. It's the '60s. Angry Young Men, Beatlemania, the Space Race, Kennedy. And Vietnam beginning. I know these things and have a sense of them, but really, I am an observer. There is a deep disconnect between me and my world.

The station I departed from was Fratton. If you are coming from London the train stops here before going on to the main station, Portsmouth-and-Southsea, and finally to the Harbor Station and the sea. About ten years before I had taken that route and crossed with my family, on the ferry, the narrow strait of water to the Isle of Wight, where my father had a job at a high security prison. Five years later, we returned to the mainland and the battle-marked naval town of Portsmouth. I felt even less at home there than on the island.

So many nights I lay in bed listening to the London train picking up speed as it went the other way, along the eastern edge of Portsea, escaping the city. I imagined the red taillights of the last carriage, rattling and shaking its way north in a kind of hard, mechanical fury.

So often it was a hard and angry world. Joining a religious order would give me a true and gentle island of belonging, a genuine refuge from an inhospitable world.

Fratton is the nearest station to Fratton Park, home to Portsmouth—or Pompey—football club. The club was famous for the Pompey chimes sung by the fans and sounding like clock chimes. "Play up Pompey, Pompey play up!" My dad never took me there. He'd long ago been excluded from any kind of major role in my childhood. Perhaps he liked it that way, but as far as my mom was concerned, as an immigrant from Ireland, almost any product of English culture was tainted, and my dad, native English as he was, never was able to break the *cordon sanitaire* she placed around her children. Or at least around me.

The priesthood was a golden shore where everything else was a grey sea. A world not just set apart, but the only real world there was. The moment I announced at the age of four that I wanted to be a priest my fate was sealed. I was anointed and special. Certainly, I liked the specialness, but saying mass never seemed to me all that great (something about the candles and vestments perhaps). What was attractive was the sense of God. I couldn't call it anything else. God seemed more real than anything, and talking to people, telling them about God, that would be my glory. Still, that too would wane in my teenage years. Priests cut a rather lonely, isolated figure, and what they said often didn't seem to make sense, or was too lofty for this world. But the need for the shore of belonging, that never went.

Rather than soccer, my major experience of Fratton was cycling to school, over the steep bridge that crossed the railway line. There was always a very stern policeman on point duty there. Because he was a British policeman, he was also vaguely the tribal enemy. I was always careful to obey his instructions, but I resented them. One time the dread sergeant came to our house because I had been caught riding a bicycle at night without lights. I was actually trying to cross Fratton bridge coming home from a Catholic youth club, and there was a police car there with a couple of bored detectives, obviously parked on the bridge. A sudden wild rebellion made me double back and try to get to a footbridge further along the line, but they easily guessed my plan and cut me off. They took my details and obliged me to walk home. Next day they sent the point policeman to my house—probably because the offense took place on his beat—to warn my parents that a life of crime awaited their son. But after an initial scare he let me off and actually became quite friendly when he found out my dad was more or less in the same line of work—a prison officer at Portsmouth Borstal. And that was the measure of things—living in an unfriendly nation with my father basically one of its hired men.

My mother had purchased a large cane-bound trunk to hold the dowry of personal items I was taking with me to novitiate. It was safely stowed in the guard's van, and contained towels, shirts, pants, socks, underwear, sheets, and toiletries, all in multiple copies and packed with funereal care. I'm not sure where the idea came from—the order I was joining did not require it. I think perhaps it was a repeat of something similar she had prepared for my older sister who herself had joined a convent some three years previously. (In those days it was quite a procession out of the Bartlett household. A couple of years later my younger brother went off to become a member of a missionary order. Their stories are no doubt parallel to mine. One big difference is I lasted a good bit longer in the cloth than they.) The big dark-brown trunk was the send-off my mother had always dreamed of, all my life packed away for the other world.

The train wheels thumped against the rails, and it was comforting in the way of trains. *Clackety, thump, thump, thump.* They would deliver me where I was supposed to be, and the inevitability was both horrible and happy. It was at the cost of my entire youth, but I was going someplace where I would at last be a real person.

It was the distant thought of this journey that had sustained me during the vacant years of early adolescence when I had no bearings in the world apart from school, church, and home. No sports or hobbies to speak of. Various slightly manic pastimes shared with my brother and younger sister, but these too ebbing as I got to my mid-teens. Then the thought of girls and a few random dates, frantic in their own way—having a kind of pro forma youth against the clock of a foreordained departure.

One day another teen who lived somewhere in the neighboring streets spoke about my unnatural way of life in words that seared themselves in my soul. There was a short alleyway next to our house, leading to a gate and an earth-topped Anderson air raid shelter currently used as the meeting place for a scout troop. A muscular, flop-haired blond boy in cotton shorts was in the alley with a couple of girls and some younger kids watching. The lusty lad was kissing one of the girls, pressing the evident flourishing of his youth hard against her. A feeling of sex swamped the alley. I must have been watching too, because the boy turned and saw me. At once he yelled, "Pretty Polly, Pretty Polly, you never come out of your cage, go back inside!" The whole situation—what the boy was doing, his visible prowess, his crowing words, right there next to my house—shamed me deeply. My otherworldly existence was mocked in a neighborhood taunt accompanied by a vivid contrast. Whatever the occasional dates I went on, I was and would continue to be a kind of caged bird, cut off in my cell, ready for another life, unlike the boy who was living his teenage life all the way, right there in the alley. I felt like a ghost haunting my own life, and I felt it terribly. Or, rather, all of life around me was a ghost, already dead, or simply fragments of a virtual, unreal world. I, for my part, was just a germ of existence still waiting for a real world to be born into.

The very thing, however, that curtailed my life and deprived it of real content was what gave it hope and promise. And hence my feeling on the train. These days when people wonder at my supposed sense of optimism in a world in crisis they do not know of my long training in a future still to come. My childhood and adolescence dug a hole in my soul as big as the planet. I was always waiting and working for a day when it would be filled up.

∽

I was met at Bristol railway station by one of the young men who was due to start novitiate with me. His name was Chris, and he took me in his car up into the Mendip Hills, to the big house where I would spend my year of preparation.

We wound our way up the steep drive between high laurels, emerging into spacious grounds, with parkland trees to the right and a soccer field to the left. Before us, on the crest, was a stately Georgian mansion, a grand house at ease in the afternoon sunshine. It had wooden porticos over the downstairs windows, a gabled entrance porch, and an extended wing on the west side. On the other side was a chapel connected by a passageway. The modern chapel was in abrupt contrast to the nineteenth-century genteel architecture. It had a sharply pitched roof like an Alpine lodge, and a huge picture window at either end. But all of it together was to be my home, with the oak-paneled hallways, staircase, drawing room, dining room, library, games room, kitchen garden, stables, and grounds.

In an instant my world leapt from a terraced house in a working-class city to the halls of the landed gentry. Of course, I was not personally the heir to this house, and the religious order itself was only making use of it. Still, here was a breadth of space and style that enlarged my horizon beyond anything I had known. Already, then, I was being given the world for which I longed, but at the same time it felt strange and even uncomfortable. Perhaps a cloth-cap reaction stirred within me, or at least a sense of irony, but I put it aside. My task was spiritual, and the Alpine chapel signaled to me where my work was to be, the sharp angle of the roof shooting upward. This was about drawing near to God.

We crunched onto the gravel terrace and the novice master came out to greet me, a peasant-framed, stocky man with a wrinkled, jovial face. His name was Angel Urrutia. We called him "Father Angel," which was about as heavenly-appropriate a name possible for a novice master. We entered by a side door and Chris helped me carry the trunk upstairs to a dormitory where Angel showed me my bed. We placed the big trunk at the foot, and I made some nervous joke about this being like a coffin, and didn't some nuns sleep with coffins under their beds to remind them always of their death? Angel blinked and chortled, not sure what to make of me. A previous contact with him had established the information about my sister being a nun. He was always quite impressed with this and brought the topic up himself more than once. He said, "Oh my goodness, a coffin, you said. Is that what your sister told you?"

After this I joined the others with whom I would be starting the year of preparation: Chris, Pete, Phil, and Joe. They had all been together at junior seminary and I'd spent a few days there earlier in the year, so we were acquainted. There was also Wilkins, who was a postulant and on track to be a lay brother, not a priest. The rest of us were known as aspirants, i.e., in the immediate anteroom before novitiate. We were looking to join a small Roman Catholic religious congregation (the correct nomenclature, but people often use the easier term "order," so I will continue to employ that). We were beginning the eight-day retreat leading to the big feast day when we would officially enroll as novices. Everything was to be in silence so at that point there was little time for conversation. The silence made everything safe and quickly I curled up inside it like a cocoon, letting the feeling of rules and piety carry me forward without focusing on the fear.

The order's familiar name was Claretians, after St. Anthony Claret, a nineteenth-century saint from Catalonia. He was a zealous priest, preaching to restore Catholic faith and practice in post-Napoleonic Spain, and later in Cuba. He gathered a wider group of priests to help him and gave them the official title of "Missionary Sons of the Immaculate Heart of Mary," so you can see why it was shortened up. I chose this order because they placed an advert for a holiday retreat on our school bulletin board and my best friend thought it would be cool to go and enjoy the swimming, tennis, soccer, and campfires. I took my friend's interest as a sign from God: essentially everything was preordained or not at all. On August 22nd, the feast of the Immaculate Heart of Mary, I and the four others donned our cassocks and sashes marking our status as novices and our entrance to the religious life.

The junior seminary where the other aspirants had been together was a place called Buckden in Cambridgeshire. I'd visited the place earlier in the year, a fifteenth-century bishop's palace, with medieval keep, gatehouse, curtain walls, and the timeless atmosphere of a noble ruin. Accommodation was rudimentary but it filled the purpose, a place where boys as young as eleven and twelve could leave their families and begin a quasi-monastic life shepherded by priests. My fellow novices came with stories of this place lost in the East Anglia fens. They told of an insular boarding school life with patchy education and populated by a cast of weird characters, both boys and priests. I came to know some of these figures pretty well, even if I'd never met them. I heard of the doings of the priests, often unedifying, sometimes criminal. But even if it all seemed makeshift and disreputable, it was also under the blessing of the church and that gave it a passing grade, a final glow of rightness, come what may. On the one hand, I was very glad I never went there; on the other, I was jealous of the obvious camaraderie it produced among its graduates.

However, for these alumni the experience of bonding was now facing a moment of maximum pressure, a beckoning world and its objects of desire. For a couple of the Buckden boys the ties created by "junior sem" would never withstand the strain. They would soon quit the band of brothers and head for an environment with richer possibilities, that is to say, girls.

Pete was the most obvious case of raging hormones. He asked me if I had kissed a girl and when I shrugged and grinned you could see both the jealousy and respect in his eyes. He used to pick on Wilkins unmercifully, shouting his name as a term of disgust and inferiority. He loved to hear me imitate Mick Jagger and Charlie Watts of the Rolling Stones, going into fits of laughter at my feeble impressions.

Joe was acutely sentimental. He had an older brother in the order and was in awe of him. During meditation times he used to screw his eyes up to try and produce a vision. He swore one morning he saw the statue of the Virgin move. He admired my haircut when I first arrived, thinking it very stylish—before I submitted to a more monastic trim.

Chris, I have already introduced. He was solidly built and determined, and looked by far the best in a cassock, tying it up in a flourish on his hip to enable him to run like a hurricane when he played a pick-up game of soccer. He was appointed as our "monitor," meaning he was in charge when our priest superiors were absent. It was his job to keep us in sync with the timetable and call us to order when conversation might veer too far in an unholy direction. He was responsible in his duties, and when he got upset his top lip would tremble.

Phil was the smartest of the bunch, good at math and languages, slim, languid to the point of indifference, a clarinetist and guitarist, and quick to complain about manual work. One time he and I were told to carry a five-gallon can of fertilizer from a shed. We labored so far, with the metal edges bumping on our legs, and then he simply quit, refusing to carry it further.

I took over and lugged the can the rest of the way on my own. Later, in one-to-one spiritual direction, Angel said he'd witnessed the incident and asked me whether I knew he'd been watching. I didn't know but I didn't need to know—my constant sense of the destiny I was fulfilling was sure any such gesture would never go unrecorded. I was not surprised when he told me that he'd seen—gratified, but not surprised. As far as Phil was concerned, I am sure he sensed the merit points I was racking up carrying the bucket, so he was entirely justified in refusing to contribute his efforts to my profits . . . but then it proved even greater dividends for me!

The house, set high on its hill, had an incomparable view, fifty miles north to the Severn Estuary. The front of the house and its gravel terrace were bounded by a stone parapet, which looked out over a lawn and the magnificent panorama below. One evening in September the sky was flooded in crimson from end to end, the most emphatic sunset I have ever seen, like a sustained organ chord. The whole community turned out to watch, standing in silent awe before the pulsing colors. It seemed like a message from God. Often throughout those early weeks the six of us would gather by the parapet at the last break time of the day, before night prayers. We'd look out where the land fell away across the football field, down over Chelvey Wood, out through the waxy night. We could see the floodplain, the lights of the coastal road, and the trains passing on the line to Weston-super-Mare. The songs of the Beatles and Rolling Stones were still ringing in our heads and I would do my imitations of Jagger with his fake Virginia accent, hand-on-hip pointing at the trains, "See them snaaa-kyy laiittsss!"

In those first dreamlike sunshiny weeks a group of workingmen from the local electricity service were laying a cable on the hill below the novitiate house. Every day during break the novices would wander down to watch them chipping deep through Mendip granite, taking as long as they needed and talking workingmen talk. They placed bets on how long each of us would last the lifestyle, and they gave me the least time of all, sure I wouldn't stick it for a month. Once again, I laughed inside: they had no idea of my hidden deal with God and its steely framework. How could they? I didn't even know it clearly myself. I just was certain of its seismic power.

But there was another thing I didn't know. We were on the cusp of an epochal change in the Roman Catholic Church itself and we had no idea of what was coming at us, of the turmoil awaiting just around the corner. When it finally hit me, the kind of ascetical success I was embracing would count for nothing, and less than nothing. My life would be changed much more radically than simply by entering novitiate. It would be taken completely out of my control, overpowered by forces I would barely understand and even less be able to manage for my own goals. I would be totally at sea, unable to find my island of belonging, the only way forward the shell of the organization I was in. The weight of the absent world that produced my strength of purpose in novitiate would become the chains that bound me to the flimsiest of lifeboats.

But that was a year in the future. In the immediate prospect of the novitiate the rules were still in place, and I was able to set my course by them, and energetically so.

All the same, in those last nights of summer on our remote hill we watched the trains and for a brief moment had a sense of missing something and yet still trying to keep hold of it, if even for a fleeting space. Then Chris would interrupt to remind us we were five minutes to the hour, and we would troop back once more to the chapel. A couple of psalms, some invocations and finally the *Salve regina*, the ancient monastic hymn to Mary, pleading she console us in this vale of tears. Finally in silence to bed, while the bright trains passed below.

two

ANGEL TALES

OUR DAY BEGINS AT six a.m. with a wake-up call from Angel, *Deo gratias et Mariae*, meaning "Thanks be to God and Mary." To which the response in chorus is *Semper Deo gratias et Mariae*, "Always thanks be to God and Mary!" Sometimes there is a salutation in English, the first part "Sweet heart of Mary!" spoken by Angel, and then dutifully answered "Be my salvation!" by the novices. Pete used to mimic Angel's voice doing the English call, the first three words harshly pronounced on a steady low note, then the next rising abruptly in the successive two syllables, producing a sound somewhere between a question, a threat, and a cry of utter distress. Sometimes we'd be woken already by Angel's puffing up the stairs, then gathering himself to knock and utter the dire greeting.

The only way to stop being totally depressed by this routine is to throw myself into it, heart and soul. I leap out of bed, pull on my pants and shirt, rush off to the bathroom, then hurry back to drag on the cassock and clip on the sash. Then I race downstairs to be first in chapel. Chris is pretty nippy himself and sometimes he'll beat me, but normally he runs a close second. Morning prayers begin at six thirty, consisting of psalms, invocations, and responses. Then there is meditation conducted according to the method of Ignatius of Loyola.

This is essentially a visualization technique. The novice master sits behind the novices spread in a row on the benches in front. He intones the written meditation, starting with a scene from the Gospels in which the reader or listener is invited to situate himself as a close observer. There follow three points developing the meaning of the scene. Finally, there is a summons to a personal response. The disembodied voice and the dogmatic language serve to make prayer seem remote, a kind of mental route march without real demonstration of the benefits. I spend a lot of the time fighting to stay awake. I rub my hands together in a fierce manner, or I simply repeat over and over a single phrase, like "Sacred heart of Jesus have mercy on me!" or "Jesus mercy, Mary help!" I am not sure where I learned this from—perhaps it was my mother who used to say things like that, or maybe I picked it up from a book—but at least the repeated phrases have the merit of a kind of self-soothing and maybe a meditation mantra (but without knowing any of the theory). After a few months of this I get a recurring image going through my mind: as I kneel in chapel there is a snarling dog continually driving me through the door, and I am keeping it at bay only by holding my frantically rubbing hands before it. Maybe I was going slightly nuts, but the point was always to keep up the maximum intensity doing what I am doing. The snarling dog had to be me, driving myself on to establish my side of the bargain.

Meditation is followed by mass and private thanksgiving. Once again, I outdo everyone in fervor, staying longer at my prayers than all the others. Finally, I head off for breakfast, always with a sense of consolation that I had won the morning championship, at least to my own mind. Now I can relax a little as the day unfolds. After breakfast there is house cleaning, a short recreation time, a lecture by the novice master or his deputy, study, midday prayer, lunch, some more recreation, a quiet time, manual work, tea, more study, evening prayer, dinner, a longer recreation, night prayers, then bed until the next morning, and start all over.

Pete and Joe were the ones who left us. Each appeared in the chapel one morning dressed not in the novice's cassock but in street clothes, and the rest of us know it's over. As always, we eat our breakfast in silence and before there is a chance for a goodbye they are up and gone; the car has taken them to the station. There is a brief sense of shock, but one is quickly absorbed in the rhythm of the timetable and the sense of those who remained keeping the higher calling.

These are Chris, Phil, Wilkins, and myself, each with his personal reasons. For Wilkins I think it was a pathway to an education. After our year together he started going to a vocational college and I heard of him no more. The remaining three became known as the "Holy Trinity" since we stayed together through novitiate and seminary, all the way to ordination. For sure, this Trinity was locked in. If Pete and Joe had been tempted by the siren call of sex, sexuality did not count so much for us, at least during that time. I liked girls well enough, but during that whole year I cannot remember a wet dream, and I never took what was obliquely (at least for me) named "solitary pleasure." It was as if women were foreign territory and I'd surrendered my passport.

There was a wealthy Catholic family that sponsored the Claretian community at Backwell and put the money up for the modern chapel. They would come on visits, including teenage daughters, arriving in a sleek limousine and quickly shepherded out of sight into the best reception room. One time we sinful novices spied from our side door on their arrival and when I saw a white-silk-stockinged leg emerge from the back seat I literally went weak at the knees. It was a pure shock, like some exotic creature, belonging to a far-away biome, visiting our remote boarding school residence. Very probably, you could say I was sexually repressed. The need I carried, and its passion, were more powerful and insistent even than sex. I was like one of those pearl divers who learn to hold their breath for amounts of time and at ocean depths impossible for most others. The Gospel story of the pearl tells of a merchant who found it and gave everything to buy it. He simply came across it and then had to have it. I did not know what the Gospel pearl was. I was diving, holding my breath, looking for something, anything by which I could live. A simple rock, a piece of the earth on which to stand, would be enough, so long as I could call it my own.

The intellectual highlight of our day is the novice master's lecture or "conference." This is the key opportunity for the religious order to pass on its lore. Embracing the tradition is the way in which we young men are to bring our minds and souls into lifelong identity with the organization. Angel was a Basque, from a region in Northern Spain that claimed its separate culture and right as a nation. His ethnic origin is in fact the key thing in this man's identity, but it is only little by little we understand this. He introduces us to what is called "the Constitutions," the legal document on which the congregation is founded. It gives the date and place of origin (Spain, 1849), the group's goals (mission or evangelization), and the main rules of membership—obedience and observation of timetable ranking high on the list. Angel has trained in canon law, which means that he has specialized in the much bigger rule book of the Roman Catholic Church covering almost every circumstance imaginable. He liked to entertain us with its abstruse distinctions. He also came out with occasional Latin tags, which interested me because they seemed to hold some kind of classic wisdom. One of them I remember only in English translation, probably because it really did contain something vital: *Nothing violent lasts . . .*

Angel also made occasional forays into the Gospels, but always in broad dogmatic or ascetical terms. The historical sense was completely lacking, as was any hint of anthropology or philosophy. So, what was left to learn from these daily monologues was the fascinating figure of Angel himself. It is something we picked up from occasional asides and remarks when he would allow himself to go off script and tell us something about himself. We saw it as semi-scandalous, a lapse into the everyday and the real. But it amounted, in fact, to an unofficial history of the congregation.

Angel had supported the Popular Front government in the Spanish Civil War, in its struggle against the insurrectionist Nationalist and Royalist forces led by Franco. He had quit his appointed position in a religious community and begun some kind of roving ministry among the militias battling for the Republican cause. He did not mention places or names—they would have been meaningless to us—but it seemed pretty clear that for a time he had left behind his religious duties and his chain of command to become a voluntary chaplain to the motley gang of irregulars at war with Franco. In particular he supported the Basque and Catalan brigades. But he ministered to others, socialists, anarchists, communists, groups hated and reviled by a great many in the Spanish church and nation. The very fact that he was now working with a pimply group of English teenagers to the far north of the Pyrenees said there were very likely some "deviations" in his past. History decided, of course, that Angel was on the losing side in the Civil War. Franco was now dictator and would remain so for another ten years. Under him the Spanish state was a monolithic institution of *patria, iglesia, familia* (fatherland, church, family), and Angel didn't fit the pattern. He used to refer to his political problems as his "adversities" and his situation as "exile"; it was plain that the religious and civil authorities had thought it far better for everyone if he were out of the country.

Later on, when I met groups of Spanish religious people outside of England, I saw how many of them fervently supported the Franco ideology. They considered *el caudillo* to be a kind of saint and sometimes when they had downed shots of thick Spanish brandy, they would sing a fascist song or two. One older priest I met in Rome boasted of how during the war he had toured Franco's gun emplacements and the officers had invited him to direct the fire on Republican positions, which he had done with relish. Angel's militant activities had been more or less the mirror image of this, but at school I had read Hemingway's *For Whom the Bell*

Tolls and I'd heard of Orwell's volunteering. My sympathies were all with Angel.

A further source of education alongside the conferences was reading at mealtimes. Soon after we began our year Angel chose for lunchtime edification the biography of a Basque adventurer, Juan Sebastian Elcano. He was a sea captain and a member of Ferdinand Magellan's fleet. After Magellan was killed in the Philippines, Elcano took command of the sole remaining ship, completing the first circumnavigation of the world. I wondered at the time what this sixteenth-century Basque daredevil had to do with our spiritual training, but now I know. It fit with everything that was humanly meaningful in Angel's life and as our "master" it was this that he wanted to communicate.

For, Angel had another story too. It was about how he had first joined the order. He told us that back in the day, around the turn of the century, priests from the local seminary used to send a hay cart about the peasant villages and farms, crying out, "Give us your sons!" If there was a child who was weak or dreamy—another mouth to feed and unwilling to pull his weight with the farming chores—the presumption was that he had a vocation to the priesthood. He would always get an education, and, in all likelihood, would stay on, get ordained, and become part of the privileged clergy and a badge of honor to the family. Angel left home at the age of *five* and he did stay on, never really knowing a mother's love. And when the church for him meant law, where was the passion of his life going to go but to his native land? His wartime adventure—only perhaps for a few months when he was in his late thirties/early forties—that was enough to give him meaning. It was long delayed, but it was his rite of passage as a man, his coming of age. Angel was Juan Elcano, just in slightly less swashbuckling dress.

Of course, I didn't really get this then. Angel was my religious superior, a devoted son to his order and the church. He was someone whose standards of piety and discipline I was keen not just to meet but to outdo. I would keep strict silence when the timetable required it, considering the others who joked and whispered to be inferior in observance and spiritual progress. As in the story of the heavy can of fertilizer I labored hard in work time and didn't shirk. During study hours I read the biggest, densest tome on ascetic theology I could find, and for light relief I studied French vocabulary. I am in competition with the entire system, believing I can use it to mount to the pinnacle of an invisible peak of sainthood, godliness, intellect, who knows what? Angel is, so to speak, my coach, the guy with the stopwatch who records my astonishing times and nods helplessly with approval.

During one evening meal I do the standard "confession of faults" for the sake of humility and repentance. I kneel at the entrance of the refectory, beating my breast and asking my brothers to pardon my pride and lack of observance. I'd asked Angel's permission to do this as a recommended ascetical practice, but after I bleat my sins for less than a minute, he waves me to get up. He is probably as embarrassed as I am, possibly remembering other occasions when the ritual had misfired. On one occasion someone knelt too far out across the entrance, sending a good brother sprawling as he marched hungrily in for his dinner.

I also ask and receive Angel's permission to wear the cilice, the little piece of chain mail about the size of your palm with little blunt spokes at right angles. It was strapped with cord around the thigh or the calf for the purpose of "mortification," applying pain and discomfort to the flesh so, by contrast, the spirit could grow. I would surreptitiously sit on it for minutes at a stretch during meditation, mentally recording my score and adding it to my overall tally of bankable virtue.

One time I accidentally broke some cruets, small vessels used in the ritual of the mass. As required, I reported the breakages, telling Angel the items were now "useless." He says, "Like you," which surprised and stung me, but I understood it is a test of humility, given my evident desire to excel. I responded with eyes cast down. I suppose pride was the spiritual fault he suspected me of, and, in a way, he was right, but there was always a deeper fault line that neither he nor any superior was able to track. I felt fairly sure he held me in regard, but at a certain point that didn't even matter. I was performing for an audience that exceeded any visible pair of eyes and so his approval was secondary.

In this spirit I carried my mortification to the extreme of going off to the woods beside the house and finding a nettle bed with which to sting my legs and forearms. I think there was an Irish saint who did something like this, and it was vital that I stay up with the leaders in the holiness stakes. So, when it came to the approval of my novice master, to the graduation report he had to give me, I had it in the bag, whatever he might think. Toward the end of novitiate, he almost put words to this. Almost, but not quite. He said that I would always be happy in religious life because I had an "intellectual approach" and this would carry me through. But he mistook calculation for intellect and as my master he miscalculated. I was like a gambler who knew that the more money he placed on the table, the more the bank (i.e., God) would become interested. And even if in the end the gambler lost everything, the bank in this case would have to somehow honor the debt. One way or another I would come out the winner. And so, could it be true, even back then, that I intended one day to rise from the table, pocket my winnings, and leave?

But who was wise enough for those times? Even just ten years earlier Angel might have been right. I would have grown a rigid personality representing a rigid institution, and I might even have thrived. But the '60s were upon us, and every material not tried in fire was doomed to collapse. Angel's own story was to suffer a yet further adversity during that year, and it was a direct result of the Second Vatican Council, which was just then coming to an end. In the spring of 1965, with months still to go of the novitiate year, he was appointed provincial superior, in charge of the five communities in what was called the Anglo-Irish Province. I remember when Angel got the news. He looked as if a mountain had fallen on him, as if he had got JFK's job the day before Dallas. He knew it was an impossible task, and he reconciled himself only by invoking the traditional idea of a cross to bear, a terrible trial given him by God.

Steve, his replacement as novice master, another Spaniard, arrived shortly after. His actual name was Esteban, and he had a large lugubrious face like one of those semi-melted creatures in a painting by Salvador Dalí. There followed what seemed like weeks of head-to-head conferences between Angel and Steve, interminable walks in the wind and rain up and down the long arc of the drive that led up to the house. I knew something was afoot and it wasn't reassuring. Clearly it was about problems in the communities, but the details were unknown. Only much later was I able to piece together more or less what was going on. It was a matter of generations and cultures, and mixed in with it all there was a vague atmosphere of sexual identity, worldview, and sensibility, something I was oblivious to and would decode only many years later. Angel had been appointed as a compromise figure, someone representing the old strict Spanish way, but having a gentle disposition. He was bound to fail. The plotline went as follows.

three

BISHOPS, NEWTS, AND CAVES

In 1962 a meeting of all the bishops of the Catholic Church was convened in Rome. It was called the Second Vatican Council, and its watchword was *aggiornamento*, a bringing of things up to date. At the time I was in novitiate the policy was still straws-in-the-wind, but it had already accelerated the desire for change. There was a roiling impatience among men who reached manhood in the postwar world, directed against elders schooled in a much more inflexible universe. And, as I very slowly came to comprehend, a lot of this was related to gay sensibility, not yet having that name to speak of itself, but wanting progressively to find for itself rights of style and recognition. The struggle for homosexual life to "come out" had not yet begun but the first stirrings of that great progressive shift were certainly underway and finding their own displaced expression in religious life. I was certainly unaware at that time, but I now believe that more or less half the men in the communities were men attracted to other men. Here was an ethos, as powerful as it was obscure, able to provide an assertive alternative to the military style of male relationship that dominated before.

Back in the '50s the Claretians had decided in a burst of missionary enthusiasm to improve outreach in England by establishing an "international seminary." Providing a corps of priests with greater cultural affinity was going to kick-start the growth of the congregation in the Anglo world. That was the theory. A number of young men, from the US and Germany, were brought together to form the nucleus. But there was a growing rift between this new blood and the old conservative ethos that dominated the leadership. The number of students did increase with new English and Irish vocations also added, but it was a case of a path half a mile long and a quarter-inch deep. Numbers were essential but the groundwork had not been laid. Men were lacking who embraced the order's spirit deeply enough and at the same time were able to translate it to a quite different culture. What resulted instead was a destructive struggle between these half-formed new generations and the old battle-hardened "Spanish" discipline that saw itself as really the one and only thing necessary.

Angel's replacement was a case in point. If I had to find one word for Steve it would be angry. I mean seriously angry. He had been sent to the novitiate evidently against his will. His main relaxation was brutal physical labor, wading deep into a thicket of nettles and briars, his clothes ripped, his face bleeding, tearing things out with his bare hands. One afternoon he sat under a front portico taking tea after work. He wouldn't look anyone in the eye but just over your shoulder, in the manner of a man who won't engage you in case he might kill you. I ask him how he is, and he gives an ugly sigh and says something in a hollow tone about "the disappointments of life." I find myself trying to encourage him, my novice master, because whatever had happened to him was now happening to me. I want to shore up that world of discipline he is supposed to represent, because in day-to-day practice I absolutely need its metaphysical assurance. But there he is, crumbling before my eyes, like Dalí's *Metamorphosis of Narcissus*.

Steve had been provincial himself and also a local superior, and was probably the Spaniard most identified as standard-bearer for the old discipline. One of the men who defied him was the then-outgoing provincial, an American named Dan. Some years later I heard Dan describe how Steve used to wait up for him when he was a young priest in a parish where Steve was in charge. Steve would sit in a chair just inside the front door like a great mythical bird seeking to instill the rules-consciousness the American was evidently lacking. Staying out late, even if with a local family of Catholics, was a violent break in the timetable and it threatened the fabric of monastic religious community. Dan, for his part, wasn't about to change, and he definitely didn't like Steve crimping his style. Most of all he had the times on his side. As mentioned, he too had been appointed to a term as provincial, because, undoubtedly, he represented the wave of the future in which the order was investing.

Steve was now little more than a dinosaur. He had, I feel sure, prompted the appointment of Angel as Dan's successor, via a stream of complaints sent to Rome. Perhaps he'd hoped he would be appointed himself, to another term as provincial, but Angel had been introduced as a halfway figure. This would account for all those driveway conversations with Steve shooting his bitter complaints into Angel's ear as they tramped obsessively back and forth along the drive. One time the novices saw them head off on one of their marches and noticed a black April storm rolling in from the north. We locked the side door and hid, waiting to see what happened. Sure enough, a pelting downpour overtook them, and it was a sad sight even if I didn't know the full background. For pity's sake, these men had fought a civil war with two million dead, and they were now being brought low by kids who had won their combat ribbons watching the Flintstones. But that was the way of it. As they stumbled from the side door to the front, with their cassocks and capes flapping wildly and the rain sheeting, they looked like nothing so much as the last members of a near-extinct species seeking desperately a final niche to hide in.

I took my first vows on August 22, 1965. They were called temporary, legally a one-year commitment, but you were not supposed to think that way. You were to embrace them with a whole heart, the intention of a lifetime promise. For me there was nothing temporary about them. The only thing that made sense was a headlong dive into the religious life, no glance back. Anything else would have resolved nothing, would have given no answer to the emptiness inside and around me.

The ceremony felt strange. I remember a phrase, something about calling all the citizens of heaven to witness my words, which seemed weird and medieval, and yet also quite comforting. It was amazing that some bunch of "citizens" should be interested in what I was doing, the members of some real, if otherworldly, city. I kept a small journal from that time, now fifty years old. I did not look at it again in all those years and only now have I reread it. Inside the fervid prose, a brute willfulness is on display: willful to command God with my zeal, willful to exceed everyone by being less than them. At the same time there is awareness and an unhappy circling around this flawed selfhood. "I love him, though how my heart can rise above the mauling chains of self-conscious and desperate self-seeking I will never know . . . I speak as in a little box, dark, self-loving, and fighting desperately for one little handhold on the infinite exterior of His Power, which only He can give."

Embarrassing, yes; the emotions are both adolescent and violent. In fact, I use the actual term, talking of my soul's "violent attempts" to excel. When Angel left us, and his dutiful approach was replaced by Steve's fierce resentment, this violence came to the surface. On a bored early summer's afternoon when Steve was away on a visit and had Chris driving the car, Phil and I captured a newt about two inches long, with its small green legs and arms waving helplessly. We wired it up, one opposite arm and leg, to an electric plug and stuck the terminals straight in the outlet. Two hundred forty volts coursed through its fragile body, its leg smoked, it opened its mouth with a heartrending scream. We were bored and mean but none of the formal teaching of the novitiate stood in the way of our being torturers and killers—only a distant pain of conscience. Rather, against the background of church centuries, the effect went the other way. Again, looking in my journal, the crucifixion was not a revelation of human violence—as I understand it now—but the ultimate deal set up by Godself to pay Godself through violence. With only the barest hint of unease, I call it "the just but negative side of Christ's kingdom—the atonement for sins."

It was not long before our killing of the newt, and in a similar mood, Phil and I carried out a mock crucifixion of Wilkins. It took place in the Victorian vegetable garden next to the house. We tied the postulant with his hands outstretched across a small rose arch and left him there under the sun with the flies buzzing in his face. Wilkins went along with it because he was so used to being picked on, and, I think, he may have even seen this as a devotional act. It may, actually, have been Good Friday.

We were unsupervised boys for sure. At that age—even with the most profound spirituality—the only thing that can be assured is discipline. And now that too was unravelling.

Wednesday afternoons are always our afternoon off. We go for a walk on the roads and lanes, or sometimes take the car for a visit to a scenic area. One Wednesday the gang piles into a car and we head off for some spelunking. The area of the West Country we were in was notable for gorges or "combes," great gouges in the earth's surface diving down hundreds of feet, and below them are narrow sinkholes or "swallets" disappearing underground. We go to one of these tunnels in Cheddar Gorge and crawl down with no equipment except flashlights. The space is not more than twenty inches high, and we penetrate perhaps fifty yards with the huge weight of the earth, its hills and mountains, only inches from our faces. At one point the passage turns vertically downward. The drop is about seven feet and is easy enough to fall through, but it is only about eighteen inches wide at the top and expands into a wide bell shape a couple of feet down. We all know it is going to be tough getting back, with nothing for our legs to brace against.

After exploring the passage some more it is time to return home. We make our way to the small chimney. Climbing it demands gripping the ledge on the top and then hoisting yourself solely by upper arm strength until you can lever an elbow onto the surface. We take it in turns and when it comes to mine, for one desperate moment, I think I can't do it. But I heave and squirm and somehow get myself up. Wilkins is last to go, and it is not good. He is broad in the beam, like an inverted cork, and he just can't pull himself upward. We yell at him furiously to try harder, but to no avail; and in the confined space it is impossible to help him. There among the dirty yellow rocks and the failing torches we become seriously frightened and decide to pray, telling Wilkins to pray too. He is saying Hail Marys furiously; I believe we all are. Then suddenly, out of nowhere, he rises straight up, just like the cork out of a bottle, landing free on the ledge! We whoop with relief, and if possible we would all have hugged him. We crawl our way out of the tunnel as quickly as we can, covered in mud and grime, but rejoicing to stand clear in the open air, beneath the sky.

Brockley Combe was not far from our house on the hill, running south and west. It was a wild place with a sense of danger and immoral liaisons, and we were thrilled to explore it on another of our afternoon escapades in the late summer of 1964. We found a big truck tire discarded on the roadside and wheeled it to the top of the ridge. Finding a clear space, we let it go, watching it leap and bound down the precipice, spinning twenty, thirty feet in the air, jumping clear across the road which ran along the bottom. We considered doing the same to a massive rock, but we were unable to dislodge it, which is just as well because it could have crushed any car passing below. What were we but a group of boys enjoying a few brainless hours together while they lasted?

So it was back in those early months, when I was still seventeen, that we received a visit from the local bishop. The strangest thing, he did not exhort us to faith and virtue, but brought an entertainment of entirely another order from exploring caves and tipping rocks. He came up our hill in his purring hunter-green Jaguar Mark X and set up a screen on a tripod in the front parlor—one of the few occasions we were allowed in there. He showed homemade movies of his vacation, and without protest we watched burnished scenes from the south of France, the Côte d'Azur, and Cannes. His camera lingered on the bikinied bottoms and tanned thighs of three girls as they strolled along a stone quay surrounded by passionate blues of sea and sky. It was a total mystery why he did this

(I still feel the shock—both poverty and chastity were outraged), unless perhaps he derived some covert pleasure imagining the reactions his images would provoke in tender adolescents. Poor Angel was mortified. He tried to explain to us that the church is full of all manner of people and occasions. "Do not be scandalized," he pleaded. "You must be ready for things like this. Perhaps the Lord allowed it as a test for you?"

four

CHILDHOOD WARS

Before novitiate there was childhood. So let me go back now to that crucial before. Let me begin again on that island south of Portsmouth. We had a holiday cabin there, overlooking the Solent, a place called Thorness Bay. It was our escape from the world.

It stood perched high on a green field that fell steeply across marl cliffs to the sea. It was at the eastern edge of a bay on the north side of the isle. The bay curled toward the west, while if you glanced across to its right over a strip of blue water you could see the mainland. Some fifteen years earlier, during the war, the British Ministry of Defense had considered the possibility the Nazis might use the narrow strait as a springboard for invasion. So, they built a guard post on the hill and gun emplacements along the cliff. Back then a squad of soldiers kept twenty-four-hour watch overlooking the sheltered channel. But now their guard room was deserted, and the blockhouses choked with bramble. The only explosions were the sounds of the cows shitting liquidly on the concrete floors.

My mother had brought us to this place at the edge of the sea. I don't know how she found it, but the effect was to remove us fairly effectively from our day-to-day setting, and this was her intention. She deeply distrusted English culture in general and hated our housing estate in particular, the one attached to the Parkhurst high security prison at the center of the island. We had come there from Gloucester in the West of England—the setting of my earliest memories—attracted no doubt by a promise of good pay for my father as a prison officer in one of the less appealing prison settings in England.

The Isle of Wight itself has the feeling of a time warp, belonging to a vaguely secret kingdom or society, separate from England. Queen

Victoria spent childhood holidays on the island and confirmed its "getaway" identity when she and her consort, Albert, built a grand palazzo there, Osborne House, as a summer home. It was the place she eventually died. A couple of centuries earlier, during the Civil War, Charles I's luck finally ran out on the island. Fleeing from London, he had thought its governor would be sympathetic, but the governor arrested and imprisoned him at Carisbrooke Castle, whence he would be later transferred back to the mainland and ultimately executed. The school we went to was Carisbrooke Convent, with the castle's brooding Norman walls towering directly above us. Alternatively, we lived under the Parkhurst prison walls. "Civilization" is literally constituted by walls. All this stone weight of history, of which of course we understood little, was still, with my mother's constant commentary, something felt, tasted, digested. How very good, therefore, to have this holiday place set in a field looking out to the sea.

My mother purchased the cabin for three hundred pounds, which, I think, back then was a tidy sum. We children called it "the hut." It was in fact an old railway carriage raised on sleepers, with a ply and corrugated-iron extension stuck on one end. It held a comforting sense of security, due to its heavy metal door and warm stuffy air, but also a mysterious feeling. It had made an impossible journey, for there were no railway tracks by which a carriage could get there. Clearly the stalwarts of the British army had used a crane to lower it in place as somewhere to sleep while waiting for Hitler. But that was never mentioned. I wondered to myself, "Had it arrived from the sky?" For me just about everything arrived from the sky.

On bright sunny days I used to climb to the roof of the guardhouse and gaze out over my kingdom. Shinnying twenty feet up the drainpipe at its corner was possibly dangerous but that was part of the thrill of my solitary meeting with the universe. I would stand on the roof beneath the heavens stretched out and glistening just for me. The whole thing, land, sea, and air, seemed a single organism, a womb aching with life. It did not have a name. Very few things had names—yes, the Isle of Wight where we were living; Thorness Bay where the cabin was; and the Solent, the strait between the island and the mainland—but I did not think in these terms. Everything was something else, a mystery and an event that could hardly be given words, and yet I could reach out and almost hold it.

Farmer Foulkes sold the cabin, but not the land on which it stood, which meant he did not provide ease of access. There was a rutted track, with an archipelago of large rocks that kept the surface from collapsing completely. The cows negotiated this path with indifference. They meandered back and forth from milking, each time plunging the lane deeper in slime. In winter and early spring, the going was a nightmare. We had a car, a noble Renault. It looked like one of the vehicles you see in Al Capone movies, with running boards, great rounded mudguards, and headlamps like onion halves. But it was French and colored grey. We called it "the old grey mare," which was an insult because its trim would have looked sexy in Paris. This side of the English Channel, however, it showed disdain for performing any duties related to transport. It was always breaking down. Really it was the last vehicle to bring up that track. When we did, it bucked and swiveled and ground to a halt in front of a huge boulder, axle deep in muck and shit. I don't know how my father ever got it back to the road, because we abandoned him and the car and continued on foot.

There was in fact a perfectly good paved road, bypassing almost all the cow track. Called the military road, the army had built it to connect to the coastal defenses. But Farmer Foulkes kept it gated and locked at all times. Likely he did not want to encourage access to the cliffs by the public, but that meant those who actually purchased the cabins had to use his highway from hell, while a royal road lay just beyond. The pavement was pristine, except for the few standard cowpats, and coming into sight of it was a supernatural shock. My brother, sisters, and I had to pick our way through knee-deep filth, which sucked at our Wellington boots so our feet shot out and landed in the freezing mire. Our mother, laden with supplies, had to keep retracing her own steps to rip the boots free. Then we saw the road and it was salvation ever and always beyond reach. I knew nothing of the doctrine of predestination, but I did know we were Catholics and the farmer was Protestant, and I felt deep down in my soul his lovely road was righteousness denied. My mother's complaints about not being given access to the road fitted seamlessly with her constant critique of Protestant culture, so it was not hard for me to conclude this implicit theology. We had come to the cabin, even in this harsh weather, to get away from the housing estate where we lived. Almost everyone there was Protestant, but we had a pretty good fix on them; it was they who were going to hell. However, Farmer Foulkes's unused road had a sudden mighty power all its own; it said we were the unredeemed ones in the mud.

Then the summer came, and we forgot about all that. May and June, the track dried out, the cuckoo played its two-note orchestra flying open-mouthed across the hill, and the jack hare sat on the field looking straight in our cabin window. My younger sister, my brother, and I set out joyfully along the hardened surface to the farmhouse, carrying coins and a shopping note. We returned with fresh milk, eggs, and vegetables. The cream slopped on the sides of the aluminum can and if you put your nose in you caught the raw, washed scent of the dairy springing straight from the metal. The eggs had flecks of straw stuck with chicken poop, and the potatoes gave off a scent of earth.

Immediately we handed over our purchases, and they were placed in the cooling bucket sunk in the earth beside the stoop, we set out. We passed in a heartbeat to another world. Always we were some kind of primitive tribe, small and surrounded by others more powerful, our existence always threatened. We hardly had a name for our enemies, they were always just there, the default of all our stories. Perhaps we called them the Blue Noses or the Red Ears, but we always beat them, always outwitted them. We would run when we had to, hide in lairs and mountains, or build ourselves temporary forts that we'd sneak away from when the enemy discovered us and gathered to surround us. We'd trek and hide, fight and escape, and on the way, we'd hunt, turn over rocks, scout thickets, and enter the blockhouses filled with a sense of discovery and wonder. All would take on meaning as treasures, as camps of our enemies, or the remains of dead and departed peoples before which we could only stand in honor and awe. We were small, invincible, heroic, with a religious respect given to each separate feature of our world.

It would not need a genius of psychology to understand the underlying drama of our games. In real social terms we were vastly outnumbered by the world of Protestantism, or at least what we saw as such. At the same time, the Catholic Church was a timeless institution, like a great mountain range that would always be there, above and beyond the vicissitudes of history. Back in Gloucester our lives had revolved around a steepled parish church, St. Peter's, and the man who was its parish priest, Canon Roche. He was the classic successful priest, originator of building projects, prolific fundraiser, confident preacher, distinguished in appearance. I have looked him up on the internet, and my memory of him certainly fits the profile. My mother loved this priest, popular and authoritative as he was, and there can be no doubt he was a paragon of long-form triumphant Catholicism. But on the island, especially the prison estate, those glory days were well gone.

The house we occupied in Gloucester was in a leafy, flower-strewn square within earshot of the city cathedral and its peal of bells on a summer's evening. No cathedral bells welcomed us in Parkhurst, only prison walls and the officers' housing huddled beneath them. Our house was a cramped, semidetached spatter-dash-walled cottage. It stood about fifteen yards beyond the prison's granite perimeter, which reared up eighteen feet like the hulk of a ship on an arctic shore. Our dwelling was surrounded by scores of other houses similarly accommodating the families of prison officials. All at once we were ringed about by the mob of children belonging to those houses and by the gangs they formed, and my mother's choices did nothing to make us fit in. Of course, we went to mass on Sunday where very few others did, but most of all she managed to get us enrolled in a convent school serving the daughters of wealthy farmers, of whom, I would guess, fewer than half were Roman Catholics. Boys could also attend the school for the first grades, and so all four Bartlett children caught the two buses to Carisbrooke Convent where we would receive a good Catholic education. The local children attended the local schools, and if our different destinations were not enough, our blazers, caps, and gym slips made sure we stood out like flags on parade.

The physical world on the estate thus came to converge neatly with my mother's psychic world. In our first summer there, as we made our slow way up the long, imperial approach to the prison gates and then turned right to follow the everlasting prison wall, there were plenty of chances for us to meet the other kids coming from their school and for our evident difference to be noted. And we were fair game: we lived in the same housing as they did, and our dad was a simple officer no higher than the rest. Why should we set ourselves apart? Our caps and satchels were dragged from us and thrown in the bushes. We were jostled, pushed over, and called insulting names.

As the weeks of this humiliation wore on, my brother and I took a particular hatred for one of the boys. This kid was roughly my brother's height but stocky in build and in the forefront of our torment. Somewhere, part of my mother's formation also involved guerilla warfare, so together my brother and I decided on a strategy. We made a plan to race out of school and get the earliest bus home so as to steal a march on our foe. We hid in the laurel bushes opposite the prison wall, our hearts thumping. Sure enough, the gang showed up, trailing one another up the dusty road. After only a couple of waits the object of our wrath could be seen lagging at the end of the column. He was a perfect target. We waited until the last of his allies turned the corner, then dashed out of cover, overwhelming him with surprise and welting him around the head with our little fists. We inflicted a sincere thrashing and ran off laughing and glorious. It had seemed so easy and the thrill of victory so intense that we decided to move up the order of opponents. We wanted to do the same thing to the biggest boy, the one who guaranteed the gang. We figured that pound for pound the two of us outweighed him and if we gave him a beating we had settled with the whole bunch. So once more we lay in wait until, again, finding our foe alone we erupted out of the bushes. But we hadn't reckoned on our victim's longer reach and solid fighting strength. He gave us the pasting we had given his friend and we quickly ran out of steam and turned tail, with him crowing loudly after us. All the same, our guerilla campaign seemed to come to an honorable draw, and from then on, the kids coming back from school left us alone.

My brother's name was Terence and my younger sister's Christine. Together we formed the tight little band that played the Iliad of the cliff tops. Back here in Parkhurst we could not let our imagination run so free. Other children would want to know what we were doing and would likely interfere or offer to fight us for real. So, we kept a lower profile, mostly inside, and spent our creativity on stories whose protagonists were plastic cowboys and Indians bought in the store, the "Little Men" as we called them. These hardened model figures played out the infinite saga of our childhood with a thousand heroic adventures across the living room floor or in the grasses and weeds of the back yard. Imagination becomes spirituality where social life is narrowed almost to nothing. The Brontë children had twelve wooden soldiers, "the Young Men," whose intricate adventures became the springboard for their literary careers. For the Bartletts there was too much actual threat and stress for anything remotely as productive as the Brontë experience. The games were a real escape, a parallel world, apart from but part of the real world.

We did also play with the other children when there was a common entertainment, searching for lizards in the dry earth or slow worms in the tuft grass, or after a downpour joining the crowd launching ships of twigs and sticks on the dirty brown torrent formed by the brook at the bottom of the hill. But it remained a risk to go out alone, or at a time when the gangs were around, or to a place too far from home.

One bright spring morning I abandoned both these rules and decided it was a good day to go looking for birds' eggs. It would require going afield, and I also relished the thrill of doing something on my own, for myself. I had a long, straight hawthorn stick I considered essential for probing nests in the higher branches and, so equipped for the hunt, I set out.

I was heading for the woods to the north of the prison but had not walked two hundred yards when a boy appeared from the bushes. He was a year or so younger than I but built like the side of a house and probably twice my weight. He demanded that I give him my stick. I recognized this boy as the brother of the notorious Allan, the leader of one of the two major gangs on the estate. So far, we had carefully avoided these individuals of evil repute, but here was a direct challenge to the joy of the morning. In the bold, fresh sunshine everything took on a metaphysical value. I refused. The young man advanced and threw a brick at me, which hit me on the ankle. Here was a direct challenge to my share of the world, and the boy's combative desire for the stick declared its true identity. Without a moment's hesitation I lifted the straight branch and whipped it around in a warrior arc, catching him on the back of the neck. He went down like a sack of stones. Almost instantaneously, as if it were scripted, a shout rang out from somewhere back along the track, "Hey, Allan, this kid just killed your brother!"

I knew at once the jig was up. The voice had come from behind me so the way back to my house was cut off. My only chance was to try to outrun the gang, heading up the hill and flanking out to the main road, then down to the approach road to the prison entrance. There was a slim possibility I could stay in front. I dropped the stick and took off up the hill. At the top there was a short row of the nicest houses on the estate, and as I got there I could hear two or three boys closing in behind me. I was terrified and my lungs already felt as if someone had poured metal into them all the way down to my stomach. In panic I dashed into the front yard of one of the houses, seeking sanctuary. The owner perhaps was already there or came out directly and I tried to plead with him, pointing to the murderous posse outside his gate. But he was fearful for his roses and his own morning, and he ordered me out, while waving the boys away from his fence. They retired to the trees on the other side, and I had about a three-yard start. Needless to say, they caught me immediately after I left safety, grabbing me from the side and behind. I wondered vaguely if the man would intervene, but nothing happened. The gang now had me to do as they wanted, and they boldly marched me out onto the main road and down the hill to meet my fate.

At the bottom of the hill, there was a bridge by which the road crossed the brook. Between the brook and the prison approach road was a field and in the field there was a small group of trustee prisoners in their familiar faded blue fatigues, under the eye of a single officer. On the bridge stood Allan senior, a boy with the body of a man, and when my escort set me in front of him, he promptly took a slug at me. But the moment my guards let go of my arms my knees buckled and I fell, and somehow Allan's blow glanced off me. He swore and told me to stand up. His lackeys pulled me to my feet and set me there again, stupidly thinking I was going to take my punishment like a man. "Why don't you stand up, you bastard?" But once again my knees creased, and his blow was ineffective. I honestly think he didn't manage to land a single true hit because whatever gang code they were operating by I was far too deep into an animal defense mechanism to abide by it. Meantime the group of prisoners in the field, about fifty yards away, could see only this savage beating inflicted by a gang of boys all twice the size of their victim. So now their own sense of code was activated and two of them, without waiting for their officer, began running hotfoot toward us.

The sight of those time-hardened men bearing down fast was too much for any housing estate bully and in a flash I was alone on the bridge. The prisoners looked satisfied, gave me the nod, and went calmly back to their gesticulating officer. I walked home slowly in an endorphin fog, accompanied by my sister Christine who at some point had started following me and witnessed the unfolding drama. Later the Allans' father came around to complain of the near-homicide of his son despite the fact that the only aftereffect was a sore neck. It was a certain exaggeration given the whole family were built like dray horses and it would take much more than my childish stick to kill them. It was also richly hypocritical considering that his eldest brute had put all us children in fear of our lives since we first arrived. All the same, there were no further repercussions. I think the idea that prisoners had my back made me someone to be reckoned with and again I was left in peace. The prisoners, the guards, and their families all had some kind of code in common, one that passed back and forth through the prison wall invisibly and without hindrance.

There were, in fact, day-to-day connections between the prisoners and the officers' families that made us an actual organic society. The prisoners would bake delicious bread every week and bring it around on a horse and cart for sale. We loved that bread. It was like the prisoners put all their denied humanity into it, and we could taste something of that truth when we ate it. There was nothing we could give back, but the very communication was perhaps important for them. They would also come around with the same horses picking up kitchen slops to feed to their pigs on the prison farm. The horses were magnificent beasts, with muscled flanks, great manes, and blinkers around their eyes. Their breath would plume in the winter air, and the prisoners collected the slop in bins in a businesslike fashion. In those moments we could easily have been in a time frame ten centuries earlier, in a feudal period, with serfs, horses, and the officers as what they were—a permanent military garrison keeping order.

My father even had his wounds to carry as part of his role. At some point he was involved in a struggle restraining a prisoner and took a heavy blow to the chest. According to a doctor this seemed to have disturbed some old scarring in his lungs and he developed full-blown tuberculosis. At that time, they had only recently found the cure and TB still had a reputation as a deadly illness. While he was waiting for admission to the sanatorium, he lapsed into depression. He used to sit motionless by the fireplace staring into the red coals, not saying a word. Still, that strange, sad feeling in the house was not completely new and although I was scared by the way he was, it was really just a further variation on deeply familiar relationships and emotions. After the birth of Christine my mother remained in bed and was dramatically different. I was a little boy and went into her room, and for the first time she was unresponsive to me. She was catatonic. Her condition was never explained, and certainly not diagnosed as postpartum depression. It's likely that the birth of her fourth child became the occasion when at least part of her soul was pitched permanently in darkness. And that part was powerful enough to communicate its effects to everybody around her. She kicked my father out of her bed and, for a good few months, he came to sleep in mine. When the alarm went off in the small hours to get up for work my father would rise and dress himself, repeating over and over in a horrible, soul-in-hell kind of way, "Oh dear, oh dear, oh dear, oh dear." I'm sure it's the reason I hate alarm clocks to this very day.

To understand all this I have to dig deeper into my father's own backstory. Charles Bartlett was born in 1914 and brought up in Chard, Somerset, the west country of England, the older of two brothers. His mother was a successful businesswoman, running a Clarke's shoe store on the main street in town. Somewhere in his youth his mother concluded that the younger brother had the better business head, and she chose him to run the store, sending Charlie to work in a tire factory at the age of fourteen. I really do not know the sequence of details after that—my father was very withdrawn about almost everything—but the period just before the war found him employed as a care worker in the Colchester Public Assistance Institution, Essex. It was in or around Colchester that he met his future wife, Julia O'Connor, who was, more or less concurrently, working as a maid at the Spread Eagle Hotel, Witham, about fifteen miles away.

I am sure Charlie felt Julia was the best thing that had ever happened to him, and she responded positively to this handsome, diffident young man who sometimes played the trumpet in a local band. Julia was a year older than Charlie and had immigrated to England in the 1930s, a second-choice destination after the US had closed the door to immigrants during the Great Depression. She was the eighth of eleven children, growing up on a fourteen-acre patch of bog, rock, and small fields on the edge of Connemara, Galway. Three of her siblings died, and four others headed to the US, while she turned to England for her future. She carried with her a deep trauma, one that was narrated to her children in the long history of oppression of her nation at the hands of imperial England. But it seems that her acute hostility to England was in practical terms nonsensical—given that she came there for work and, ultimately, a husband. Or was it the case that, little by little, the land of the Saxons became a stand-in for a wound much deeper and more personal, something that the stresses of childbearing had somehow provoked into life? The visceral force of her anger—especially as I weave all the threads of the story together—has more and more convinced me of the deeper explanation.

In order to get married my father converted to Roman Catholicism. The alternative was a "mixed marriage" with permission from the local bishop; but my mother, I'm sure, insisted. This would be the minimum she'd require. She could marry an Englishman, but never a Protestant. Part of the deal was also Sunday mass. My father was faithful to this, in a desultory kind of way, at least for the early part of the marriage, and always with what seemed a slightly terrified, uncomprehending attitude. The only payoff was the good graces of my mother, and when these disappeared so did attendance at mass. A less apparent part of the deal was the prohibition of birth control, something I'm sure was mentioned but I am equally sure my father never understood or reckoned with. As a teenager I never understood it myself, so I can fully empathize with my father. But there was much more to it than its philosophical explanations—the abstruse Aristotelian teleology invoked by the church to demand that every act of married sex had to be "open to the possibility of procreation." It was a matter of who ultimately had control of the relationship, the couple or the church.

I have spoken about my father sleeping in my bed. The fundamental reason for this was my mother did not want any more childbirth—it was a serious risk to her health and experienced as a threat to her mental existence itself. In which case there could simply be no sex. Plain as that. When we got to the Isle of Wight there was discussion of the church's sole permitted approach, the so-called "rhythm method." It was in the air. I can't remember exactly but I remember the words and I am certain it was talked about by my parents. The rhythm method involves a careful monitoring of the woman's ovulation cycle, using calendars and close recordkeeping, in order to figure out the probable days when she is not fertile. Then and only then would non-procreative sex be permitted, because, paradoxically, there was still a remote possibility of conception according to the "ways of nature."

So, there was a time, soon after our arrival on the Isle of Wight, that the tension in our house ramped up unbearably. Whatever efforts were made with the rhythm method came to nothing. I can imagine my mother slamming down the calendar the moment my father expressed any kind of distaste for the process, or indeed if he did anything to upset her. At some point there was a total shutdown on sex.

I came down one morning and walked into the kitchen when my father was just about to head out to work at the prison. He had been trying to bid goodbye to my mother and as usual he was saying he was sorry for something. There was that familiar horribly tense yet dead feeling, laden with anger and desire. When he saw me, he convulsively grabbed his black officer's tie with both hands and tightened it around his heavy blue cotton shirt, making a gasping, choking sound as he did. I really thought he was committing suicide right there in front of my eyes and I screamed uncontrollably. It was both terrifying and perverse, intended, perhaps, to mock my own symptoms of asthma. My mother told me to take no notice, he was just pretending and trying to frighten me; in any case it worked.

It was one of the last times that my father ever responded with evident passion. It was around about the same period he smashed the Sunday dinner to the floor, prepared for him with torturous care by my mother. The perfectly cooked greens, roast potatoes, and joint of lamb said she was discharging exactly her responsibilities, but they did not include the one he most wanted. Hence the food mocked him, and hence it landed on the floor. After these occasions, and over time, my father seemed to change, to become even more withdrawn and, at the same time, harshly content, like a prisoner who has done his crime and is prepared bitterly to do his time.

There was a convenience store on the road into Newport, the town at the center of the island. The store was only about a mile or so away from Parkhurst. My father used to stop there to get cigarettes, and one time he took me in with him. He laughed and joked with the woman behind the counter, in a way that seemed to me quite amazing. I had never seen my dad that free and relaxed with anyone. I wished he could have fun with my mom like that! I have no certain evidence, but I think it was this woman he had some kind of affair with. Even before I logically thought the whole thing through, I had a niggling feeling about that place, like a truth I somehow always knew. Still, I may be mistaken. Overall, it makes no difference whether it was actually her or not; the evidence of my mother's rage is incontestable: if it was not this woman, there had to be someone. Many years later I asked my brother about it, whether my mother had ever spoken to him of an affair. He said, definitely not. Then in what seemed a faintly casual (if not callous) aside—as if the issue had indeed somehow come up in the years he lived with my mother as an adult, after her husband's death—he added, "Maybe it was prostitutes."

In that period my mother's emotions went from dull self-defense to apocalyptic anger. She would speak with a kind of animal growl, coming straight up from her guts, uttering that they could persecute and torment the Irish, but "they will never break our spirit." She would intone that God was a witness to everything and indeed "God is not mocked." I wondered what it could possibly be that had caused such offense—yes, my father was English, but how could he suddenly become responsible for all that ancient history? A particular name she called him, and with especial venom, was "blackguard," a word with an archaic tone, of contempt and hatred, and even possible racism, which again seemed somehow incongruous. These thoughts, only vague and ill-formed, passed through my mind, helpless to take coherent shape before the white-hot stream of invective pouring from my mother.

She found the family Bible, neglected in the ordinary Catholic way, and cracked open the book of Exodus. I don't remember exactly the sequence in which she read things, but the crossing of the Red Sea and the giving of the Ten Commandments at Sinai were certainly introduced to me at that point, their drama taking hold of my imagination. The figure of Moses emerges, majestic and druid-holy, someone absolutely not to be trifled with. The threat and enactment of stoning to death are introduced to the open-mouthed amazement of her children gathered around her feet as she reads from the armchair, seated, as it were, in the chair of Moses. So, a scene is emblazoned in memory. We are clustered around the hearth with her sitting to its right. My father comes in from the kitchen and stands just inside the door, his eyes fixed on my mother as she reads from the holy book. A communication passes between them, one I do not understand. There is no doubt my father is under condemnation—my mother has all the moral firepower on her side. Yet he does not seem cowed. Instead, I remember his glittering blue eyes looking at her in a mixture both of sorrow and triumph. It seems certain that, whatever he is accused of, something inside of him is glad that he did it—even in defiance of the Bible. I am astounded.

Now, all these years later, the only plausible explanation for it all is the church's outlawing of contraception, and my mother's eager embrace of the teaching, for reasons of her own abhorrence of any more sex. Later on, she told her daughters that she used to take a large safety pin to bed to keep her husband at bay. So it is, my dad decides in desperation, "I will show her! I will assert my manhood, and then where will this precious, incomprehensible teaching be?" Once she finds out—no doubt helpfully informed by the whispers of estate gossip—my mother in retaliation goes back to the origins of law and punishment, to the incontestable authority of Moses. And that is where the matter stays, an endless stalemate between my father's half-repented sexual offense and my mother's biblical rage. But even this does not seem enough to explain it.

What was the energy of the terrifying shaft of fury flung from out her soul? What was its primal psychic force? For sure, there was the poverty of her childhood and the trauma of the British forces in Ireland when she was a child. But there was more to it, I am sure. The poverty would have counted for nothing where there was love and safety at home. And in the War of Independence the rural population always had a relative strategic and political advantage. In the end they won, eventually establishing the Republic of Ireland. No, there had to be something deeper, a wound too profound for naming, let alone healing. I heard it in her voice, its desperate hurt and manic displacement, although I did not understand it at the time.

When my mother was a young teenager, she had a brother about two years older than she. His name was James and he died when he was sixteen. A wild, headstrong kid, it was hinted by my mother that the disciplinary belt-thrashings he got from his dad, my grandfather, had something to do with his death. James would skip school, and with a band of tearaways like himself he scoured the countryside playing practical jokes and upsetting the neighbors. His father obviously felt his own reputation was at stake and laid in unmercifully when he collared his son after a complaint. Purportedly James died from cancer, but when the local doctor came to visit the dying boy, he pointed ominously to a bruise on his upper arm and declared, "There, there, that's where the cancer began." The evident disconnect of this statement plus the heightened look of significance in my mother's eye as she told the story (all within a context of the father's beatings) sharply intimated that the truth of it was somehow other. And when my own brother and I visited Ireland as adults, we found out our cousins also knew the stories, and basically believed James had been killed by a blow or blows from his father. My mother loved James intensely. She mourned him all her life, as a kind of Adonis removed by implacable gods from natural life. In her sixties she had a headstone carved and erected over the family grave in Moycullen. The epigraph named her parents lying there, then followed with the line: "And their son, beloved James . . ." The three-syllable personal endearment pops from the stone with a biblical passion, right out of Solomon's ecstatic poetry. It was her love letter, written so long after the fact, but the flame never dimmed.

It seems to me that almost everything in her crisis behaviors can be explained as a displacement of the terrible violence she experienced surrounding her brother's death—in it, because of it, and as part of it. Because, in fact, she loved her father too, with almost the selfsame passionate feeling. According to her, he was a paragon among men. She would speak of him with vibrant daughterly devotion, of how hard he worked, of the respect in which he was held, and his strength and courage in confronting those who wronged him, or of his violent, dangerous task of dynamiting rocks on the hillside to create grazing land. I hardly ever heard her speak of her mother—she never described her. It seems evident that her mother was emotionally absent from both her and from her father, and all my mother's emotional investment was in these two male figures. How conflicted then was her soul at this root level! A tangled mix of love, pleasure, guilt, shame, anger, violence, collusion. It was into this maelstrom of history and emotion that my father walked. And he himself would not come out alive.

five

VISIONS AND SAINTS

DURING THESE EXPERIENCES I fell in love with time. Christmas came and I was given a watch. As the day degenerated into the usual mix of deadness and rancor, I went to bed early and stuck my head under the pillow to gaze at its fluorescent dial. I watched the big and little hands, and their bright green pointers marching steadily across the black abyss, and something in me stirred. It seemed to me that there was an infinite goodness in time. That its purposes for good could not be turned back and that one day the hour would come when all would be well and all this misery would be ended. I could not have put it in so many words but that's certainly what I felt, and I don't know where it came from. I fell asleep with the watch under my head, comforted by its truly limitless spaces of goodness and hope. To this day I hate alarm clocks, but I love watches.

Perhaps to explain this love of time it should stand in contrast to my infant sense of eternity. Normally the latter means the perfect spiritual being of God rather than the transience, corruption, and futility of the material realm. This classic Platonic and Augustinian point of view I received at my mother's breast and from the standard preaching of Catholic priests. But it morphed in me into a fear, even hatred, of eternity, by merging seamlessly with a very contemporary sense of absolute violence. In one of those childhood dreams that have stayed with me throughout my life, it is all condensed in precise terms. I think I am about six years old, and I am flying in a plane that is increasing to impossible, diabolical speeds. The pilots of the plane are having an uproarious time and laughing hysterically as they continue to drive up the velocity. I attempt to stop them but too late. Everything explodes in a blinding flash, becoming a kind of white glistening nothing that goes on forever: an infinitely expanding, eternal moment of destruction. I wake up screaming, of course; and there is no doubt that some information about the atomic bomb is being processed.

The general knowledge of terminal war was background radio, so to speak, to those earliest years. The V-2 rockets introduced by Germany at the end of the war, targeting the general population, left a scar in people's minds, a lingering threat that went on to gain altogether new life in the 1950s' arms race. One time, when I was barely over three, I'm sure, there was a firework display in a local park. My mother and my aunt, who was visiting, did not know about it and hearing the heavy shocks began screaming in terror up the stairs to my sister and me to come down and shelter under the kitchen table. They were sure that Hitler had survived and was attacking us with his supersonic devices. My sister and I were in the bathroom, going to the toilet before bedtime. The black-and-white diamond shapes of the linoleum flooring are forever branded in my mind as I come stumbling up from the potty and down the stairs with my pants still around my ankles. The actual atomic bomb was dropped on Japan a year before I was born and introduced the world irretrievably to the thought of time's annihilation: Augustine plus the bomb! So, my secret love affair with my watch is without doubt a personal pledge that human time would ultimately triumph over the mixed-up terrors of absolute violence and eternity.

Meanwhile, for a brief interim of childhood, there was maybe a promise, a hope for change. As I mentioned, my father contracted TB in the prison. It was sometime after those early experiences of fury and alienation, because, as I say, there was hope for reconciliation. He spent months in the national sanatorium in Ventnor, Isle of Wight, taking treatment and recovering. My mother did her duty, visiting her husband regularly. It was a tolerable form of relationship, as she did not have to share a bed with him. Back home, during the whole period, an unwonted peace reigned, as if we were now in good health after recovery from some horrible kind of infection. But, as the time drew near for his return, there came a sense of growing dread. Would things be different or go back to how they'd always been? When he finally came home, we held a celebration, with food and gifts all around, and I stood between my mother and father holding their hands begging them to make up. My mother gazed at my father with relentless eyes, hovering between victory and unyielding recrimination. My father gazed back at her with repentance and pleading, thrilled at both his physical recovery and a chance of rehabilitation.

I had my own pulmonary condition, one that seemed, in its own way, to parallel my father's. Chronic asthma was part of my life, following me on our various moves, until it seemed eventually to stand as the dominant theme of childhood. My wheezing started back in Gloucester, an autoimmune reaction in the lungs, triggered somehow by the environment. I remember the weird folk remedies I was subjected to. My father took me to the city cattle market and on a cold winter's evening held me over a sheep pen to inhale the breath of the huddled ewes. I looked into their glassy eyes and tried to suck in the steam from their lungs. All that resulted was a pain in the stomach from leaning over the metal bar and, of course, a general sick feeling. Another time he took me to the cooling pond of the local gas works to breathe the cocktail of vapors it gave off, sulfur, ammonia, tar. After some years a more scientific approach established that I was allergic to pollen and cats. The latter was a problem because we had a pet cat that really loved me; in fact, it was given my middle name, William or "Willy," because of its obvious attraction to me. I had to try and shoo it away once the cat antigen had raised its probative bump on my skin; which was a problem both emotionally and practically—I had to touch it to keep it away.

During my pre- and early teens I missed a quarter to a third of my schooling. Where other kids excelled at sports I excelled at disability. Hunched over, gasping and wheezing like a bagpipe, I moved about the room by holding onto the mantelpiece, tables, and chairs. I was like someone who can't swim hugging the walls at the deep end, trying to keep from drowning. Over the years everyone became used to my illness, and it seemed the normal state of affairs. Christine would say that hearing me wheezing in the next bedroom was always a comforting experience. Years afterward my older sister, Maureen, asked me whether I did not continue to get asthma attacks, and she seemed genuinely shocked when I told her that with modern inhalers it was completely controlled.

The principle of magical cures was much more part of the children's pharmacy, because, of course, it was much more fun. At one point it was decided that what I needed was a massive sharp shock; only thus would my body let go of its hurtful indulgence. So, one fierce day in March on the Isle of Wight we took the journey to the hut and the sea. The sky was a rack of cloud and the wind gusts on their own took your breath away. I was escorted down the hill by a posse of my siblings and my father, all eager to see the effect on my body of the frigid ocean. I stripped down to my swimming trunks, a pathetic figure in the bullying wind. My elder sister and father took off their shoes and socks and waded in with me, then propelled me on my back into the next big wave. It was a brutal baptism and when I came back up, I thought I would never breathe again. It was one of those experiences when you look around at the world, at the trees and the sky, and you know this is it, this is your last look at everything. But, finally, my breath came and I went back up the hill with excruciating slowness, stopping every other step to drag in the sliver of oxygen my lungs could permit. I was supported on either side by only a slightly mortified family, sorry perhaps that the experiment had not worked, confirmed in their ready sense that this was a much harder nut to crack than might first appear.

The flip side to this was my privilege. According to my aunt, I said I wanted to be a priest when I was four, and I believe it. I don't remember a time when I was not saying this. The declaration advanced me at once to aristocratic status, something that stayed with me through my teens and twenties, until in fact I was ordained. My siblings had gotten used to it as a fact of life, and vaguely one of divine origin. But there were two sides to the coin, and part of their acceptance of my status was, I think, a deep understanding of my role in the family system—sucking up the atmosphere of violence in the house with my lungs. I believe this because the horrible relationship between my parents was never a matter of real comment. It was just the way things were, and my chronic inability to breathe seemed part and parcel of the same inevitability. Moreover, my status eventually outperformed my asthma. At the point of my getting ordained I more or less overcame the condition completely. And it was not by accident that at that time resentments against me actually came to the surface, especially among my sisters. In other words, at a certain moment I stopped paying my substance into the family system, and it happened, naturally, at the place when I came into my destined inheritance. At that point collusion turned to anger.

Ultimately, however, this is nobody's fault. We were all caught up in the same cycle. I feel so much regret for it all now, especially how I usurped the importance of my father. But you cannot hand a child power without them taking it, especially when it is presented as divinely sanctioned. And the thing is complicated. At the same time the status of future priesthood was corrupting for me, spirituality was also a real thing. I was invested in relationships of the spirit from very early on and, therefore, paradoxically, the priesthood was made for me, or a highly individualized form of it. I suppose, in my own way, I also seduced my mother. In a world as alienated as hers, how could she resist a firstborn son so quickly confident in affairs of the soul!

When I was very little, probably no more than four, I had a kind of vision that you could say sealed the deal. Surely it was a kind of dream, an apparition arising in my body in full daylight. Whatever it was the event stands there in its own right, without prelude, without explanation, and as vivid today as the day it happened. I was sat on the floor playing with my colored bricks. I can see them, the yellow, the blue, the red. My brother is opposite me, and he seems very little, less than two years, because he is wearing diapers and sitting straight-legged on the floor like very young children do. Across from us is the flight of stairs from the upper floor, coming directly down into the living room. A door to the kitchen is on the right and through it there is my mother at the sink peeling potatoes. At first, I see Jesus' feet, sandaled and golden, descending the staircase. Then his robe, a royal purple reaching to his ankles, belted at the middle by a white cord. And then his head, crowned in gold. He is well over six feet and has a face of incandescent beauty and majesty. He doesn't look at me but at my mother who is shocked and frightened. When he has her attention, he points toward me. Then he turns on his heel and walks out the front door. That's it.

For certain, it's mediated by Catholic ritual and its vestments: the colors and the cord. And there's the role of my mother who very likely did mention to her little boy how great it would be if one day he were a priest, the noblest thing on earth. But the dream wasn't of me being a priest, or any priest being a priest, or indeed Jesus being a priest, but about a man of immense beauty and authority who had urgent business in the next town and wanted me along. The connection to my mother is in fact inverted: Jesus asserts authority over both her and me, and she seems genuinely shocked from her wits. A psychologist might say my infant ego was appropriating to itself the key symbol of power and meaning in its world, but even if that is the case the symbol acted reciprocally. If my psyche engaged with Jesus it was a two-way street. The person of Jesus took my heart and continued to command it for the rest of my life.

It's also hard for me not to celebrate my mother's loss of power, because it's truly not possible to overstate how much of it she wielded through religion. Just the fact that three of her children went off to join religious orders—and subsequently left their orders—must confirm this.

In terms of her background, the domestic scene that she presided over was molded by three hundred years of resistance to imperial oppression. Since the 1600s Ireland was stripped of its remaining Gaelic aristocracy and social structure. Catholic identity, practice, and priesthood became surrogates which preserved the culture itself, in a displaced, priestly, otherworldly, sacrificial, soulish form. My mother came to England from the west, from a desolate paradise of rock, bog, and water between Lough Corrib and the Atlantic. Memories of Cromwell still burned hot, of how the Lord Protector with his New Model Army had driven the Catholic Irish from the arable land, sending them "To Hell or to Connaught." Cromwell's ethnic cleansing deprived the Irish peasantry of land suitable for cattle or diversity of crops, forcing dependence on the potato, which then imploded into blight and famine in the middle of the nineteenth century. As a child my mother was only a couple of generations from genocidal starvation and mass forced exile. At least one of her brothers was in the original IRA, and her parents' cottage was a safe house for their fighters on the run from the British force recruited to suppress them, the notorious Black and Tans. My mother was seven or eight years old at the time. She told the story of how they hid two or three IRA men. She remembered how their feet were sore and bloody and how they had bathed the feet while they gave the young men food and sustenance, finally sending them back into the night. She remarked on how beautiful and bright those youthful feet were as her mother washed them in the enamel basin.

Later in life, when we were in Portsmouth, and after the fury of anger between my parents had settled into routine rancor, my mother used to keep a photograph, first on a mantel and then by her bed. It was of a man named Patrick Pearse, an Irish teacher, writer, poet, revolutionary, and martyr of the 1916 Rising. In many ways this was the man of her life, an obvious affront to my father, but saved from worldly infidelity because Pearse had achieved a kind of sainthood that removed him from the natural realm. In preparing Ireland's soil for the Easter rebellion, Pearse had nourished an ideology of holiness and nationalism, identifying the bloodshed of war with the sacrifice of Christ, and celebrating both together. The trope of Christlike death for the sake of national salvation flowed seamlessly through my mother's own Catholicism, and helped supply the spigot of her spirituality. It did no harm either that Pearse adored his mother, remaining unnervingly celibate throughout his life and writing especially to her in his last hours before execution at the hands of the British. During the same moment, he wrote a famous poem,

"The Mother," spoken in his mother's voice as she contemplated her son's imminent sacrificial death.

If I had to identify one single practice that kept alive the flickering power of this whole cultural tradition, it would be the nightly recitation of the rosary around the family hearth. Even if there were no priests left to say mass—the metaphysical engine of religious independence—the rosary echoed and rehearsed it over and over on the level of the people. Halfway between a mantra and a statement of doctrine it literally went around in a circle—the rosary is a circuit of five sets of ten beads. On each bead the same prayer was said, the Hail Mary. This prayer celebrated the unique status of the Virgin Mary and was at once an offense and challenge to Protestantism. Almost every night of my childhood and adolescence, shortly before going to bed, the family would kneel down and dive into the recitation. I mean dive seriously because everyone would lean on a chair, and as children, and older, we would often fall asleep with our heads buried in a cushion.

At the end of the five decades, my mother would launch into a further long prayer, which was a catena of biblical quotes and invocations plus intercession for an endless list of relatives and those in need. My mother's actual set of beads had a big brass crucifix attached and the whole thing had a mysterious feeling of passion and power. And she used it expressly as a talisman. On one memorable occasion the engine of our ill-willed Renault caught fire while it was laboring up some country lane. As my father got the hood open and tried to smother the flames with a cloth, she grabbed for her rosary, hitting at the dashboard in a kind of anointing or voodoo. It was frightening and painful to watch, because it was both crazy and humiliating to my father's physical efforts to put out the fire. He succeeded, thank God, but it was always a definite mental exercise to distinguish what happened practically and her claims of a miracle.

No doubt I lived in a fervent atmosphere of Catholic imagery and resistance, and my boyhood imagination was imprinted with so much of its passion and symbolism. But the human spirit is a mysterious thing, and it is almost guaranteed that it will also supply its own take or twist on the symbols given to it. Moreover, the figure of Jesus himself is perhaps the most guaranteed to shift the framework in which he is packaged. Another image that came to me a little later suggests that this figure is ultimately engaged in overturning the violent human systems that make use of him.

The year after we first came to the island it was time for my first communion, at the age of seven years. According to the church this is the time when the child attains the power of reason and so is able to "discern the body of the Lord" once it is explained to them. In the months before the big June celebration, I suffered from horrible nightmares in anticipation of my encounter with the church's most sacred ritual. There were wild animals attacking me and explosive colors attached to them, raining down on me like Chinese dragon and tiger paintings. I had a terrible fear that I was not worthy of the communion bread, and the terror of the dreams repeated and played out the fear of this holy thing. It was as if the wafer I was to receive was a sacred material that would react like cosmic acid on my sinful humanity and annihilate it on the spot. When the day came, I was sick to my stomach and stumbled through the service and celebratory breakfast as a man half dead. Photos from the joyous occasion testify to my sorry physical and mental state. Nothing happened, of course, but my body did retain a strange two-dimensional feeling as if all the blood had been squeezed from it, one that continued to reappear in religious services for many years after.

But then there was a dream, surely the most powerful of my life. As astonishing in its condensation as its clarity, somehow it managed to reveal everything that was at stake in my terror of "holy communion." It happened on the Good Friday a couple of months *before* the first communion service. It is a waking dream, because every detail is fixed in memory. I'm standing behind a rank of Roman soldiers who are clad in leather and armor, with javelins in their hands, the famous pilum of the Roman infantry. It is lethal looking, taller than their heads, but it's actually their helmets that fix my attention. These have a smoky, brassy flare, as if the light from a sooty flame is reflected in their surface. Beyond the soldiers on a raised platform there is a man sitting in judgment. He is wearing purple, silken robes, his hands spread juridically upon his knees. Next to him, also facing the rank of soldiers, is a tall, brown-skinned man in a white robe, his hands bound in front of him. His head is down. His hair obscures his face like Velazquez's *Christ Crucified*. I wake up screaming.

At the time and for years after I had no way of figuring out what it meant—my mother thought I'd seen a genuine vision. But now it seems crystal clear. The dream is the inverse of my first meeting with Jesus, and its dreamwork is a separating out of the original priestly imagery. Jesus' purple robe has been switched to the figure seated in judgment, i.e., the

Pilate, who has been given the typical dress and posture of the priest presiding at mass. And the flare of the soldiers' helmets is the brass of the altar candlesticks giving off the smoky reflection of the candles themselves. Helmets are not made of brass, but altar furniture is. Jesus' face is unseen. He is no longer free or in command. Intense violence threatens. He is the victim of a judicial and military apparatus that is mirrored exactly in the ritual of the mass. Freud marveled at the ability of dreams to condense complex relationships into symbolic form. All the terror of holy communion I experienced was the ferocity of human violence packed into the "sacrifice of the mass"—the theory of medieval theology—but now sprung loose by virtue of my mother's constant angry rehearsal. It would be almost another fifty years before I would unpack the violence of medieval theology, but already, right back then, the figure of Jesus was revealed as the victim of human violence given a gloss of divine inevitability. This was what was truly terrifying.

I must have had an inkling of this meaning because I felt somehow the dream was blasphemous and pushed it away from me. I felt, in fact, I was somehow part of the gang victimizing Jesus, and not in any kind of pious sense of Jesus bearing our sins. This was real victim-making, and I was horribly part of it. But in my waking life I was far too locked into concepts and relations belonging to the church to be able to think of things in such a radical manner. The more I went on in my vaporized social context, stripped of any meaningful engagement, the more the Catholic Church was the only possible way ahead. I may have said at the age of four I wanted to be a priest but there was nothing in succeeding years to offer any competition. British institutions—educational, political, practical—were all hopelessly contaminated and so their world was dead. The Anglican church itself was the haunt of demons. Back in Gloucester, the family had once visited Gloucester cathedral, a triumph of English perpendicular style. As I marveled at its leaping forms, my mother kept up a running commentary on the diabolical character of Henry and Elizabeth's Reformation. That night the inevitable dream symbolization took place: I was inside the darkened cathedral and a great agile devil leapt from the organ loft, swung across the nave, and darted obscenely among the pews.

In contrast, the Catholic Church, in any of its settings, was a place of safety and purity, a site we returned to as often as possible—for weekday mass, devotions, or any special function. We were like refugees, continually fleeing to this location while the rest of the world was burning around us. Even when I was suffering an episode of asthma—and perhaps particularly then—my mother would try to take me to mass. She carried me on her back, bearing me down the long avenue from the prison gates to the bus stop, like Aeneas carrying Priam from burning Troy. As I wheezed on her back, I felt the complicity between us, but I did not have the strength to break free. She bought me a special gift—there was nothing comparable for my siblings—Butler's *Lives of the Saints*, a multivolume set telling the stories of the saints from ancient martyrs to modern Catholic paragons, male and female. Where other boys got hearty annuals on sports cars and football players, my focus was directed to heroes and heroines of holiness. The actual books were large, richly bound, with heavy, creamy, thick-grain paper and ancient, inky typeface. The whole idea was that I should imagine myself between those musty pages. As always, I found myself both attracted and repelled.

six

HEAD BOY AT A CONVENT

Because of Catholicism not every English cultural setting was of evil omen. The castle that overlooked our convent school must have had its share of wretched stories, but it became for me an emblem of protection and peace. The violent histories of the Normans did not impinge on my childhood under its walls. Instead, the battlements seemed to reflect safety, as if entering the convent grounds under the gaze of the twelfth-century motte-and-bailey said my future was secured by this ancient stronghold. If I were an outlaw on the prison estate, I had tenure at Carisbrooke.

As I say, it was a private school for girls, with boys to the end of elementary. Really it was an old-fashioned upper-class arrangement where the better sort of families sent their daughters to be educated by nuns. Only a percentage of these could be Catholics. The rest were daughters of wealthy farmers, shop owners, and doctors who didn't care about religion but liked the idea of virginal women providing that hint of value-added to their girls. At my infantile level, I enjoyed the company of these well-turned-out girls: Elaine, Diana, Anne, Janet. For my elder sister, Maureen, I think it was a purgatory. We were not rich. In comparison to many pupils at the school, we were definitely poor. Maureen did not join the school at a young age like the rest of us but at a level when friendships and alliances were often well established, and she suffered among those little debutantes from the shire. On the other hand, Maureen was never part of my family gang of children. She kept herself aloof and sought her own friends. She did ultimately find them at the convent school and unsurprisingly avoided my adventures. She was seldom in my company. Just about everything about me must have been toxic in her struggle for her own identity. You can imagine how my automatic birthright would have seemed for someone who had to pull herself up without title or status. And yet I think I helped her. She sheltered in the shadow of my massive role—all the dysfunction and its desire and danger went in my direction; she was left largely in peace.

At first the nuns did not give me any special individual treatment, but that didn't matter. I was a boy and in that traditionally patriarchal setting it gave me a default sense of privilege, muted but always there. At the same time, boys were in a minority and did not stay long; a lot of them wanted to move on to other schools which weren't, in their opinion, so sissy. So, I quickly got to be one of the oldest boys in the school population. This meant I was able to take on an unofficial role as play-leader for children younger than I.

One time I found a length of rope from somewhere and tied a stout stick off on one end. Out of sight of the nuns, I slung it over a high branch of a tree and recruited a bunch of children as muscle. With the team all pulling together on the rope I gave turns to individual kids and hoisted them fifteen feet off the ground. They loved it, hanging there from their arms among the leaves and the sunshine, but they could easily have broken their legs, or worse. Finally, one of the nuns discovered us and put an abrupt stop to our circus act. Not all my escapades were successful or made me popular. On a dreary, wet day in late winter, I got a gang of boys to build a dam. A small stream had appeared in the ditch running along the top of the big field that was our playground, and it was too good an excitement to miss. After an hour of intense industry in the mud we all trooped back to our classrooms and then the teachers for the younger classes went berserk. What happened to get you all covered in filth? Your parents will be furious. What were you doing? In answer: Anthony Bartlett told us to . . . In a literal sense I had not told them to do anything, but in little-boy-speak, confronted by a towering nun, it was the only honest answer. I was hauled before the head mistress and she said, is this true? Just as certainly, confronted by Sister Francis looking for someone to blame, I denied it. I did not want to lose my status as a boy on a higher plane. No, they did it themselves.

There was a revolution: the group of boys never played with me again. But in the process, I had protected my sense of being someone of destined virtue, a feeling that had come back to me as a shock when I thought I might lose it. And it's true, little by little I was garnering a distinctive role in the convent's life. I eventually got to be the chief altar boy and leader of all the religious processions, of which there were more than a few. This ended up as something beyond being the oldest boy, a boy surrounded by a couple hundred girls in their sky-blue cardigans and checkered dresses. It became a feeling of ecstasy, of something out of this world.

    There was landscape around the convent, a kind of paradise touched by fingerprints of a Maker. The castle stood tall on its looming mound to the south. In a shivering winter's afternoon, the red ball of the sun hung close beside it, speaking of kingdoms and passions an ocean away, beyond the present frosted land. Then in springtime the trees around the field would erupt in a riot of leaf and blossom. There were elms and chestnuts whose great white-and-pink candles illuminated the air, doubling the light of the sun. Our field was a boundless pleasure garden where boys and girls danced and laughed, they too, like blossoms, drifted in the sun. Over to the right of the field beyond an avenue of trees there was a tennis court and just beyond that a narrow lawn surmounted by a bank. Here the nuns had built a grotto, a replica of the cave at Lourdes where in the story the Virgin Mary had appeared to Bernadette. It was a place of devotion with a statue in white and blue and as unremarked and easy as the trees. In the first few weeks of May the whole school would bring baskets of flowers to the grotto, daffodils, tulips, primroses, and forget-me-nots, and decorate the space in front of the statue, singing hymns in honor of the Virgin. The event was always incredibly joyful, thrilled with the scent of blossoms and the triumph of a woman.

    Later there would be a big procession to crown the queen of the May. We could carry another statue around the grounds and end up in a garden in front of a chapel where the statue was replaced on its usual plinth. Then one of the girls all dressed in white would mount a platform and place a crown on its head, a weave of baby's breath and lily-of-the-valley. One year my sister Christine was the girl who placed the crown, but it seems I was always there at the head of the procession. I carried a ceremonial cross, and beside me there were candle-bearers. And behind, a party of flower girls dressed in white dresses strewing the way with petals. By now the sun was hot, all the leaves of the hedges and trees were glossy, and the perfume of flowers was pleasure itself. Every sense was flooded with beauty, and I overdosed on it.

    And after May came June. Again, I was the leader in the procession and this time we carried a statue of the Sacred Heart and the petals the girls threw were crimson. The rose petals were warm as ever but the scent they gave off was thicker and even more dizzying than those of May. The color of the Sacred Heart was the color of blood, but the feeling was different from that of my Good Friday dream; it was one of passionate love rather than cruelty. This time the procession would end up at the chapel. It was a place of regular worship we were familiar with and one that had its own layer of mystery.

It was a pinewood structure at the far end of the convent, tucked away from the school grounds. Every Friday afternoon at the end of the week all the Catholic pupils would assemble there for the service called Benediction. The priest would take a large host consecrated during mass, the bread that was Christ's body, and mount it in a golden and glass display called a monstrance. The monstrance was placed high up on the altar, incense was offered, a couple of Latin hymns sung, and then the priest would wrap himself in a golden veil, go up to the altar, grasp the monstrance through the veil, turn around, and bless everyone with the consecrated bread. No surprise, of course, that I was one of the altar servers on these occasions. Our job was to carry the incense burner to the priest so he could make the offering, or at the proper moment fetch the golden veil and throw it over his shoulders. Playing music in the background was an old pump organ, which would wheeze into life pedaled furiously by one of the nuns. You could almost see her legs working away and it was strange to think of a nun's legs, as they normally seemed to be just independently mobile black shoes pretending to be connected to some ethereal material floating above them. It was the chapel, in fact, that brought me closest to the lives of the nuns. Listening week after week to the asthmatic organ and hearing their convent voices leading the singing, I had a dim sense of the forces that ruled their lives. Much later when I was a priest, I learned that communities of women tend to synchronize menstruation and sometimes when you went to say mass for them you could tell what time it was of the month. But back then it would have been hard for me to think of nuns actually bleeding, especially in that way. If they might provide signs of ecstasy and beauty out in the sunshine, in here where they gathered there was only the wax gleam on the pine boards, the forms of the ritual, and then something other. It was something without color or liquidity, something dark like gravity itself, something ancient, unspeakably holy and scary, not far from the terror of my dream.

Eastertide was coming. I was eleven years old and on my way to the prestigious Catholic school across the water in Portsmouth. My mother and the nuns agreed that the robes of the priesthood were looking more and more a suitable fit, and so I could be regarded as something of a little priest for the purposes of the season. The Easter Vigil is the service taking place late, close to midnight on the Saturday, celebrating the moment of Christ's resurrection before dawn. In order for the nuns to hold the service, there had to be an altar boy to assist. So, the plan was made that I should stay overnight at the convent, be there for the midnight ceremony, go back to bed, and then get up early on Sunday for the morning mass. In payment I would get a large Easter egg. Once again it was the thought of privilege that was seductive, so, embracing my role, I agreed. I was brought to the convent, fed supper, and bedded down for the two or three hours before the main event.

My bed was a cubicle in the nuns' dormitory. The dividers were white linen panels on metal frames and, in the dark, there was a dull glow from the loose sheets of white around me. I don't think I slept. And then quickly I really was terrified. At some point the nuns got the call to rise in the night for the service and I saw them all. They were lined up dressed in white ankle-length gowns with caps on their heads and carrying white jugs. Later I supposed they were going to the bathroom to pee and to empty the water from the wash basins they each had by their bed. But at that point they looked like they were dead, dressed in shrouds and lining up for some endless ritual dead people did. I had stumbled into the realm of the departed and I got that feeling of bloodlessness, as if my skin and flesh had detached themselves from the world and I was just an empty two-dimensional thing. My stomach was a knot and sick and yet I had to get up myself and go through the liturgy with the priest, the reason why I was there. I don't know how I did it, and I really have no memory of what happened. Everything was a procession of the dead. But where did that feeling come from? What exactly created it? It must have meant that my body understood at some level a great deal of the significance of what was going on. It was all about sacrificial death, my death. I certainly was not the first child to be somehow dedicated to the gods and to have had their blood drained out before their very eyes.

And yet the strangest thing happened. After the service I went back to bed, and I think I slept from exhaustion. Next morning when I got up, I still felt like hell. We did the morning mass and then the nuns provided breakfast. This was the big payoff. I got to sit at the same table with the priest, rich white linen now spread before me and covered with fine china, a sparkling silver teapot, eggs, bacon, toast, and, of course, my

Easter egg. I suppose all this did help me feel better but what really hit me was the little display of primulas and daffodils at the center. It's not possible to describe the excitement and vibrancy communicated by those flowers on that Easter Sunday morning. It was like the whole world had taken a giant leap. All the death that was inside my stomach shrank to a vanishing point, and I was alive again. It was as if in one bound, I had left the surface of the moon and I was on planet earth with the rosy dawn awakening in the human eye for the very first time. There really was no more death, no more pain. I drank in the sensation, breathed the fresh air with all my lungs. I was a child of a divine plan. No question, no big deal. This was it. Christ had risen.

If only for this, I have to thank the nuns and love them. Who knows for what reasons they endured their living death? Did any of them have stories parallel to mine? Was the world burned out for them the moment they learned to speak and understand? Were they disappointed in love? Were they fearful of love? Did any single one of them have a genuine overriding experience of God? All of these questions would be unleashed on many, many convents within ten years of that Easter. The Roman Catholic Church would go through a massive upheaval and full hurricanes would blow through those sepulchral dormitories, scattering the sheets and ripping the nuns' shifts to the four winds, leaving so many of them naked before themselves. Carisbrooke Convent was one of the first to go. But that hardly matters. While the nuns were there, they opened a space in the landscape where the deepest promises of this earth could briefly be glimpsed.

For me, Sister Moira was the best. She was tall, graceful, smart, and unemotional. She was my teacher in my final grade at the school, the year when I did the exam called the eleven-plus, which qualified someone for grammar school. I had no idea whether she liked me or not, but I had plenty of interaction with her as she often had to lean over me to show me something on a math question or sentence comprehension. She had a strong warm smell of carbolic soap coming through the black cotton of her habit. That warm smell accompanied me during the exam and helped me succeed, no doubt.

Carisbrooke came to an end, and so did the Isle of Wight. We were set to move to Portsmouth, once more across on the mainland. Before we did, however, we produced a surprising grand finale to the whole Parkhurst episode. My father's brush with TB and his return from the hospital gave birth to a daring escapade. A pilgrimage to the Catholic shrine of Lourdes in France would be a fitting act of thanksgiving, and a parallel work of penitence from my father. Another couple was recruited to share the driving, and for them it was the road trip that was the attraction. Both the cooperation and the daring involved seem amazing looking back, but the connection to my father's return from the sanatorium helps explain our French adventure. Religion, sex, and guilt are powerful motivators, and they were all involved in getting this project underway. My dad fitted out a Morris goods van with windows and extra backseats and when the summer came, we linked up with the other couple. We all set out across the Channel, four adults and four kids, plunging south through the French countryside on its long warm roads. French loaves and their great, big red tomatoes bought and eaten on the roadside were a revelation. And the smell of coffee in the morning! Lourdes itself was impressive, with its throngs of shops and hotels, its pulsing, green, sediment-rich river, the fervent devotion, hordes of beggars, and a lingering sense of nineteenth-century rural poverty as a portal of the divine. My father acquitted himself well, breaking into tears at the Grotto of the Apparition in evidence of a changed heart. I felt the force of devotion myself and, not to be outdone, I made my own grand gesture: the low-value but high-denomination French banknote that had been given to me for spending I handed over entirely to a North African woman begging with a child. She looked so much like Mary Magdalene!

The French interlude seemed somehow out of sync with everything else, opening a wider world and bringing me for the first time into contact with Latin and southern culture. It was very enjoyable and established a precedent I would follow in the rest of my life. But in the end, it made no difference to our family. A trip taken a year or so earlier provides a much more accurate portrayal of its core dynamic. My mother decided she needed a vacation away from home, choosing just me to go with her as her squire. We traveled to the east coast, to Clacton-on-Sea in Essex, staying at a boardinghouse, sitting down at a breakfast table together, walking along the front, and in the afternoon going for scones and jam in a tea shop. But the idyllic escape was marred by my getting a murderous toothache and my mother needing to find a dental office in town. A ferocious row erupted when the dentist declared it was her fault for not teaching me to brush my teeth properly. Whatever the reason the decayed tooth had to come out, and did so with unforgettable pain.

seven

TEENAGE THEOLOGIAN

We moved to Portsmouth in September of 1958. The family rented an apartment close to St. John's College, the school I was to attend. The world changed for us when we came to Portsmouth. We lost the cabin and all its open spaces. We lost the closeness of nature we had at Carisbrooke and even on the estate at Parkhurst. And I personally lost the romance of the convent and my role there. Instead, we were plunged into the anonymity of an industrial city, one of the oldest in the country, and one with a grimly real military flavor rooted in British history. The rigging of Nelson's flagship, the *Victory*, in which he defeated the French at Trafalgar, stood over the dockland and mentally over the city. All young lads were taken on field trips to see it, and even at that age we had to watch our heads to get around belowdecks and between the gunports. Our teachers reminded us with gusto at what cost of cruelty and blood British sea power was attained. At the same time the panorama of the city had anything but a victorious feel. The scars of German bombing raids were everywhere, giving off that sense of modern war and people's nerves shredded to exhaustion. A pall lay over the city (as indeed over every major industrial city in England), one that would not begin to dissipate until the Beatles broke into the charts, and even they could not lift it completely.

The reason why we came to Portsmouth was to follow the trail of my education and that was what made sense of it all. My mother enrolled me in St. John's College, a private Catholic grammar school run by a men's religious order called De La Salle Brothers. The family followed along, my father getting a job in Portsmouth Borstal, a prison for young offenders, Terence joining the elementary school attached to the college, and my sisters enrolling in yet another convent school, at the north end of town.

My mother, I'm sure, always wanted to get off the estate in Parkhurst but it was the next step in my path of formation that gave the cue. And I think we stretched things to the limit to do it. The apartment we lived in was comfortable enough, but we were there only four months, September through December. During this time my parents signed for a mortgage on a house on the north side of the city. The plan was we would take the ferry one last time to spend Christmas on the island and then return to Portsmouth, moving into our new house in the new year.

The journeys back and forth, and the lack of a permanent home, made for the bleakest of Christmases. All disposable income was used on the deposit and removers' expenses. And so, for the holiday, it was gifts of shirts and pants for school, in a temporary dwelling stripped of memory and comfort. The Christmas holiday I found more and more depressing anyhow, and especially since the previous year. It had been Christmas Eve and I was returning alone on the bus from Newport, from shopping for gifts. A harassed-looking mother, carrying a large basket and multiple bags, was getting off at the stop previous to mine: the Albany army barracks. The bus was one of the traditionally open platforms you could jump on and off, and she, cumbered as she was, launched out before it had come to a halt. She completely misjudged her step, betrayed by the weight of her purchases, and she crashed headlong. While both hands were tied and unable to save her, she struck her head directly on the concrete. The life drained from her visibly as I watched. She turned blue, her careworn face twisted in a last defeat.

And now it was one year later, temporarily returned from Portsmouth, and I was again coming back from town. It was pitch black and I was following the long prison wall I had walked under so many times before. Five meters of Dartmoor granite rose vertically from the gloom, its geological crystal glinting dully in the light from a distant streetlamp. Now as I skirted its length for a final time the threads of prehistoric mica suddenly reached up and swept the stars from the sky. The power of the distant suns was undone, and I was plunging with them into a bottomless pit. I was twelve years old, and the universe was collapsing. This was not the dance of ghostly nuns scaring a child, but the cosmos itself dying in my brain. I prayed to Jesus, a conscious desperate prayer for life, for sanity, my only hope in an infinite darkness. I said I would give my life completely to him if he saved me from this abyss. In response there was nothing, no Easter revelation, just my own footsteps one in front of the other and the prayer itself holding back the night.

After the wretched celebration, my father went to the mainland to take possession of the new house, and finally we followed on. When we arrived at our new home in a row of city houses, there was a woman sitting by the fire in the living room, like she owned the place. I'd never seen this person before, and she was introduced as a certain "Mrs. Cook." In truth she was a deranged and needy person, and I don't know how my dad fetched up with her. Apparently, she had helped clean and prepare the house, but, for sure, my dad was making a point and it wasn't lost on me. Was this going to be Dad's new live-in wife? After an hour or so my mother threw her out, and I was mightily relieved. But the situation was clear. The fault line between my mother and father was now located at the foundations of our new home.

It was 1958 and '59, my teen years were approaching, but rather than speeding up, everything settled into a dull, lifeless rhythm, one that was not going to change essentially for the next five years. My parents' relationship was fixed in an exhausted stalemate, without the fierce drama of the earlier years, but without reconciliation either. My father developed small routines of comfort. He visited the local pub, for company as much as drink. He lost himself in study of the sports pages of the newspaper and placed bets on the horses every weekend. And he did the "football pools," a weekly national competition with huge numbers of people supplying small cash stakes to predict the Saturday match results, hoping for the big payout. Every Saturday evening the BBC announcer would intone the scores for the four national divisions like a solemn working-class liturgy. My father would tick off his guesses, looking for the elusive amount of eight correct results, the minimum for a prize. He never won more than a few shillings, but really that wasn't fully the point.

My mother kept house, kept distance from her neighbors, and kept her children in the orbit of her church, her tradition, and her own personal sense of culture. Although it was official schooling that had dictated our move, she possessed her own sense of learning, especially literature and poetry, and she shared it continually with all her daughters and sons. She read the contemporary Catholic authors, Chesterton and Belloc, but she also knew and spoke of Swift, Shaw, and Wilde, the poetry of Byron, Walter Scott, Robbie Burns, and Yeats, the novels of the Brontës, Dickens, Mark Twain, and the plays of Eugene O'Neill and Terence Rattigan. The Irish trend is not hard to spot, and her own words could be beautiful in their own right. Sometimes she would fill the house with them. But far too often they were harsh and angry. All the physical poetry of the Carisbrooke landscape, and the childhood odyssey of Parkhurst and Thorness, all that disappeared, and all that was left was the angry fortress of our house and the potent words that reigned within it. Inside this cultural bunker I was like one of those dogs held in the yard by an invisible fence: the world beyond would always have the taste of a sharp toxic shock in comparison with the domain of the home and the words that circumscribed it. If I was in any way to engage with the outside, it would have to be on paths built and approved by the church; everything else would carry a kind of nervous electrocution.

In my first year at St. John's our form teacher, a man rejoicing in the name of Brother Dennis Mary, always covered the first period, a class devoted to religious education. Our topic was the Sermon on the Mount and he read it to us in its entirety, commenting as he went along. I don't remember a thing he said but the words from Matthew's Gospel detonated in my head like a galaxy in space. If my prayer in the darkness beneath the prison walls was not answered directly, within months it was answered in my classroom. Listening to and reading those words I could see and taste the sky over Galilee. It was literally as if someone had turned on the light of the sun and the switch was the language of this man. I must have heard some of it before in church, but there it had been lost in a world of religion. Now rather his words were direct, focused, earthy, and crammed with life.

I wondered how anyone could dare to speak like that, with such authority, such passion, and at the same time with acute sensitivity and beauty. It's only much later that I ask myself a follow-up question: How could mere written-down words—the actual physical words by which the whole thing is reported in the Gospel of Matthew—carry the message anyway? What is the mechanism by which they have their contemporary effect? Unless I want to spiritualize everything, I have to say there is a function hidden in words or signs themselves. It is mysterious and hard to trace, but it is real and human, and the gospel mobilizes this function so that it transforms the world. The gospel casts its net of words over humanity and draws it, together with all its historical junk, into an entirely new place, a new world of meaning that is itself the making of a new earth. But I digress.

Back when I was twelve, I recognized only the effect, and did not analyze the means. But it was the major learning experience of my whole time at high school, coming right at the beginning, and more impactful than anything I learned in grammar, math, physics, geography, history, or literature. I did well enough in these subjects. I regularly brought home the glowing red tickets among the different colored "testimonials" distributed at the end of each week—white for fail, through green and blue, up to red for hot stuff. But no teacher and no subject ever grabbed me the way that first class on the chapters from Matthew's Gospel did. I learned most of them by heart and wrote them all straight back down again in the end-of-year exam. Dennis Mary commented on the exam paper that since I had delivered to him verbatim the words of the Lord, he had little choice but to give me a straight A.

Really, I had started down the road of theology and it's perhaps less of a surprise, therefore, that I did write some actual theology later in the summer of that year, although it was prompted by the promise of a free trip to Italy and Rome and another foray across the Channel. There was a competition posted on the school notice board inviting essay submissions on a religious topic, one of which was the Virgin Mary. I went to a local church library, got a pamphlet out on the Immaculate Conception, and then more or less put down in my own words what I'd read there. I can't remember exactly what I said but I know it gave me a feeling of a kind of logic I had managed to grasp and successfully repeat. I wrote the essay in the summer break, visiting the school on a deserted afternoon to check the entry requirements. Then in January the headmaster came to our class to make an announcement. Brother Edwin was tall, thin, and seemed to harbor a deep sadness; he was rumored to have survived a Japanese prison camp. He said it was a pleasure to come to a class to celebrate something nice rather than address a problem; then he announced I had won the essay competition. It felt like destiny: I was going to Rome, Rome of the martyrs, in Italy of the Romans. And Rome and Italy being all these things, and so many others too, which I did not know at the time, how could it not end up as destiny?

I traveled that Easter with a group of youth from a London parish, a teenage pilgrimage with chaperones and leaders. I'd never met these people before, but I got on well enough and really had a lot of fun. In its way this was my major teenage experience, happening like the educational one, right at the beginning, but ending almost as soon as it happened. Taking the train through France and across the Alps to Italy was like suddenly overcoming a chronic illness. As described, the year earlier the family had gone on a road trip to France, and although that had its own sense of adventure, everything was shaped by my mother and her overall religious purpose. Here for the first time a different world really did unfold, especially when we crossed the Alps. We awoke in the morning after a long night rattling through the tunnels, feeling the hard thump as we changed engines at the mountain stations. Now there were strange cries and at once a feeling of life already going on. We rushed to the windows and the southern light filled our eyes. For someone from northern Europe there's nothing to compare to that first taste of a Mediterranean world. The mountains are brown where before they were snow covered, and the air is fragrant where before it was sharp. The fruit and juice vendors thrust their wares into the open windows in a direct, uncomplicated way. The eucalyptus and plane trees seem culturally older and more at home with humans than the wilder oaks and pines of the north. I have taken the same train a dozen times since my first trip, and that morning stop south of the mountains always has the same electric effect.

And the feeling got only stronger the further south we went. At first the train hugs the coast, and you can see the houses standing right on the shoreline in their pale blues and pinks, and there are kids and dogs playing in the yards. Then as the terrain flattens it becomes farmland and there are cream-walled farmhouses with red ridge tile roofs and sentinel trees. The surrounding vineyards seem to breathe the air in and out, giving it a sensuous liquid quality. It's as if the first kiss was discovered here and has been going on ever since. I stood enchanted at the window and could not pull myself away. I drank in the sensations, trying to remember everything I was seeing and feeling. I had left behind a world steel bound in a history of wrong, and now suddenly I found myself in one that clasped me, and everyone, in free, passionate embrace.

In Rome we stayed in a convent guesthouse. Nothing like our convent at Carisbrooke, its terrazzo floors and walls and faint sweet smell of herbs made it seem like a palace. We visited the usual tourist spots, catacombs, basilicas, Vatican Museum, Sistine Chapel. Here Catholicism was vivid, its blood had become art: Raphael and Michelangelo. These men, I marveled at them; they seemed to be sent directly by God to put eternal truth on canvas. At the Easter Vigil we lit the fire of resurrection in the backyard of the convent, and the flames glittered and rolled with primal energy. Easter morning came and we were at St. Peter's to see Pope John XXIII carried into his great church on a shoulder-high chair flanked by Swiss Guards and ostrich feathers. After the mass we went out into the piazza to await the blessing in multiple languages. As it happened, my sister Maureen had signed up for her own school pilgrimage before I was given the prize, so she too was in Rome that morning. I knew that she would be in the piazza so I set out to look for her. It didn't take long to spot the group of schoolgirls in their green blazers and boaters. Was she pleased to see me? I'm not sure, but I was proud to have found her in a crowd of fifty thousand. But then again, I had no doubt I would. St. Peter's Square belonged to me, its sunshine, its colonnades, and the pope speaking to everyone. Here was what I was born for. Those ancient pilgrim-worn stones would lead me straight to her and straight back again to my group.

We took a bus trip to Assisi and saw the Apennine hills against the cobalt blue sky. We stopped at a restaurant with a spectacular view over the plain. To celebrate Francis's taming of the wolf they had captured a red fox and placed it in a rough cage set up under an oak tree. The animal ran back and forth frantically in a four-foot space and there was something terrible and true about the scene in the hot afternoon. I was discovering what so many English writers have felt and made use of—the closeness of cruelty and blood to the southern surface, unlike its more distant and mechanical northern forms. It was the opposite of what Francis had done, but the harsh contradiction still somehow made sense. The suffering of that animal remains emblazoned on my memory.

I had gotten to know some of the older teenagers and been accepted into their group. When the time came for the return trip, I traveled with them in their compartment and left the chaperones in theirs. There were six of us. The leader of the pack was a guy funnily enough called Peter. He was a Teddy Boy, with the high, slicked-back hair and the dangling quiff in front. He wore drainpipe pants, an open neck shirt, and a fancy waistcoat. I'm not sure if he was all that good looking or it was just there was no competition, but he had a chin plentiful with pimples and stubble and a girl permanently on each arm. As the train worked its way up the leg of Italy and we got ready for the nighttime crossing of the Alps, a clear pattern evolved. He sat on the opposite couch and one of the girls kissed and petted him with unflagging zeal while the other one sat there patiently, waiting for his possible attentions, with his free arm draped over her. On the couch on my side there was another girl called Jean. Obviously, there was no free space to get involved with making Peter happy, but she was not to be abashed. She recruited me to her right hand and another boy about my age to the left, and she put an arm around each of us and bestowed her kisses in a mirror image of Peter and his nymphs. The only difference I think was she kissed me and the other boy with impartial devotion, without the preference Peter seemed to show. I was thirteen years old, and this was Italy. The passionate feeling that had been outside the carriage on the way down had joined us on the inside for the journey up. Jean was well formed, warm lipped, and confident, and I think that was the most erotic twenty hours of my entire life. I was not sexually mature, but I had enough going on to spend the whole trip, all the way up through France, floating in a dense fog of pleasure. A lot of the time I had my eyes closed, pretending I was asleep, scared less I seemed too interested and Jean's generous attentions would dry up. But they didn't, and I can almost smell the feminine narcotic of that railway carriage to this day. When we reached the ferry to take us across the English Channel, I felt a cold wind buffeting me back to reality. All the same I was still staggering when we said our goodbyes on Victoria station in London and I rejoined my family who were there waiting for me. I knew I was never going to see any of those kids again and my only thought was to win another competition so I could go on another trip just like that.

But I never did. How true it is, you never step in the same river twice. After that trip, and the writing of theology before it, nothing really creative or life giving—nothing really Easter-like—happened to me for another fourteen years; not in fact until I returned to Rome in 1974. My life was now vacuum packed, sealed, set aside for its single purposed goal—to be ordained a priest. Going to school at St. John's College was in its own way a form of seminary education and it closed around me as intimately as the airless atmosphere of home. None of its activities meant much to me; everything was achieved in the single passage it supplied, the one toward priesthood.

Back home normal routine reasserted itself, and with a vengeance. There was nothing else but school and home, and more home than school. I continued to suffer from asthma and miss long stretches of attendance. I didn't play sports—a combination of asthma, lack of strength, and fuzzy timing on the ball. So, I was rarely in the company of other boys apart from the actual school term. Our little gang—I and my younger siblings—continued to play, but not with the same conviction; or perhaps sometimes with too much. I did some crazy things in our narrow backyard, buying an air rifle and shooting at starlings in the neighbors' trees. Fascinated by chemistry that blew things up I even made an experimental explosive, using store-bought fertilizer and narrowly missing my sister's head with a chunk of shrapnel. I frightened even myself with this event and stopped my experiments. Neighborhood kids, of course, got to notice us and once again me and my brother got picked on because we attended a school different from the local one. There were obscene gestures, names called, and offers to fight that could not be backed away from. I maintained my honor as best I could, then after a while, just as before, we were generally left alone.

It's impossible to overstate the endless boredom and lassitude that took over the house in some of that time: long January evenings staring at the pictures in Christmas comic book annuals; vacant summer afternoons running out of things to do in the confines of the home, lacking pastimes on the outside. In comparison, our time on the Isle of Wight was filled with drama, romance, meaning. Portsmouth instead was a dead end where we were completely separated from local kids and their lives. And my school, of course, was boys only, without the relational stimulus and interest of girls. Once a school friend came to the door and invited me to go and play tennis. He said it would be good for getting to know girls. Aside from fear of not being able to hold a racquet with any strength, the invitation seemed to come from a world where I just did not belong, tennis whites, membership clubs, people with socially appropriate parents. I refused, leaving him standing at the door, ducking back inside with my existential shame.

Everything for me was on hold, looking only to the day I would join a body that would immediately be able to provide the true world I lacked. I would become part of something concrete and important, the church, in which all the missing reality of my life would descend and fit around me like a glove.

By the same token, the speculative side of me ran unchecked. During the many weeks when I had asthma and stayed at home, my mother and I had shared a little routine. After my brother and sisters left for school, I would wheeze down from my bedroom to sit by the fire. She would tidy away the breakfast things, make herself tea, and then bring in the day's newspaper to read it together. We'd comment on the latest news and gossip, the British loss of colonies in Africa or the scandals surrounding Princess Margaret, that kind of thing. We couldn't wait to begin talking down the hypocrisy and small-mindedness of the British establishment and the arrogance and decay of their empire.

While my mother provided me with much of the information, my role was to summarize it in conceptual formulae, to achieve that lofty moral reason that struck the knell of a regime and culture whose time was up. There was certainly something of "shocking the bourgeoisie" in my attitude, a militant sense of superiority to all that was small-minded, Victorian, and phony. I don't know where I got it from; I had certainly never heard of the French Decadent poets, but Wilde, and Shaw, and Chesterton, for sure. And, then politically, Hitler's denunciations of the English as a "nation of shopkeepers"—which my mother liked to repeat—clung to the clouds above our house, along, of course, with the Soviet Union's contempt for all Western culture and institutions. The twentieth century's revolutionary and ideological enemies of England were all on our side and, without doubt, I bathed in their metaphysical absolutes. Most of all, however, it had to be the Irish Catholic homegrown rebellion against Protestant untruth that nourished my righteous thought. The cruel falsehoods of the latter could never be pilloried enough.

The abstract practice had a huge effect on my writing, which did not go unremarked. It skewed my sentences into long clausal and adjectival affairs, which sought to trap the universe in a sentence. Some of the brothers who taught me couldn't believe I actually wrote what I wrote, and in my first or second year one young up-and-coming teacher with a killer instinct took me aside to try and prove I'd been coached. I used the same lofty attitude on him, and he retired angry and frustrated. Later, when they had gotten more used to me, my teachers said I wrote like a Latin writer and chided me on lacking a common touch. I rejoiced in the criticism because it meant, as I saw it, the absurdity and pettiness of their world had been shown up by my classic usage. But, no doubt, the brothers were right to suspect my approach: I was practicing an otherworldly literary snobbism, far too high and holy for this world. I did have some defenders, however, and was once or twice given English prizes. I think at one point the school even included one of my metaphysical rants in the school magazine, but it was so painful to most I was not asked again.

Meanwhile, the one social constant in our lives was priests, connections with them and to them. There was always a parish priest or curate to think about, talk about, and sometime get a visit from. They had the role of angels flying close by us, sharing their proximity to God; but then, shockingly, some of those angels flew a little too close for comfort. There was one, a Father Clare, who used to visit us, sent by his order to raise funds and promote its special spirit and devotions. He always arrived in a massive vintage car, a wonderful beast, with a flexible hood and imposing hunter-green-and-red coachwork, gleaming chrome, and barely touched bright green leather upholstery: a Lancia or Bentley or something insane like that. The Riviera conveyance must have looked highly incongruous outside our plastered cottage under the prison walls, but that was the point. My mother treated him like royalty, making piles of carefully cut egg sandwiches, jam tarts, moist currant buns, and lashings of tea. He used to hand out little "holy cards," especially to my brother and me, encouraging us to keep the devotion to the saint depicted. It was a young nineteenth-century Italian boy, thin and wan, in a jacket and yellow waistcoat, with pale light shining from around his head. He was a model of purity and piety, and I always felt my chest constricting asthmatically when I looked at the image. Father Clare himself was nothing like him, corpulent in his clerical black, with a puffy cherubic face above his collar and a shock of white patriarchal hair. He would overawe us children, taking my younger four-year-old sister on his knee and fondling her in a way that was definitely not fatherly. I thought, "That's wrong, he shouldn't be doing that." But at the same time a hapless collusion was set up. "But it's Father Clare, and, look, he does exactly what he likes!" And for sure, my mother was in the kitchen, blissfully preparing sandwiches, distantly colluding herself. Nothing was ever said.

My mother was not quite so passive later when something happened to my older sister, now a teen. Maureen herself told me of the circumstances. She said the parish priest in a parish we used to attend cornered her in the sacristy. He pushed her up against one of the big armoires where they kept the vestments and pressed himself against her. She was able to make her escape, but not before her sense of safety and trust were deeply violated. Our mother moved us from that parish to another, abruptly and without explanation. It was only when Maureen told me of this event that an explanation fell into place. I somehow feel that our status as a sacrificially surrendered Catholic family made us vulnerable to these episodes.

As adolescence went on there were situations with more usual occasions of youthful sexual experience. Catholic youth clubs were acceptable and when they offered dances for young people I went. Out of this I was able to date girls once or twice. I even got to kiss and cuddle a little, but there was always something unconvincing about it. I was young and few relationships are serious at that time of life anyway, but I was also refraining from being serious at a much more fundamental level than the average teenager. I think the word went around fairly quickly that I was just skipping stones, and girls fairly soon lost interest. By that point, my connection to most things was purely speculative. I was working on borrowed time, and sex, no matter its fascination, was just skin deep, and even less, compared to the one real center of gravity in my life.

I was orbiting that dark well in ever-decreasing circles. I had a best friend at school, a boy called Terry O'Reilly. Apart from the certified Irishness of his name he always had the top grades in the class, and we became best of pals, hanging out together during break times and on bus rides home. When an advertisement appeared on the school noticeboard publicizing what was called a "holiday retreat" to think about the priesthood, out of the blue he suggested we go. I'd seen the advert earlier and avoided it. Then when he called my attention to it and said we should send our names in, I felt the voice of destiny in my ear; and the circle of my orbit suddenly shrank to within a few feet. Terry wasn't interested in the priesthood, just the holiday, but I knew where this was leading. What could I do but agree?

The group that had sent the advert to the school was a religious order with a choice location right on the south coast of England, an ideal spot for young lads to swim, hike, play sports, have a good time, and possibly think about a divine calling. Terry and I went that summer, but it was I who carried with me the stated wish to become a priest. Around this time my sister, Maureen, asked me why I didn't want to join the Jesuits. I told her the Jesuits put me off with their history of power and influence, and underneath I think I was terrified by what I felt was a reputation for forming people in a lifelong metal jacket. The order that offered the retreat was small, with a goal of preaching and spreading the gospel, and by using, as they said it, a flexible approach. I think I believed it would allow me to express myself ultimately with a freedom for which, deep down, I longed. The man who led the retreat was an American priest by the name of Joe, and when it came to my end-of-week interview he leaned across the table and told me I would make a great addition to his religious congregation. That, more or less, did it. I was theirs.

This was my fifteenth year, and I went back for the same summer retreat the two following years, including the year that I joined up. Somewhere at this point of my mid-teens Maureen herself left home to enter a convent as a trainee nun. It was a bit of a shock as she had never mentioned that kind of thing before. We were walking along Chichester Road, the route we always took from our house to where the buses passed. I asked her why she was doing this. She answered as if she was spitting a very bad taste out of her mouth: "Why would anyone want to stay here?" I don't know if my mother expected the turn of events, but she was immensely happy and proud when it happened. Maureen joined the convent, but then about ten years later she left. My mother could not accept it and treated Maureen like a piece of chipped tableware, never the same good quality as before: but that's another story. We used to go visit Maureen in her convent in South London, always a special occasion for my mother who got a tremendous amount of affirmation from the Mother Superior and the older nuns. But it was probably the most incestuous moment of our whole family history, with everyone playing a part inside a collective maternal dream. The only thing that carried us forward was time.

My own sense of the fast-approaching date with destiny led me to disconnect from the urgency of school and study. The enormous gravity of my future planet was pulling me, and everything in me, toward itself, and nothing would stop it. There was nothing for me to contribute, so I stopped studying and concentrated on experiencing as much of life as I could this side of my imminent plunge to my priestly fate. I took jobs in cafes washing dishes, in a funfair ticketing rides, in a dance hall picking up glasses. I hung out with fellow teens, listened to Manfred Mann, the Dave Clark Five, the Beatles, the Stones. I tried to dress sharp, went to the movies, and checked out the girls on the seafront esplanade. But the crushing weight of planet X made everything else simply an exercise in going through the motions.

In the springtime of my last year, I paid a visit to the order's junior seminary to meet some of the other young men who would be beginning novitiate with me. It was fun, but also a strain, halfway between letting them know what a cool guy I was and a first real encounter with the separate inner world of the order. When the visit was over I returned home on a suburban train, halting at a dozen commuter stops on the way back to London. Drained of nervous energy I drifted between sleep and a strange, altered perception of everything around me. The small carriage crawled down the line, throbbing with an idiotic excess of heat and noise. The people, exhausted by their lives, bore it indifferently, slumped in their seats, or staggering off at their stations. They seemed intensely unreal, mere vibrations, ropes of fractured air. The whole universe was now two-dimensional, and I felt the absolutely futility of every human life. I think I was at the borderline of two worlds and indeed of my own mind. My weak grasp on ordinary human existence had been broken and my new existence was not yet fully mine. I and everything else seemed like flies buzzing against an infinite glass with nothing on the other side. Scared for my mind and my soul I hung on desperately until I could get back to the relative safety of my family.

In the summer I heard other young men talking of going off to college, getting jobs, beginning pension plans. I was horrified. The gap between me and them was unbridgeable. My mother bought the traveling trunk I was to take to the novitiate, huge, ribbed, like a coffin. It really did feel like the kind of thing they would do for a boy Pharaoh being sealed up in his pyramid. We went to the railway station, the porter stowed the trunk in the guards' van, and we made our farewells. I was fulfilling my scripted role, "going away" to seminary. Yet while I felt trepidation, and faintly sick, I did not feel loss. Even if my life was set up this way it was what I also truly wanted and needed. Joining a religious order was my pathway to life and I had to grasp it with my whole being. I knew that even if I was playing a role, I would play it to the hilt, and ultimately it would lead me to my destiny, whatever that would be. God was guarantor of the deal, so ultimately there was no way I could fail. For sure I saw that in quite traditional terms, even possibly of sainthood! But, deep down, the mechanism remained a deal, so gauging by what I was putting in—everything—it was certain, whatever the plot, I would come out the hero.

So now, before I depart on that train, a final scene to wonder at. It's not long before I go and it's a weekday morning mass, before school, an occasion when sometimes I would accompany my mother. I feel worthy doing this, yet after a certain point patience runs thin. The mass ends, and my mother makes her devotions, but these do not finish in the pews. Once her prayer there is done, there is the lighting of candles before the statues of the Virgin Mary, of Saint Anthony, perhaps for the Holy Souls, and then the greatest relish kept for last, prayer before the pietà of the Sorrowful Mother. This is a full-size plaster image of the Virgin Mary with the dead Christ spread across Mary's knees. I always dread this. It fills me with unease and suspicion. I know there is something unhealthy about it, but I cannot say what. She kneels on the greasy crimson kneeler, her face taking on a look of horrible harsh collusion. It is necessary this son die and suffer brutally in the process. She reaches out to touch a painted shoulder, lingering sensuously over the contours of the image. The desire and libido are evident, but it has to do with the dead, not the living. I stand there willing her desperately to withdraw her hand, wanting her to come back to the realm of life. She must know my revulsion, but she keeps it up, even perhaps for that reason, to hex me into her world of death. At last, reluctantly, she lets go, slowly, lingeringly, removing her hand as if from the grasp of a lover, playing out these pleasures with a molded block of chalk. We walk out of the church into the fresh air. But that was not Jesus she was touching in her caress. No way. He would not have allowed it. It is her deceased brother James she was embracing, for sure, her sixteen-year-old beloved, done to death in dark circumstances involving a father's righteous rage.

My mother had many very admirable qualities. She was smart, courageous, hardworking, undaunted. When she was in a good mood she could fill the house with song, laughter, life, and love. The fact that God, hell, and the devil were the most frequent words in her lexicon had little to do with free choices and everything to do with the world into which she had been conceived. If she detonated like a bomb in my life—just one of all the splendid bombs invented in our time—there was something that I also picked up around her that would continue to lead me on the road where in the end all violence is overcome. In the last hours of her life when she had to face those demons that had haunted her throughout, I am sure she did so with her courage undimmed. My hope is that the sunlight of a soul-changing compassion would have broken through the habitual dark clouds and melted her true but unhappy heart even as she breathed her last.

eight

LUCRETIUS

I ARRIVED AT THE Claretian major seminary from novitiate in the summer of 1965, and the revolution was in full swing. I was like a man carrying a diploma everyone wanted to tear up on the spot. For my part, I was not about to throw it in the trash. It was still the only thing that made sense of my life, and I was pigheaded enough to want to defend it. There was a conservative cardinal in Rome named Ottaviani, notorious for blocking changes proposed by the reforming pope, John XXIII. A little to my own surprise, I was given his name as a nickname. One of the priests spoke it to my face. This man, Father Dennis, was one of the representatives of the order who had recruited me. He had conducted the holiday retreats I had taken part in and also visited my home in Portsmouth, charming my mother and encouraging me to remain committed while I finished high school. As it turned out, he would be one of the many priests to leave the order in those years of the '60s (he joined a diocese in America, I believe). I did not regard myself as a power-loving Vatican cardinal; I felt I was very much one of the people. But I also wanted there to be some recognizable ideology and mode of life with which I could identify and negotiate.

The place where the seminary was located was in fact the same setting where the holiday retreats had been held: Highcliffe Castle. I'd enjoyed it well enough during those first visits. I remembered it having a faintly happy smell, like a beach camp—salt air, sweaty washrooms, fresh milk, bread, and margarine served for breakfast. But I learned to hate it with a loathing I've never experienced for any other location in my life. It came to represent the end of my illusions, and even something more than that. It became a disaster, a sinister ruin in both a physical and spiritual sense, as close to a place of evil as anywhere I would encounter.

There were seventeen students (including Chris, Phil, and me, newly arrived), plus one Spanish seminarian. We still wore our long cassocks, black frocks that made us look like a bevy of giant crows when we came together in a cluster. We did this every morning, after the first study period, when we made our way to the end of the corridor to the area outside of the prefect of students' office. He would come out, stand on the bottom step of the stairs, which led up to the priests' rooms, and distribute the mail that came in that morning. There was a special buzz about these musters, with lots of joshing and bantering, and the feeling of excitement centered particularly around this man. His name was Peter, affectionately known as "Wacker." A Liverpudlian of simple habits and sincere belief, he demonstrated alternating layers of dourness and gentleness. He had been called on to take the job of prefect after the student body had refused outright to accept the authority of the previous priest in charge. Wacker's clear remit was to be progressive and apply a looser rein where the man before had been rigid and inclined to the bit. Wacker, in fact, was someone who would play the role of religious superior for almost all my time in the order. The other man, the prefect before Wacker, was named Michael. I always felt a sneaking sympathy for Michael's story and a decade later he would become my best friend in the order.

Michael was a stick-thin asthmatic Dubliner mocked for his reedy, nasal voice, prudish attitude, and (initially) slightly pompous manner. He addressed the students as "gentlemen," pricking his thumb and forefingers together to make his points, and one of the key things he insisted on—very much like Steve with Dan in the parish—was the timetable. Under Michael's command it was essential that students restrict themselves to bedtime silence directly after night prayer, which could have been as early as nine-thirty. A story told about Michael was the occasion when one student had asked, and received permission, to go and retrieve something after night prayers, and in the process had to pass in front of the door of the prefect's office. It was a pretext to fool him. Instead of the sole student walking by, three students marched in unison by the office, spooned front to back like a comedy troop. I do not know the intended destination of the brotherly procession, but it entered the lore of Michael's failed term in office, causing sidesplitting merriment whenever it was recounted. Another chestnut was his use of a piece of cardboard held in front of the TV screen when anything salacious appeared during the permitted times of viewing. It usually happened in the course of the immensely popular Sunday evening show *Sunday Night at the London Palladium*, especially when the Tiller Girls opened the program. Michael's cardboard shielded the innocent eyes of the seminarians during the girls' pulse-rousing routine.

The crisis came to a head when Michael sent the student body to bed at an offensively early hour one midsummer's night. As I said, the time could have been as soon as nine-thirty, or even before, because the complaint was the sky was still light and the calls and laughter of the young people still on the beach below drifted in through the open windows of the dormitories. A howl of protest exploded from the seminarians, addressed to the provincial superior, Dan. Probably because he sympathized from his personal experience, he and his council dismissed Michael. By the Christmas prior to my arrival, Michael had been replaced by Wacker. Wacker was therefore a minister for change. He was the government in a time of revolution, and had the near impossible task of giving the forces of rebellion their head without letting them destroy the whole enterprise. Ultimately, Wacker found the path of least resistance was the easiest. If freedom was what people demanded, then who was he to stand in the way? He let things run their course, and the rest was up to the inscrutable counsels of God.

To understand the drama of Highcliffe you have to visualize the place. At its most westward point, the same island where I lived as a boy, the Isle of Wight, tapers off into three jagged rocks known as the Needles. The Solent comes to an end there, the sun-splashed channel where the upper classes held their annual sailing regatta, a stretch of water that would mesmerize me when earlier I gazed out from the island shore. I did not know it at the time but across on the opposite coast, past the headland to the west, stood Highcliffe Castle, my someday home. More than a stately house it was a nineteenth-century fantasy, an exquisite architectural romance made of polished Purbeck limestone. Preening on the cliffs over the sparkling sea, its pillars gazed at their mirror reflection in the chalk bluffs just across the strait. It was conceived by a British aristocrat, purchasing and rebuilding a property once belonging to his ancestors. He ferried French medieval stained glass and carved stone across the English Channel in barges, and a great oriel window from a noble house in Normandy. The window had belonged to a room where the father of a king had died, and for that slender reason it was known as the "king's window." A parapet running along the top of the central section, connecting the two wings of the building, consisted of a huge pediment of carved stone letters expressing a perfectly pagan notion. It was a quotation from the Epicurean Lucretius, in classic Latin, from his *De rerum natura*, "On the Nature of Things." It ran: "How sweet it is during a storm to look out from the safety of the land at the desperate struggles of those at sea." The mood that gave birth to this place, and still lingered on its walls, was the "nature of things," effete, victimizing, cruel, and little by little during the year I lived there it left its barb in me.

Not many years previously the order had purchased the place at a bargain price from a businessman who had acquired the estate from the original family. The bold capture of the castle was to provide a base for the order's triumphant further growth in England. But to staff the place adequately with professors, while paying for its upkeep and running costs, would always be a challenge, without taking into account the revolution that was weakening the order within. The year I joined the seminary at the castle was to be its last. By the end of the following summer the whole seminary moved entirely to Oxfordshire, attaching itself to a Jesuit-run college for the purposes of education. This proved, in fact, a great boon to me, offering a genuine academic setting. However, my first and final year at the order's own major seminary would be an experience of unparalleled collapse.

At Backwell, the novitiate house, I still had about me my teenage years, my recent time in the world of weekend and summer jobs. I went on a date with a pretty girl with whom I shared the work of the pot sink at Southsea ballroom. We met a bunch of her friends who were "rockers." She proudly told me afterward they would have beaten the tar out of me if I hadn't been wearing jeans. But none of it counted for a thing there among the older seminarians at Highcliffe and in the subtly gay ethos that almost unconsciously controlled the place. The unconscious bit was mostly as far as I was concerned, for as I remember it now, there were multiple hints of the reality of this ethos. It was my fierce need to affirm the traditional "spiritual" identity of the religious order that, instead, masked it from me.

Something that should perhaps have disembarrassed me more than anything was the treatment meted out to one particular individual. His name was John. A seminarian in his final year, not long to go before ordination, he was universally despised and mocked. On one occasion, I saw him physically attacked and tumbled to the ground, but mostly it was constant ridicule behind his back and to his face. He had a slight speech defect, slurring and splashing his words, going too fast. He also did the worst thing any scapegoat can do, which is to talk back at his tormentors in ways that never shut them down and only gave further excuse to sneer. But he was intelligent, eager to work as a priest, and actually a very good guy. So why was he so loathed? I did not understand it at the time, but I believe now it was because he was overly emotional and sentimental about women. His mother was devout and effusive and claimed a public role in his life: there was a lot of obvious transfer going on, but as evident emotional relationship it was far from any kind of repression. Once ordained he quickly became unorthodox and hung out in a hippy-style commune. Then he moved to Australia and got married. These two things were clear: he liked women, and he was definitely not part of the in-crowd at Highcliffe.

I continued with my determination to be first at prayers and longest at devotions, but very soon I understood it got me nowhere. No one cared! Not long into the first semester we began regular community meetings discussing the content and structure of our daily life. This was in response to the Second Vatican Council's call that we renew our religious community in the spirit of the order's origins, and in relation to our contemporary culture and time. It was the second principle that energized the discussions, far and away outstripping the first. Who really understood what motivated a group of patriotic Spanish churchmen in the middle of the nineteenth century? In comparison, everyone had a vibrant sense of what was happening all around us in the '60s, the huge upwelling of freedom and selfhood in that era. Out of that tempest of life arose a dominant principle of the self-determining, monadic individual.

In meeting after meeting, retreat day after retreat day, the voices for change chipped away at the distinctive collective structure of religious life, until literally nothing was left. The person appointed to call everyone to rise was one of the first things to go, to be replaced by alarm clocks. Regular TV watching was introduced, and the time and space allowed for it gradually extended. Obligation to timetable, including common prayer time, was progressively slackened. The practice of doing silent meditation in common disappeared, and spiritual reading at meals went the same way. Ultimately it was entirely possible for individuals never to show up for community prayer and not be thought in any way derelict. All of this didn't happen at once, of course; it took a few years. And it was not that anyone was negating the community entirely. No, the community provided a setting, a club, a camaraderie in which individuals found affirmation. But what could possibly be the cement holding a bunch of individual guys together once any collective form of spiritual practice was gone?

I repeat, nothing happened all at once, but I am someone who picks up quickly on first principles, and I found myself taking positions against majority opinion on just about every decision: on the timetable, prayer times, and even the morning wake-up call. I did not have the knowledge or language to make good arguments, and I was often tongue tied and clumsy, but that did not stop my trying. Hence my reputation as an Ottaviani. Little by little I began to understand the futility of my position and, as I did, I retreated into myself. Slowly and painfully, I sought to carve out a new persona, but there was no material for the sculpture, just thin air.

One early morning, covered in shame, I took my cilice down the cliff steps, down to the sand and the beating surf. With a pair of wire cutters I chopped the instrument of torture into a dozen fragments and threw them, pieces by piece, as far as I could into the ocean. I wanted to prevent any future researcher dredging it up and pondering what on earth was its foul purpose.

I threw myself into my studies, leftover duties from high school. There I'd taken three A levels and passed in only one. I'd done very little study in preparation, and now I felt the need to reverse the situation that had been humiliating. Plus, study was a pathway entirely separate from the community; it would serve in my emerging, deep plan to succeed in the world of Christian religion entirely by myself. I would work hard in whatever was given to me and then one day people would recognize my value and I would be proven right. I studied for A levels in English literature and Latin, and also worked for two lesser exams in Spanish and logic.

Weeks and months wore on. Christmas came and we had a more relaxed schedule, with private morning prayer and not so many study hours. Free time for me was divided between reading Jane Austen and listening to the Rolling Stones. I did not have close friendships, but I joined in the festive mood as well as I could. Chris and Phil were much more part of the in-crowd, taken under the wing of a particularly dominant personality named Matt. Matt was one who led the charge for change, a powerful and decisive voice. There was an unbridgeable chasm between myself and this man. I knew he saw me as playing the martyr. Yet I half wanted his approval, even as the other half hated his overweening influence. These days, when I look back on that time, it's the impact of this individual on my life I resent the most—a depressing, corrosive effect, dismantling my sense of the world and my place in it. But in the last analysis I also believe I must be grateful to him. I was in a cocoon, one stitched around me by quite particular family circumstances, and one from which I would surely never have emerged if the way of things had remained unchanged. It's conceivable that I could have grown into a rule-bound hypocrite, with destructive behaviors in parallel. Because of Matt's impact I was forced to begin to reevaluate everything and engage in a process of rethinking that went to the roots of my being. Matt was the phenomenon of the Vatican Council rendered personal and overwhelming for me. There were other factors too, obviously, but none more direct and forceful than him. It's fitting, therefore, that when I finally came to leave the order, it was on Matt's watch, when he had finally emerged as the provincial superior. He tried desperately to stop me, but the process he set underway in me had by that time gone far beyond anything he was able to call back. He had released the genie from its bottle!

In the meantime, however, my personal identity was invested entirely within the given structures of religious life in the Roman Catholic Church. I was in the horrible situation of hanging on to the shreds of a chaotic organization in order that one day, magically, it would somehow deliver my true self in the world.

Pop music was an interest we all had in common. I developed a liking for Bob Dylan. Amazingly it was my mother who told me about him. During a family visit in the fall, she fished out of the car a vinyl of *Bringing It All Back Home*, holding it up and telling me I really needed to listen to this. I was astonished at her invitation to embrace something in the outside world, but after all it was the '60s and she too had caught Dylan's poetic intensity. And the moment I saw the album's cover, smelled its cool don't-think-twice vinyl scent, and of course listened to its songs, all of it blew me away. The stark alienation of the words, the folk style but biting delivery, and the mixture of sexuality and nuclear angst depicted on the cover, it all seemed like a foreign language that I already knew perfectly well.

Another thing my mother brought, this time on my request, was my old air gun, a large .22 lever action affair. With a couple of other guys, I developed the habit of dashing out during midmorning break to shoot as many squirrels as we could see. We shot scores of them, more or less clearing the property. I used to go out on my own to shoot pigeons, listening for their passionate cooing, silently fixing their shape in front of my sights against a translucent sky. They came down easily, shot through the crop or the wing. If it crossed my mind that what I was doing was killing, or that it might stand in some kind of contrast to a spiritual calling, it was the briefest consideration. Eventually, some years later, the air gun wore out and couldn't hit a thing; pigeons roosting a few feet away were perfectly safe. It began to dawn on me slowly and finally that random killing was, perhaps, after all not part of the order of things.

The grounds of Highcliffe really were strikingly beautiful, filled with tall trees, plane, beech, and stately pine, an undergrowth of rhododendron, and a large, hidden bamboo grove. I think the original gardens had been laid out by Capability Brown, and what was left certainly had some of his timeless style. The vista to the Solent, framed by trees, offered an artifice of paradise. The young men gathered in the seminary were oblivious to the degree of cultivation, but I don't think any of us were indifferent to the undertow of sensuality. One of the seminarians was a bird spotter who spent a lot of time on the cliffs with his binoculars. Perhaps he was actually searching for something else, for what he saw one day had a huge impact on him. He came back to the house flushed and breathless to tell how he had spied a couple having sex in a secluded spot among the pines. After the deed was done, he witnessed money changing hands. It wasn't long after that he left the order.

Personally, I felt the sensuality in and around the house. One of the older seminarians gave hints about the cellars as a place where on occasions certain of the brethren had met for sex. He was another who left at the end of the year, and when I met him later, he said he personally couldn't stay in an all-male environment because it was too much of a temptation. As the spring term ended and full summer returned, the house grew warm and seemed to wink at the secrets it held, Mona Lisa fashion. Some of the older guys roomed upstairs, unlike us younger ones who had dormitories in a purpose-built extension on the ground floor. Once in the summer I had occasion to go up to their area and I was surprised to find they had set up a roof space where they had armchairs put out to lounge on the lead roof listening to the Rolling Stones and Herman's Hermits. I was taken aback by the sudden sense of organized good times in contrast to my Spartan concept of the religious life.

The original great hall of Highcliffe was a neo-Gothic vision of vaulted white stone. It had grand staircases on either side, sweeping up to a gallery that gazed down into the hall. To convert the place into a chapel the priests had removed the twin staircases (using them for steps down the cliff to the beach), and a giant statue of the Virgin Mary sitting enthroned was placed on top of the gallery. This is where we said our community prayers and held mass while Mary, our patroness, gazed down benignly. After mass I would sometimes make my devotions by walking around the building, out behind the library, along the winter garden, and back to the side looking toward the sea. The library had a bad reputation among the seminarians, not because they didn't like books, but because people said it was haunted. Going there late at night was deemed not a good idea. Was it perhaps because it was also a trysting spot that the rumor served to keep private? At any rate, I can never be sure whether I was too impressionable, but on a couple of occasions walking by on the outside, past the stone of the library's mullioned windows, I had a sense of indescribable evil. It was as if a creature of real malevolence was locked there, powerless to hurt me, but permitted to show me its hate. I've never had that feeling in any other place.

At the end of the summer the library books were packed in boxes and transported to our new location in Radford, Oxfordshire. Some furniture was also taken there, but not very much as the place we were moving to had housed the seminary of another order and kept many of the things we would need. Meanwhile, Highcliffe remained filled with items, beds, tables, chairs, desks, bric-a-brac of all sorts. I was worried in my mind how all these things would be disposed of properly, simply because it seemed the competent thing to do. It was the responsibility of the house treasurer, the priest put in charge of the monies and possessions of the community. But it all proved too much of a challenge and in the end the whole thing took on the character of a rout. A lone priest was left in charge as caretaker while the building itself was yet to be sold. The priest's name was Albistur, a smart, good-looking guy, and I felt sorry for him down there in that decadent pile with only his flashlight and ghosts for company. As it turned out I didn't have to feel so concerned. Albistur was seeing a woman in Bournemouth and subsequently got married to her. I don't know whether it was during his tenure, or whether he had already formally quit, but it wasn't long after we left that the news came of a fire. It was set by vandals and seems to have been started in the chapel area, which was badly damaged, including the great statue of the Virgin.

The context was of a group of local businessmen who wanted to purchase the castle for development, using it for apartments and upscale houses on the grounds. The local government body, Christchurch Council, instead wanted the castle to be bought entire, as a stately home, and they refused development permission. A strong suspicion emerged that it was the businessmen themselves who had somehow prompted the fire, to force the council's hand. This was strengthened when a second fire swept through the castle the following year, after the businessmen had, in fact, bought the property. According to its Wikipedia page, the castle then "deteriorated into a ruin."[1] Ultimately, it was compulsorily purchased by the council, and pictures of its sorry state were used in a poster campaign against socialist political administration: "Here is the kind of neglect you can expect from these people!" It was not until almost thirty years later that, with the help of English Heritage, repairs were begun, acknowledging the castle represented a significant heirloom of British culture and history.

The Claretians escaped the castle as it burned to the ground and for the better part of two generations it slipped into decay. Lucretius's epigram was turned against itself and against us; indeed, it seemed to mock us for ever having nested under its sneering Latin. It may be this is all simply coincidence, the tale of an aristocratic building coming to grief and a religious order using it temporarily as a stepping stone. But it seemed to me we were tripped even as we stepped, and the fate of the building was at least partially connected to our own story. Four seminarians left at the end of that year, and this was the beginning of a rapid decline that would see our numbers reduced to just three over the next three years. In terms of setting, the castle provides an extraordinary dramatization and visual imaging of what was happening to us spiritually. My seminary experience began with an epic disaster, like being born in a time of war and flight, and it never recovered. I lost almost all confidence in my superiors. In my heart I thought they were lacking leadership and even practical common sense. They were like refugees themselves.

So, of course, the question has to be asked again, why did I stay? It was 1966 and in July of that year England played host to international soccer's World Cup and won the championship for the first and only time. The heroes of the national team, Bobby Charlton, Geoff Hurst, Gordon Banks, and Bobby Moore, were immediately household names. The whole country felt a surge of euphoria and general good will. Everybody was smiling. The thrilling final in which England beat Germany 4–2 was on Saturday, July 30. The next day I needed to be out among the public; the incredible sensation of unity among everyone seemed

1. "Highcliffe Castle," Wikipedia, last edited Feb. 2, 2023 (https://en.wikipedia.org/wiki/Highcliffe_Castle).

like a breakthrough, a spiritual passage not to be missed. I walked along the beach from Highcliffe to Christchurch to be in a place where there were as many people as possible. It was a blazing hot day, and the holiday crowds filled the esplanade between the harbor and the sea. People's faces wore a dazed, happy look, but nothing had changed. The distance between me and the public was still there and, if anything, worse. It was as if I was in some kind of a bubble and actually invisible to those around me. Instead of unity I felt rejection, even hostility. It was no good. The only thing to do was to return to my community. I was in a fundamentally different world from everyone else and my only true and safe place was there, with the Claretians, whatever the disaster the experience itself might represent.

I was in a prison of time and spirit, with nowhere to go but through. My walk along the beach that July day was in its way my first essay at freedom. Almost twenty years later, when I finally did leave the order, a superior in Rome would refer to my "long search," and it is telling that already that morning I walked to Christchurch seeking some kind of human breakthrough. But if I had to continue to journey through twenty years, in order to get to the place where freedom was finally possible, it cannot be those years were entirely useless. All along, fiber by fiber, I was building the muscle strength to make the leap. Priests and religious orders talk in terms of personal vocation, a specific spiritual call by God to take on this way of life. Was my vocation then to become a priest in order to consequently leave the official priesthood? Was my calling to attain the personal identity of an ordained priest in order then to quit the institutional form in which it is set? Really, I would much rather it had not worked out that way, as it appears devious. But it seems hard to avoid the conclusion. On the other hand, as will be seen, the ordination itself was almost a total farce. Its institutional value was practically nil to me, and it would not be long afterward that it collapsed completely. It's possible to conclude, then, that it never really happened, but that it simply provided a forced rite of passage to the birth of identity, the identity I was always seeking, but which, to that point, the official role of priesthood had effectively distorted. All the same, every now and again I am tempted to question whether there was indeed something crucial to that identity in the priesthood itself: Something I might perhaps still and always carry? If so, it has to be of a quite different order from the standard clerical form from which I broke.

I did not really grow intellectually in that year. The one exception was the occasion when a guest speaker introduced us to the thought of Pierre Teilhard de Chardin. As recently as 1962 the writing of this French Jesuit and paleontologist had been censured by the Holy Office. The "monitum" or warning exhorted religious superiors and bishops to protect the minds, particularly of youth, against the dangers represented by his ideas. The same Vatican authorities had forbidden the publication of his books during his lifetime, but after his death in 1955 there was no longer the possibility of blocking them. Moreover, in the '60s a number of Catholic theologians had begun to endorse the value of his thought. At any rate this was the first time I heard about the "Omega Point" of human evolution, which coincided with the figure and nature of Christ, a place to which all humanity was yearning and leaning. This seemed to me a thoroughly excellent thought. I can remember to this day the flip chart of the speaker with its colored lines, words, circles, and ideas. I asked some kind of question and afterward people questioned how I possibly understood what he was talking about. Obviously, this was not your standard scholastic framework, but I took to it like a duck to water. In the realm of ideas I was thoroughly at home, and to some degree this would prove my salvation. At least it helped save me from being a complete scapegoat, as happened to John. Little by little it would also serve to build an independent conversation to the church's institutional control over the meaning of Christianity.

nine

DEAD NUNS

The building we moved to was in Radford, Oxfordshire, again nineteenth-century Gothic revival, and again with aristocratic connections. (By now I was getting used to our hand-me-down association with the upper classes of England.) But the building's spirit was dark, religious, and austere compared to the hedonism of Highcliffe. Its roots went back to a Catholic aristocracy, which had continued to support enclaves of Catholicism and the ministry of its priests after the Protestant Reformation. In this case, it was neighboring Kiddington Hall, belonging to English gentry and still home of the riding-to-hounds sort during our time at Radford. In the first half of the 1800s, a Roman Catholic chaplain from Kiddington set up a presbytery and church on a parcel of land in the southern lee of a Cotswold hill. The sign at the crossroad read "Radford Only" and nothing so well expressed both the neo-Gothic seclusion of this Catholic outpost and the despair that seclusion would inspire in most of the Claretian community.

Fairly soon after the presbytery was built, a convent of nuns was established. Their purpose was to create a Catholic school for the area, and also conduct their own novitiate there. The nuns had been gone some time, and we moved into their old convent building like characters in an apocalyptic movie finding an abandoned house. It was really quite a pretty place, featuring creamy Cotswold stone and an enclosed loggia fronting onto a garden with a flower-encrusted well. Attached to the church there was a cemetery packed with the graves of former nuns.

I spent three years in Radford and, I swear, I would often feel more fellowship with those dead sisters than I did with living brothers.

At the beginning, however, things were hopeful. The whole point of being in that part of the country was to be in proximity to the Jesuit institution of education known as a Pontifical Athenaeum. Here there would be A-list professors and a first-class library, resources that a small order like the Claretians could never supply. The lure of quality education brought us additional students from abroad, including two Spaniards, an Italian, and two Asian Indians. We also added another English member, Peter, joining us from novitiate. These additions masked our previous losses, but there would not be a fresh novice entering the order for a dozen years, and our foreign additions would soon abandon us, repelled by the damp and gloom of our convent and the general sink-or-swim attitude of our superiors.

The Jesuit college was named Heythrop, after the nearby village. It was set in yet another grand house, but this time bigger and grander than anything before. It was a genuine baroque palazzo constructed in the eighteenth century in the heart of the Oxfordshire countryside. Where Highcliffe had the feeling of a rich man's folly, Heythrop was the real thing, massive, classical, assured. Its huge facade gazed out on pastures and woods with a look that said, "Come back in a thousand years and we'll still be here." The sun was honored to shine on it. In addition to this magnificent palace, two smaller houses of much more modern vintage had recently been built on the estate. They were put there by other religious orders at the invitation of the Jesuits and together with the Athenaeum they constituted an overall campus. When the band of Claretian students arrived at this place from our convent in Radford it was a rude culture shock. The Jesuits were in a class of their own, completely beyond us in wealth, cachet, and style. The two other orders with their purpose-built houses on campus were obviously richer and better organized. And there were members of still further orders who made the trip out every day from prestigious houses of study in and around Oxford.

Who, then, were we? In what way could the Claretians stand out? The decision was made, by lead voices in the community, that the quality that set us apart and put us above and beyond the rest was the virtue of hospitality. We were the ones who did not stand on pious ceremony, who were not too heavenly minded to have a good time, who knew, in fact, how to throw a party. So it was, Radford became the place where the swinging '60s hit Heythrop's collected seminaries. As dark days of October drew in, our dining room was turned into a buffet and the small parking lot next to the cemetery was illuminated and equipped with trestle tables. Platters of hors d'oeuvres, pastries, sausages, nuts, and fruits were distributed and a grand tureen of generously proofed punch was set up on a table not far from the moldering nuns. Everyone was invited. There was a grand atmosphere of excitement. The Claretians, or rather the lead figures among them, were masters of the feast. This inner group also gathered to itself a few like minds from other orders, people who had the same unstated sensibility and approach to life, including a couple of habited monks. Together they set the tone of festivity, the heart of the party, while the motley group of seminarians, including the Jesuits, mooched along for the ride. I don't think any of us at the time noticed the Fellini-esque scene and its irony: that the only women present at the party were dead. At least one of the brethren experienced an epiphany: a heavyset man, he was normally of a nervous, prickly disposition, but he went around the company, beaming at everyone, bursting into giggles, while regularly replenishing his glass of punch. After he'd sobered up the next day, he resumed his normal persona, but he continued to ask when might be the next Radford debauch.

But these were interludes. For the rest, Heythrop meant serious study, with the Jesuits as our models, both as teachers and peers. Every day we would set out in our fourteen-seater minivan and drive the single-lane roads to the great house in its park. Once through the portico and inside the arcaded hall we went our separate ways, to attend lectures or study in the library. Chris, Phil, and I joined the first-year class in philosophy, composed of a scattering of outsiders like ourselves and something like thirty-five Jesuit students in their distinctive gowns and rectangular wings. Some of these young men had already gone to university, perhaps read classics at Oxford. It was daunting sitting in a lecture hall with all of them, to hear them question a professor with confidence, knowledge, and logical skill. At the same time, it was like being thrust into a first-tier university without taking qualifying exams and I at once felt the opportunity and joy of higher-level thought and reflection.

Courses included ancient philosophy, metaphysics, epistemology, philosophy of science, psychology (ancient and modern), sociology, ethics, and history of philosophy. Our professors were all prepared and most of them impacted me in the formative way teachers are supposed to. Frederick Copleston, the world-renowned author of the nine-volume *A History of Philosophy*, taught us medieval thought and was also the examiner of my final thesis. We used to take tutorials in his room where he worked away at his little typewriter completing his monumental project.

He had a face that was as educational to look at as his books were to read, lined and troughed like some amazing, storied landscape. He used to smoke straw-thin rolled-up cigarettes and did so continually as he was forced to listen to the imbecilities of his twenty-year-old students. The furrows on his face were assisted by his tobacco habit, I'm sure, but they also seemed to replicate all the lines of thought plowed through the centuries by philosophy and followed faithfully in his volumes. This man had read everything, understood it all, and the creases above his eyes were a map to his wisdom and knowledge. Many of the young Jesuits who fancied themselves as philosophical thinkers smoked handmade cigarettes, seeking to be like the master. True intellectuals smoked rollies. When I hit the habit some time in my three years of philosophy, I did the same.

I was identified by a couple of professors as having some capacity for this kind of thought. Father Lebacqz, who taught us metaphysics, chose me as one of the handful of students worthy of his coaching. He was a tall, irritable Belgian who insisted passionately on the reality of higher concepts. I personally enjoyed thinking about the "analogy of being" with him, wrapping my mind around its distinctions, but some of the young Turks among the Jesuits despised metaphysics, and one day I would learn to do likewise. At that time, I was in a kind of dream and all abstraction came naturally to me. So, I thought it was pretty mean when later on Lebacqz was tragically killed—stepping out inattentively in front of an automobile somewhere in Belgium—and one of his Heythrop detractors commented, "Now he'll know whether what he taught was true or not!" Of course, the comment also contained metaphysical assumptions, but that did not matter: it was the harsh assertiveness of youth speaking. It was also a little bit the manner of English Jesuits, the cut and thrust of Oxbridge, and the hint of blue blood running somewhere in the veins of the English province.

Whatever the rarified atmosphere of Heythrop, returning to Radford was always a coming back to earth with a bump. The road there continued for about fifty yards past the convent, dipping down sharply and coming to a dead end in front of the great hill to the north. There were two or three cottages there that, together with the convent and presbytery, made up the hamlet of Radford. Shortly before the convent, on the road, there was a pretty farmhouse and a track to the right, which wound down steeply on an eastern flank to a stream and an abandoned mill. The track continued alongside the stream, eventually coming out beside Kiddington Hall. During the student recreation periods, a big gang of us would often walk down to the mill, with Chris skipping along backward in front of the group like a young colt, and the conversation invariably orchestrated by Matt. I never said very much when Matt was there. I could never match his wit, and basically he ignored me. My most animated conversations were separate, with Paddy, Phil, Colin, and others. We'd talk passionately about theology and religious life and how all the institutional structures were helpless in the task of relating to the modern world. It wasn't long before most of them left the order. I became still more isolated and the walk to the millstream became a solitary ritual, something I did to get away and seek to discover, somehow, who I was.

I would stand beside the waterwheel watching the wooden buckets fill and tip into the pool, endlessly turning. The wheel was no longer connected to the gears, but the huge grindstone was still in place inside, and it was dry there with a lingering scent of must and wheat. A feeling of weathered life and humanity hung about the place. It was easy for me to imagine the lovers' trysts that had taken place up in the loft among the sacks of grain. However, it was all just echoes and fantasies and I could never be part of it. When the second winter came, I would go down after mass in the mornings. I would search among the black, empty branches of the apple orchard with a weak January sun poking through. I hoped and prayed somehow God would come out of his divine hiding and show himself to me, but all I felt was absence. My deal with God had collapsed entirely. I was running on fumes.

I took up actual running. Nature has given me flat feet and in the past I'd suffered from asthma, but the college organized cross-country competitions and there was an annual "Heythrop Run" in which everyone took part, including professors. I found it a lot of fun, pounding along the wooded paths, across the deep glistening furrows of the fields, up over windy crests. I was certainly not among the first home, but neither did I come in last, and when I crossed the finish line, dropping from exhaustion and covered in mud, there was a wonderful feeling of euphoria. I would also run on my own. The tracks alongside the millstream were a favorite circuit. One early autumn morning I headed in the direction of Kiddington Hall and as I came over a hill I arrived directly at the muster of a hunt. The riders on their gleaming thoroughbred horses were gathered in a field just below the track, with the great house appearing between the trees in the background. It was a scene right out of *Downton Abbey*, men and women dressed in hunting velvet bending from their saddles to lift the stirrup cup ladled from a silver tureen by liveried servants. It was also in total contrast to my drab convent life, such that it had an unreal, dreamlike quality. It was only later I found out that the aristocratic society on display that morning was, in fact, the reason I was running that track. It was the antecedents of this group who established the Catholic enclave at Radford.

The dominant voices that decided the life of the community belonged to Matt, to another student called John, to Dennis who was a lay brother, and to Wacker, our superior. Wacker was a voice really by default. He was the superior and made the final announcement, but often he seemed to defer to the others, and whatever their version of the community's latest urgent need, that is what he did. It was as if Wacker played the role of a pliable king ruled by the whims of courtiers. One decision this group came to made a direct and disastrous impact on the seminary. It happened in our first winter at Radford and it locked my spirit up deeper in its solitary prison without hope of reprieve.

The inner council felt that we were far too insulated in our Cotswold convent, and it was imperative to break out into the real world of the happening '60s. So, we all piled in to our minivan and a couple of other cars and traveled to Soho, London, headquarters of the sex trade in England. Here were the strippers, the prostitutes, the backstreet burlesques, sex shops, and peepshows every English schoolboy had heard about but few had seen. Now the Claretian seminarians were to get a firsthand encounter.

We began with a meal. Dan, whom I have mentioned before—the young priest who subsequently became provincial—was now parish priest at the same parish where he had endured Steve's oppressive vigilance. It was in a town called Hayes, not far from London airport. Dan was used to making the trip to Soho. He was a regular patron at an Italian restaurant situated somewhere on the fringes of the red-light district, and he was obviously part of the plan to complete our unsentimental education. He met us there and treated us to a sit-down meal, with veal and dessert. Afterward we took the walking tour. We made our way down among the dives and strip joints, past gaudily lit windows hung with alluring images, by bright doorways framing visions of frilly lingerie on creamy British thighs. As we did so all the teaching of "custody of the senses"—the advice to avert the eyes from anything that might trouble the spirit—arose up in confused revolt. What exactly were we supposed to be paying attention to now? At the same time, none of us went inside the establishments or talked to the workers. We just wandered aimlessly on the sidewalk, to the annoyance of the doormen and contempt of the come-on girls on duty. On the way home, on a frozen winter night, with the heater cranked up high and our hormones both stirred and suppressed, conversation died, and each twenty-something man entered his private world of agony.

For me, it was a knife to the heart. The sexuality I had given up had nothing to do with strip joints. It was to do with girls, lots of them, and the brimming possibilities in connection to them, in all the freedom and fun that the '60s were beginning to allow. The experience of Soho seemed to say instead that sex was dirty, and what we had to be aware of rather was its vicious defiance to chastity. The face of sexuality would always be a bitter one, always close at hand, with no escape, ready to leap out and ensnare us at the slightest opportunity. I was really pretty naïve back then about what it all meant—but I definitely felt something. I felt helpless and weak, disgusted with myself, with the world, with life. As our van turned onto the Radford road and its headlights picked out the boles of the trees, petrified in the freezing night, all reality was removed, and the trees were forever made up of emptiness and nothing. I was cast into outer space, and I knew with certainty that I would never get any affirmation for my eager religious virtue. From that point onward I was on my own and any reality would have to come from within me. Today, from the perspective of forty years and a revolution in sexual attitudes, where homosexuality has come storming out of the closet, and healthily so, I ask myself who could possibly have set up such an experiment. It seems to me it could only have been a group of deeply ambivalent men, ambivalent about the all-male community they were in, wanting somehow to put everyone, gay and straight, on the same level playing field of seduction and power. Really the nomenclature of "gay" and "straight" is not correct. The whole thing belonged to a very specific subculture within the church's institution of celibacy, at a moment when it was able to give itself more freedom of expression than before, but always under the cover and construct of the religious life. A revolution in attitudes since then has very probably rendered it transparent to itself and everyone else around. Very likely the whole experience was specific to those seismic '60s.

Whatever the truth of this analysis, the experience was a definite blow to the group. I noticed how a bunch of the young men, including Paddy and Colin, progressively set themselves apart in adversarial fashion, and by the end of the following year they were gone. The foreigners also went, quickly returning to sunnier climes and better-run seminaries.

I too seriously thought about leaving. But where? None of the other religious orders attracted me. Even the Jesuits did not offer an alternative: despite their obvious excellence in so many fields, there was something soulless about their existence. Each man was isolated in a private fortress of discipline, and I'd had far too much isolation already. But then, why not abandon the goal of the priesthood altogether? Easy to say, but unthinkable in practice. There was no other place for me to stand but this narrow world called seminary, the only world where I belonged and where I could become a man. It was never a matter of simple religious obedience to God, it was always where and whether I could survive at all.

It was a morning in May, and I was on my way through Berkshire, down into Hampshire, to visit the parish priest in my hometown Portsmouth. Perhaps I would join a diocese under a bishop—that was my plan. As I drove, I saw two or three foxes moving around in broad daylight. It was evident a hunt was being prepared and the huntsmen had gone around stopping up the dens, to prevent the fox going to ground. I identified with the persecuted fox, without a home, forever on the run. My interview with the diocesan priest did not go well. He was patronizing and smug, somehow even more cut off from life than our nineteenth-century convent. I recognized this avenue of escape was also blocked and I headed back to Radford defeated. I prayed desperately for something, anything, to help me settle on a way forward. The big Heythrop chapel was formerly an indoor tennis court, converted for sacred purposes by a laminated molding, giving the seeming of green marble. As I sat in this simulated space, I felt that, despite all the problems, the Claretians were the only people with whom I had any kind of relationship. There was a kind of love there, and where there is love, there is God. I seized on this as an answer, partial and opaque, but nevertheless an answer. Wacker had heard of the intention of my visit to Portsmouth to speak with a diocesan priest, and he called me in to ask what I'd decided. I told him I was staying, and it was because I loved the Claretian community. He was taken aback and seemed embarrassed, but said it was good enough. He could not know that my island of belonging had turned into a shipwrecked life raft desperately needed to save me from drowning. That is all.

Time unfolded with the slowness and vacancy that only the luxury of youth can provide. Really, I was doing nothing until I was ordained; studying, yes, but with a dilatory interest, not with the discipline of a profession. At the same time, I sought out as many new experiences I could, instinctively trying to broaden my horizon. I was elected treasurer of the Heythrop Student Union and attended the National Union of Students conference in Leicester. On the way to the conference venue the news came on the taxi radio of the assassination of Martin Luther King Jr. We held a minute's silence in Leicester's huge De Montfort Hall, presided over by Jack Straw, the student union president who would subsequently become home secretary in the Tony Blair government. The killing of the US civil rights leader seemed par for the course in a country steeped in inexplicable racism and at that time more and more deeply mired in the murderous Vietnam adventure. Sitting in the conference hall surrounded by a couple of thousand unruly university and polytechnic students, it seemed only a matter of time before we'd settle the account for MLK and bring imperialism and militarism crashing down. About a dozen or so rows behind me the communists set up camp. They were certainly the most unruly, calling out political insults and frequently quarreling among themselves. Their evident leader was a stunning girl in a tight red dress and lush folds of black hair. She would stalk around like a *passionaria* of the Spanish Civil War, distributing leaflets and showing fierce contempt for the lily-livered lack of militancy among her comrades. She was the best show in the hall, and I spent my time looking over my shoulder to observe her. Ted Heath, then the leader of the Tory Party (and later to be prime minister himself), came to address the conference. I can't remember anything he said, but the girl in the red dress was beside herself with fury and scorn: the group of Marxists had been unable to mount any kind of serious protest against this prince of capitalism and she bitterly castigated their failure. I was reminded of how my generation in the church were always lashing ourselves for our inability to respond effectively to the modern world.

At the end of the conference there was a big party I really wanted to go to. One of the girls a few seats from mine eagerly invited me to attend, pressing her body into mine as she passed in the narrow row. A good bit of me saw this as my chance—here was my opportunity to join the massive fun time going on all around me, just for the sake of the experience, and afterward no one would know anything about it. But I just couldn't bring myself to break the ten p.m. curfew in the religious house where I had lodging during the conference. I didn't want to be the one to scandalize an older man, someone like Steve, who had spent his life observant to the timetable. And, truly, the prayerful world that older man valued still meant a lot to me.

But, oh, '68! The Tet Offensive had already happened, the Paris riots, *les évènements de mai*, and the Prague Spring were all just around the corner. Revolution was in the air, but my revolution was on ice. I returned to Heythrop where the urgency of the time quickly dissolved in the hazy vistas of the Cotswolds and dreams of Greek philosophy.

But later that summer I went to France. Together with fellow student Peter, a religious brother named Kevin, and my natural brother, Terry, I went to the South of France to work in an organization building houses for immigrants. We ended up in the Alps, east of Grenoble, high above the city, with the Grand Chartreuse somewhere on the western skyline and tiny peasant churches in the folds of the hills. We were given a mixed hut to sleep in with the girls' beds directly opposite, occupied by a group of female Dutch volunteers who didn't think twice about parading in their underwear. One of our group objected and said if we didn't move out he'd inform Wacker when we got back to England. More than a little grudgingly I requested alternative lodging. Why shouldn't I look at girls with whom I could also be friends? Under duress I did my duty, and we were given another hut, much to the amusement of the girls and the male Dutch volunteers also at the camp. Later "les Anglais" compensated for their lack of testosterone by climbing an alpine peak. With the help of a guide, we summited the Croix de Beldonne, trudging the last mile through an actual glacier. It was a fantastic experience and when we got back we felt superior to all-comers, in particular a group of precious Belgian youth who had arrived in place of the Dutch. When we made our way home via Paris, the place still held the whiff of the barricades about it, covered in graffiti and scars from the riots of May.

The escape of going abroad was now fully settled in my soul, and two years later I would visit Germany for six weeks, a much more substantial episode. In the meantime, I finished the degree in philosophy. My grades were counted, and I took the oral exam, the viva, as it was called. On the appointed day I returned to the grand entrance hall, the bright early summer sun splashing through its lattice of skylights. The results were posted and listed in order of merit. I shared the top space with another student, ahead of all the Jesuits, summa cum laude. I was exhilarated, but there was also a fair bit of luck in it. The students had been divided among two panels, one of which held a recently appointed Dominican professor, an expert in Heidegger. We really hadn't studied the German father of ontology, and the Dominican used the opportunity to settle intellectual scores with the Jesuits. He victimized the young scholastics, showing up their ignorance. Of course, I was interviewed by the other panel and *Sein und Zeit* never got mentioned. Many, many years later, I would meet one of that Jesuit class of thirty-five men, and he told me there were only three still in the society. My victory of that time has to be gauged against much more serious challenges beyond the control of any religious order. However, as I looked at that list with my name at the top it gave me an immediate sense of inevitability. I would cherish the astonishing fact of having outdone the Jesuits at their game. It was the predestined meaning I'd always believed in and a token of further vindication to come. It proved my long pilgrimage to be worthwhile.

By the end of that year (1969), there were only five Claretian seminarians: Matt, and Peter (who would soon leave), and of course the "Holy Trinity" of Phil, Chris, and myself. Wacker had just been appointed provincial superior, in charge of the handful of Claretian communities in the UK. No one else was willing or able to take on the job of prefect of students, and so, given our fewness in numbers, it was decided Wacker would double as provincial and prefect. The discussion then evolved as to where we would live. Wacker had developed a distinct allergy for Radford, its cold, damp corridors and chapel, its monastic isolation. His brother, Joe Wareing, was actually the priest in charge of one of the independent religious houses on the Heythrop campus. It belonged to the Montfort Missionaries, another obscure continental group that had somehow found its way to England. They were the ones who had occupied Radford before us but took the step of building their own residence on land close to the Jesuits. They had rooms to spare, and it was mooted we all move in with the Montforts, with Joe as doppelganger for his brother. Wacker would live elsewhere, doing the work of provincial, while visiting the students every month. Matt erupted with indignation: it would be over his dead body that his very own personal order would corrupt his identity by making him live in the house of another. I myself favored the idea, believing it would give us the kind of discipline and order I thought we so badly lacked. Wacker had the casting vote and his need to be out of Radford trumped Matt's righteous principle. As a concession, Matt was given permission to move at once to Hayes and finish his studies there, while the rest of us would crash with the Montforts. Possibly Wacker was pleased to be rid of me. He could never quite get a handle on me, on my simultaneously dutiful and rebellious approach. I had upset him, I know, with some of the sixties-ish student-rebellion poses I struck, and he was never comfortable or happy around me.

That summer then was the last at Radford. It was the place where I completed my degree in philosophy, got the news of Robert Kennedy's assassination, heard "Hey Jude" the first time. I saw a real March hare dash up and down like a genuine crazy thing in the dew-decked grass of the orchard, saw the mayfly live its single day over Kiddington stream, heard the giant C-141s make the heavens shake as they came in at the US base at Upper Heyford, on their way to and from Vietnam. Through it all, the nuns in the cemetery did not stir. Neither did I. Although I had the advantage of physical life I was in a cocoon of time and feeling that was little more than a coffin. Revolutions rose and fell around me, but I remained personally cut off from their impact. Now, finally, some of that would begin to change.

ten

HIMMELFAHRT

That Fall Montfort Hall became our lodging: orphans with another religious order, the children for whom Mom ran off and Dad could not stay. That's how it felt.

For it turned out that I could not be more wrong about the sense of discipline and order. Matt was right: a different religious outfit was always going to be somebody else's discipline, and at once when we got there it felt like oppression. In this other organization, with this other dad and mom, the sense of being abandoned was always present, and the answering spirit of rebellion very quickly grew. Maybe I could say that here is the true point of origin of my eventual leaving the priesthood, but that event was not going to happen for another fifteen years, and so the connection cannot be direct. What I should say, I believe, is that the situation fully confirmed the suspicion that any formation would come from myself, and not the order. And so, quickly the conclusion may be drawn—even if I did not formulate it as such at that time—one day I would assume necessary independence in the matter of religious meaning and life. And that means, logically enough, this is not a story about leaving something, but about the growth of a new spiritual identity altogether.

We were mixed up with a new bunch of young men, mostly from the north of England and Scotland. They made us welcome, and to some degree we were heroes, shuffled off—as the image so easily presented itself—by our own family, struggling to survive on our own. I made friends there and was even popular, and I began to become more overtly angry and resentful under the impact of the situation. One time I came down to breakfast, and I was humming a song to myself while I collected cereal and scrambled egg. Wacker's brother, Father Joe, was sat enthroned at his head table and as I took my place, still singing, he hit his little announcement bell and told me to be quiet in his harsh Liverpudlian accent. Of course, it was a mournful Irish tune and of course I really couldn't sing, but who on earth was he to tell me to shut up? A towering rage rose within me. I paused for a moment, pushed the food away, then stood up and left the refectory with all the dignity I could muster, seething inside. It created quite an impression. Joe said nothing more to me. Some of the students apologized for his brusqueness. I discovered in myself a sense of self that was a surprise, even a shock. For the first time I'd openly defied religious authority.

All the same I obeyed. I grew a Frank Zappa mustache, fashionable at the time, and a sign of my dissidence. Wacker showed up on one of his monthly visits. He said at once, "What's that?" referring to my facial hair as if it were some kind of obscene thing that had crawled above my mouth. I mumbled something about wanting to try it out and he didn't let me finish. "Get it off!" I went straight to my room and shaved away the offensive growth. I still didn't truly know who I was and needed to be ordained a priest.

At the Christmas and summer breaks we Claretian students had to go to any of our own communities that would take us. Buckden was the obvious choice, with plenty of room plus familiar ghosts from the Claretian seminary past. It also had its own historical catalog of ghosts, from a story stretching back, this time beyond the nineteenth century, way back to the late Middle Ages. Michael, the failed prefect of Highcliffe days, was now the superior here, slowly trying to restore the property, as well as his own priestly career. He was fighting the good fight. The Roman Catholic Church was currently gripped by controversy associated with the publication of *Humanae Vitae*, the papal document reaffirming the ban on artificial means of birth control. Michael, as parish priest of the local parish, was embroiled with a group of Catholics in their thirties and forties who, moved by the spirit of the times, objected passionately to the Vatican line. Michael had become something of a hate-figure for this group, just as he had to the students at Highcliffe, but he was resolved to defend the church's position with all the zeal required by his job and its setting. After all, he was custodian of a fifteenth-century bishop's palace in which Catherine of Aragon had been imprisoned for refusing to agree to Henry VIII's demand for a divorce. But even that noble association could be turned against him.

One of the practices of the group of young Catholics was the throwing of fairly risqué parties, taking place in the so-called King's Room. This was the big banquet room on the ground floor of the "Towers," the three-storied crenellated keep that provided the unmistakable landmark of the property and indeed of the whole village. Michael needed whatever rents he could charge on the rooms in view of maintaining them and all the buildings in his charge. So, on the one hand he battled the group of defiant Catholics for doctrinal reasons and welcomed their carousing for economic ones. They, on the other hand, gained an added thrill to their license by doing it in this noble building, and under Michael's nose, and by extension that of the whole hierarchy.

When the students from Heythrop arrived in Buckden we were quickly adopted by this progressive group. They had a couple of leaders, one of whom was a woman very publicly dissatisfied with her then husband. The man in question was a tall, rakish army officer, clearly as self-absorbed as she was emotionally hungry. To my youthful mind she seemed a femme fatale, intense, blond, and needing to be rescued. There was a priest in the community in a state of deep disillusion with the church and desperately in love with her. She did not reciprocate because she had something better going with a local farmer, someone she would later marry and then, later, also divorce. Back then the students would troop off with the lovesick priest to her house and she would make tea for us and talk in a Harold Pinteresque way about her life and ours.

The big party in preparation was for New Year's Eve and on the one hand I despised the whole thing—the self-important class of people and their indulgent desire for pleasure and fun. On the other, I was just twenty-three years old and strongly attracted by the wayward passion on display and the dim sense that I could share in its freedom. On the night of the party, they built a roaring fire in the great hearth, shut the lights except for a few red lamps, supplied lashings of alcohol, and played lots of very loud rock and pop. The army officer grabbed a petite woman, placed her on a chair, and carried it with one hand while smooching her with the other, waltzing all around the room, much to the amusement of the crowd.

Phil and I put in an appearance. I am not sure what happened to him, but it wasn't long before I joined the fun. I found myself dancing with a dark-haired farmer's daughter in (again!) a red dress, and soon locked in a slow-dance embrace. She suggested we go back to her house where there was nobody in, and although I understood it was a conquest she wanted, one she could boast about locally, this time I was fully prepared to go. The only thing that stopped me was the fact that Terry, my brother, had turned up unexpectedly. He was very thin, and his hair was huge and wild and flecked with straw from his work in an industrial pig farm. The previous year he had been sent home by the missionary order he had joined in Ireland, and they told him not to try to join any other group either. He still had not found his way and was bitterly depressed. He was wearing a long black greatcoat, drinking heavily, and looked suicidal. I was keeping an eye on him and then suddenly he disappeared. I told my new party friend I had to go to look for him but would be back right away. I found him up on the roof of the Towers looking over the battlements. We talked—just to make sure he was alright; inside I was desperate to get back to the tryst—and he seemed grimly satisfied that I'd come to see him. After a few minutes I excused myself and scooted back down the spiral staircase to the King's Room, but the farmer's daughter was gone. I'm sure she thought the brother thing was just a pious excuse, or, just as likely, it was just the excuse she herself needed.

It wasn't long after this party, or maybe shortly before, that I masturbated for the first time in my life. It wasn't the party. It was the whole situation of Buckden Towers, its gloominess, its coldness, the collapsed, embattled state of the order's leadership, and, of course, the inviting atmosphere of sensuality, all that broke my wall of reserve. Whatever the morality or psychology attached to masturbation, the fact that someone takes a vow of celibacy certainly seems to make it hypocritical for that person: you're doing in your imagination what you have renounced publicly by vow. I felt horribly guilty and begged God to give me the strength to resist, but too late, a bridge had been crossed. Beforehand, I was so deeply embedded in my sacred world, and its negation of the profane world, the thought of self-pleasure was, well, unthinkable. I was able to reject something that 99 percent of young men seem to engage in more or less automatically. When that changed, I started on a path that made me the same as everyone else. In the circumstances was that a good thing? Or was it a failure, a fall? I was no longer fully absorbed by a world of rules and observance, like a child in the womb, like a bug burrowed in the bark of a tree. Now, perhaps, the purpose of the visit to Soho three years before had been achieved. For better or worse my desire reached out beyond my cocoon into the actual world, into average mental fantasy and simulacrum sex.

My brother Terry had become my friend after a few years of estrangement between us. It happened the winter before our trip to France when he visited me in Radford. We stayed up late together, and he introduced me to J. D. Salinger, an author who spoke to his own feelings about life. Later when I read Salinger myself, I came to understand and appreciate Terry better. In very many ways Terry was more in contact with the actual world than I was. I learned from him, and now he was seeking with so much difficulty to find his own way. I admired him and began to imitate his independence and general attitudes, even to his way of talking. Many years later I came to understand my brother was gay, something that made sense of the fact he never married, and a number of other things too. He drank heavily all his life and died far too young. Later in his life he related he had been sexually abused by a lay teacher at the De La Salle boys' school we both attended in Portsmouth. But he would not pursue the matter legally as became common at the beginning of the twenty-first century. Terry was a very smart and perceptive guy, and it was he who also alerted me to patterns in our mother's birth family that suggested a history of sexual abuse of the children, basically beginning after the last child was born (when sexual relations between the parents would almost certainly be terminated). He eventually, in fact, became a social worker, specializing in child protection and leading a team, and it was in the thick of his involvement in this kind of work that he offered his analysis. But he talked about it only once, building a case very persuasively, and then dropping it. That was the way with him. He would mention something pretty devastating, and then become elusive if you wanted to discuss more. Despite his keen insight, full revelation and disclosure seemed to be something he wanted to avoid.

During that year with the Montforts, I began studying theology, an introductory course, and I understood very little. There was something about it I didn't get and after my triumphs in philosophy it seemed esoteric, even snobbish, a kind of secret language you had be initiated into. It frustrated me and it was only much later that I discovered the source of my frustration. Theology is vastly concrete, rooted in history and humanity. Its mixture with the philosophical tradition is a kind of alias it travels under. Once you figure this out you can begin to make sense of the two poles, the concrete and the abstract, and the constant friction between them. Back then my philosophical mindset had covered over my first experiences of the amazing concreteness of the gospel, and I simply did not get these elements mixed in with what seemed so highly speculative. It would only be step by step I would restore the priority to the concrete.

The final year at Heythrop was a transitional year in every sense. The decision had been taken to move the whole institution, lock, stock, and barrel, to London, transforming it into a constituent college of London University. It was another instance of the huge upheaval of the era, reimagining everything that had been handed down from prior worldviews. Rather than a monastic enclave lost in the countryside of England, a priestly seminary should discover itself in the heart of the secular city, surrounded by the stress and reality of modern life. A few of the Jesuit professors resisted, unconvinced, but it was a done deal, and that summer would be the last for "old Heythrop." A particular tragedy was Father George, the college librarian, an ox of a man passionately devoted to his bright, spacious, purpose-built, and recently completed library. He had supervised the transfer and ordering of the books into this ideal setting and was now required to crate them all up and take them to cramped quarters in London. It was more than a man could bear. I don't know the details, but it spelled the end of him, and I never saw him again. In any case, Heythrop had drawn us to itself in the first place and now it was drawing us onward, whether we liked it or not, to London.

All these fraying ends meant more and more freedom for me, as indeed for everyone in that time. Encouraged by one of our Benedictine comrades I applied to the Youth Department of the Council of Europe to take a summer language course in Germany, all expenses paid bar travel. The railway station at Cologne breathed an atmosphere of great journeys east, full of human destiny. Beneath its vaulted glass and steel roof there was a youthful Germany, bustling and bright, eager to leave the recent past behind. The *Frankfurter Allgemeine* shouted from the kiosks, and Milka chocolate with its friendly cow symbol was on sale on the counters. My seat reservation took me into a compartment with an oldish couple, a child, another gentleman, and a vivacious young woman with a merry mouth and tight jeans. The conversation was friendly and energetic, with everyone taking part, but the young woman was the center of attention. As nighttime came the couple took charge and supervised the stretching out of our seating into a continuous platform occupying the whole space of the compartment. It had a faded red terylene surface, and I must have looked slightly unnerved because the older lady explained to me in broken English that I shouldn't worry, they did this kind of thing all the time. The young woman looked eager to bed down and I spent the night with her next to me, inches away. I don't know if I was remembering my adolescent Italian train ride, but I couldn't sleep, longing to put my arm around her. I felt sure she wouldn't have minded, but I didn't dare.

Kassel was my destination, a city more or less in the center of today's Germany, but at that time about one hundred kilometers west of the border with East Germany. Allied bombers had pulverized most of it and the city center had been rebuilt in the '50s style of harsh concrete spaces, but there were red tiles on the roofs of the houses and the walls were plastered in pleasant tones of cream and dull pink. I lodged with Frau Glöckner, a wonderful lady in her sixties. Her husband had been captured by the Russians and died in a prison camp after the war. Her son had been shot to death, she said, by the Royal Air Force while parachuting to safety from his crippled plane. In order not to be consumed by grief or bitterness she had dedicated herself to giving hospitality to young people of any nationality, anyone who might show up in Kassel for a language course or for any other reason. She wanted to create the bonds that would ensure nothing like the Second World War would happen again.

For six weeks I had a fantastic time. For the first, and, actually, last time, I was with a mixed group of peers in their twenties who were simply interested in hanging out, watching movies, smoking cigarettes, eating, dancing, and sometimes having sex. This was a point at which my own youth came fully flush with other youth but despite the joy and the fun I still knew with metaphysical certainty that at the end of it all I would head back to seminary and the religious life. There could be no debate. These were two things happening side by side, or one after another, but religion would always win out over youth. However, for a short span I was totally prepared to put up with an active tension between the two.

I made friends with a young Turkish man by the name of Umit. He displayed an unbridled passion for life, to which I was hugely attracted. We became inseparable. When we were not in class studying the German language we explored the city, the cafes, and bars, went to museums and festivals in the parks, and most of all hung out with the girls. We spoke French together, both equally ungrammatical, but making perfect sense. French was the natural common language for everyone in the group, given the predominance of Belgian and French youth on the course. It didn't hurt either that by far the prettiest girl in the program was a Belgian by the name of Jacqueline. She was also personable and smart and inevitably became the most popular girl, the one around whom all the cool kids congregated. And wherever she was, Umit wanted to be. For me, just one look at her and I knew she belonged to a completely different planet, something called the world. At the weekly dances I never went near her and hung out only with girls with whom I thought I had something in common. For example, there was a girl from Malta who knew I was training to be a priest and talked warmly about the Catholicism of her native island, but that didn't stop her dancing intimately with me when the occasion presented. All the same Jacqueline eventually became quite friendly to me. When I got good grades in class she complimented me enthusiastically—"*Tony, tu es formidable!*"—and one time when we were all at a cafe somewhere she started feeding me food from her plate with her fork. It was very flattering, but she did it to make Umit jealous, I'm sure, and it worked. He snarled at us, "*Qu'est-ce que c'est, ça? L'amour avec la fourchette!*" (What's this? Love with a fork?). I was pretty innocent, and an easy foil for whatever more complicated games were going on between my peers.

We took a trip to see *die Grenze*, the border between West and East Germany. We viewed it running through a wooded area, with cleared spaces on either side of the razor wire rearing up twenty-five feet in the air, and a watchtower rising even taller every half a kilometer along. All of us gathered with the fence behind us and we had our picture taken, a bunch of Western kids casually demonstrating our political defiance by flashing victory signs and smiling for the camera. At the end of the program we went to Berlin, which involved traveling through East Germany. In Berlin we rode the Metro to the eastern half of the city. While we wandered around the parade ground spaces, we were always in sight of the huge TV tower with its characteristic "Sputnik" bulge in the middle, the propaganda symbol of communist success. We were also always in view of a couple of Stasi agents, or at least that's what everyone said they were. They wore the regulation trench coats, walked in step, and looked bored out of their heads. The fact that they were tailing us didn't seem to intimidate a couple of East Berlin youth who came up to us and asked to buy our jeans. I suppose the deal was we would have worn their pants in exchange, but nobody wanted to strip off, certainly not with the agents watching. Nevertheless, to have someone beg me for my jeans made me feel the height of cool.

The day before we were due to go our separate ways we attended a Berlin Philharmonic performance of Beethoven's Symphony no. 9 conducted by Herbert von Karajan in the vast auditorium of the *Philharmonie*. The sudden simultaneous rising of the full choir to intone the *Freude* was breathtaking, and Beethoven's rolling thunder of human confidence filled us all with a sense both of the wonder of life and its terrible fragility. Outside, brown leaves of autumn were already skating in circles in the corners of the walkways and as we climbed aboard our bus to return us to our hostel everyone felt something akin to desperation. It was necessary to grab this moment before it disappeared forever, and so it became essential to pair up to make that happen. I had become affectionate toward a French girl by the name of Martine, enough to catch the attention of Jacqueline. She took it on herself to warn me against Martine. She said, really she was a social inferior, she didn't wash, she was dirty. "*Elle est sale.*" Certainly, I could do much better.

As we were getting off the bus Umit gestured toward a smoldering Italian girl who was friendly with Jacqueline, suggesting that I should get together with her. What neither of them understood was that I was still hanging on as best I could to my vow of chastity. Martine was a loner and disconnected from the pushy, status-hungry youth around her. And it was true what Jacqueline said. Martine's fingernails had dirt underneath them, her hair was rat-tailed and her clothes poor. By pairing up with her, in something of a class-identity way, I felt relatively safe. There was no need to prove anything around Martine. I actually enjoyed hanging out with her.

I got off the bus and Umit disappeared. I talked with Martine a while, smoking a cigarette; maybe I kissed her, but I know I went to bed alone. The next day we had one more event to attend, a movie, I think; I don't remember, only the darkened seats and Martine sitting on her own. I went in beside her and we kissed for a long while. I liked the salt taste of her lips, and the slightly musty smell of her skin. The experience was a chaotic mixture of the end of our brief season of youth together, when it was impossible to be alone, and my own frayed identity in the religious life, torn to tatters over the last five years. Then it was over, time to leave. Umit and I took a taxi to the station and boarded a train for Frankfurt. We had a compartment to ourselves and collapsed on the seats, sunk in hormonal paralysis. It was long gone midnight when the door crashed back, and a harsh voice yelled. We awoke to see two jackbooted East German guards demanding to see our passports. My heart lurched in my chest. It was like we were on the run and had been arrested by Nazis. Their faces were contorted by anger, but they let us go, warning us to keep our feet off the couches. We waited until we knew we were safely out of the DDR and back in West Germany, then we curled up again.

We arrived in Frankfurt, found a hostel, went to the book fair and a rock concert. Later we ended up in a night club that was celebrating the life of Jimi Hendrix. He had died just that week. They played all his hits with strobe lights and morphing oil shapes pulsing on the walls. They called it Jimi Hendrix's *Himmelfahrt*. That's how I learned the German word for Christ's ascension into heaven.

eleven

TIN AND OTHER METALS

THERE NOW BEGAN, WITHOUT question, the worst three years of my life. I have stayed in touch with Umit and he called our experience in Germany a *belle époque*. If it was, it lasted precisely forty-three days (six weeks plus an extra day in Frankfurt). I came back from Germany to Hayes and its parish, which I have mentioned before. Here was to be my new home, in an industrial suburb of West London, location of EMI and Nestle and other giant factories. George Orwell once lived there and gave this as his opinion: "Hayes . . . is one of the most godforsaken places I have ever struck. The population seems to be entirely made up of clerks who frequent tin-roofed chapels on Sundays and for the rest bolt themselves within doors."[1] I'd have to agree, except instead of tin-roofed chapels there would be the massive copper-roofed new church built by the Claretians in 1961. And in addition to the clerks, there were the Irish immigrants who came for work in the factories and with their pay packets helped fund the new building. The Claretian community lived in yet another Victorian dwelling, Botwell House, adjacent to the church, and this was to be my new home. Once Heythrop had made its exodus to London and we were pursuing our studies in its new setting, it was the obvious choice, the Claretian residence with nearest access to central London and with the most rooms to spare. And that is what it felt like, a seminary by default, a crash pad for students. It was overseen by a parish priest with his mind on his parish and very little sympathy for the routine and role modeling usually associated with houses of formation.

1. George Orwell, *An Age Like This: 1920–1940*, vol. 1 of *The Collected Essays, Journalism and Letters of George Orwell*, edited by Sonia Orwell and Ian Angus (New York: Harcourt Brace & World, 1968), 105.

From a general common-sense perspective, the story of this time would seem to be a moment when the truth of my situation would finally at last come clear. I was getting closer and closer to ordination and these proximate years should seem to be the point where I would at last wake up and come to a conscious, coherent decision. But the opposite is the case. These three years in my early to mid-twenties are a fog. I was sleep-walking toward the sacrament of orders. Or, more accurately, I was a ship adrift in a broad and murky current, without power of engine or rudder, capable only of passive or, at best, erratic movement, always in the same opaque stream. The fact that directly following ordination, with my desperate request granted to spend a year "away" in Rome, I did finally come to an entirely new place of meaning in my life only increases the impenetrability of those prior years. In the time before those three years, I still had a certain green idealism and belief. After them I was based in an entirely new experience of independent spiritual strength. In between there were these three years of famine, of nearly complete confusion and pain. In all truth I declined, slipped, fell, and collapsed into ordination. It was a mess. And the "church" around me allowed it to happen, without ever offering any kind of alternative pathway to permit my life to develop more naturally or truthfully.

Because of this, because of the gloom of those years, I will run through them as sparingly, while honestly, as I can. The Holy Trinity of Phil, Chris, and myself were of course still together and it was for us that rooms at Botwell House were made available. Every day we would travel back and forth for lectures at Heythrop College's new site at Cavendish Square, W.1, just north of Oxford Street. We took a train and the London Underground, joining the toiling masses of commuters as they fought their way to work in the morning and straggled weary home at night. Those journeys were filled with the stench and constant throbbing of the trains' diesel engines waiting to depart from Paddington and the shock and batter of the doors as the guards shut them behind the last sprinting passengers. My only consolation for this soulless ritual was to find a pretty girl to stare at, hoping she would stare back at me. This pattern of behavior became a kind of default. Just like the train, I was on a set of rails. Making eye contact with a girl would establish, just for a moment, the fantasy of another existence. The communication that traveled between us, however fragmentary, was like getting off at another stop and not continuing to my foreordained destination. Because, of course, I was always going to return to Hayes and my routine of religious life.

First thing in the morning, Phil and Chris and I would gather for prayer. None of the priests would ever join in, except sometimes one elderly priest resident in the community. We were in the peculiar situation of sustaining a core practice of religious life when those in authority never bothered. The implied and sometimes stated argument was that busy parish clergy could not be expected to abide by a regular timetable, hence it was only students who were obliged to scheduled prayer. As a result, it felt like we were the children trying to hold the family together, or perhaps the old-style family was itself a fiction and we were fools to believe otherwise. We were holding the roof up but there was no floor to be standing on.

After we arrived home from Heythrop, we would gather for the evening meal, almost always the only time the whole group was together. The full community consisted of us three students, four priests, and an ancient brother named Abundio. Dan was the parish priest and superior, the elderly priest I mentioned was called Arthur, and then there were Matt and John, only recently ordained or, as the saying was, with the oils still wet on their palms. Four priests in a parish was something of a luxury, but this was the flagship of the Claretians in England, the Parish of the Immaculate Heart of Mary. The plant was huge, including the big modern church, the old one that had been converted into a hall, an extensive "men's club," an older club used as a youth club, scout huts, a very large primary school with playground and field, a secondary school about a mile away, and, of course, Botwell House. Mass attendance on a Sunday was two and a half thousand, and there were scores of groups and societies meeting every week. What with masses and confessions, marriages, baptisms, and funerals, there was always more than enough to keep the priests busy, but it was also great fun for the boys! When they gathered for dinner, prepared by our housekeeper, there would be stories galore, with an enormous cast of characters to talk about and running plot narratives like a soap opera.

I used to dread these meals, but I had to eat. Dan presided, worldly and disabused about the trustworthiness of human nature, while Matt as the family raconteur kept up a more or less constant parade of anecdote and banter. After dinner there would be perhaps some television. Often, I would go to my room to study, then come down for the news and a later program, and afterward go to bed. But exactly at that time, around ten or ten thirty p.m., after the parish doors were locked for the night, there took place a spontaneous kitchen gathering, a mini-festival in the midst of the workaday where the guys were free to be themselves. Everybody apart from Brother Abundio and the elderly priest was usually there. Sometimes I forced myself to stay, more often I also disappeared. But I could not get away.

Streams of animated conversation laced with hysterical laughter burst upstairs and onto my senses as I lay in bed. What was wrong with me? Why could I not join in? Why were Chris and Phil able to be down there at the center of the party, and not me? Dan, the parish priest and superior, was often present and lent to the proceedings both a stamp of approval and a frisson of boundaries transgressed. If the superior was there, enjoying himself after hours, then the structure of religious life had suddenly become much more flexible, much more of a boys' night out, or, if we had been in the States, a fairly tame, if weird, frat house.

Between Dan and me there was now, more and more, an underlying current of hostility. He held fairly standard US Republican opinions while I took a decisively left-leaning anti-imperial stance. But really it was his lifestyle that I hated the most, something I couldn't debate but was forced to share in. He liked nice things and nice times and the possibility of indulging himself with them, while for me a religious superior should lead the way in abandoning the world. Dan was more or less the inverse of my religious ideal.

The younger priests of the parish were almost always present, and as always Matt was the leader of the rout, the *magister ludi*. Really, he had now gained everything he had argued for at Highcliffe and at Radford: there were no more taboos to be demolished, all the doors he wanted were open. He was a big personality in every sense, expansive, talented, imposing. He could hold a packed house for hours with jokes, stories, and imitations, and it was his voice that played the longest in those late-night funfests. Chris and Phil were very much under his sway—almost as if they were clients of a great patron—but truth to tell, just about everyone was affected by him. I could not help but admire Matt and want his esteem, but the way he was able to swing everything to how he wanted spelled disaster for me. While he was around, I had little control over the content of my own existence, over its affective reality, and all I could do really was resist him internally. Down there at night it was like they were all gorging on a great big chocolate ganache, to which, unfortunately, I was completely allergic.

Meanwhile, Dan imposed on the students a labor that took a great deal of time, detracted from studies, and in the end was a big failure for me. He announced that as we had three students in a parish house, the obvious thing was that they should make themselves useful and run the parish youth club. Completely without training we opened the old men's club as a weekly venue for parish teenagers. Boy, was I in for a surprise! I thought my general friendly approach, of being one of the guys, would be enough to make the thing work. Chris was involved, as treasurer, taking care of the candy store, keeping it supplied and handling the receipts. Phil was present, the same as me, making friends, keeping order. But it always seemed to be me sorting out the crises. A favorite entertainment turned out to be throwing the main circuit breaker, handily exposed in a small corridor between the two connecting halves of the building. In the resulting pitch black, the smooth, almost half-pound balls from the pool table were flung across the room, windows were broken, and amid the chaos and screams of terror, supplies and money from the tuck shop were stolen and often somebody would be hit from behind to settle a score. I would struggle my way through the darkness, bumping into bodies, to get to the control box and turn the lights back on. When they did there were girls complaining that they'd been hurt, maybe somebody was bleeding, and most of the boys were not looking at me but each other and laughing uncontrollably at the huge fun they just had.

I would try to find out who was responsible but, of course, it was impossible. Soon, however, it became evident that all the trouble revolved around a youth called Eamon, with the improbable nickname of Lacky, a tall, sly, mocking teen with a hint of real violence about him. After more than a year of trying to deal with him and his threatening cohort of sidekicks, we came to the conclusion that the only way was to ban the lot of them. I thought I was going to get badly beaten up, but when it came down to it, they didn't seem to mind very much—perhaps it was the reputation they were aiming at anyway. But then things actually got worse. By this point Phil and Chris rarely put in an appearance and little by little I let the door policy slip, letting people bring their friends in without having to become members. The atmosphere was, in fact, much more peaceful, but what you might call "greasier," the major group attending in dirty jeans and leather jackets rather than Lacky's gang's snappy two-tone. A parishioner then figured out that these new people were not actually Roman Catholics and he or she complained. I was called on once again to institute a membership requirement, i.e., this club is for RCs and others vetted for membership. One wretched rainy evening in late winter I stood at the door and told my leather-jacketed non-Catholic friends they could not come in. They came in anyway and began an altercation.

I insisted they had to leave, then one of them picked up a chair and threw it at me. At that moment something snapped inside of me, and all those idealistic years of love and peace were instantly abandoned. I launched myself at the young man and began beating him for all I was worth. The sheer surprise of the onslaught carried me forward, while a friend of my adversary jumped on my back and began scratching my eyes. But I was so out of control, I did not care until I had thrashed and pushed the supposed Protestants out of the building, out into the night and the rain. I shut and locked the door behind them, and a couple of the girls who were in good standing came up, clearly impressed, and solicitous for my cuts and bruises. They told me what a hero I was, taking on those guys on my own. But that evening was the end of it, of two years and more of running a church youth club. I had become a wicked shepherd, beating the sheep. When I went back to the parish house, I handed in my notice directly. I can't remember if anyone was surprised, or even cared. Certainly no one tried to dissuade me.

Something snapping inside me became a characteristic of my life in that last year before ordination. Around the same time as the final period of the youth club I became involved in the running of a football team. I was assisted by a young man called Martin. I am not sure if he suggested it, or maybe the kids in the youth club, but the two of us started a team that played in a local part-time league. To make up a full eleven we had to bring in friends of the original group of boys, and friends of the friends. It was the same problem as nonmembers at the youth club, but it really was a problem this time. Martin and I recruited the most thuggish, undisciplined, and untalented team of soccer players in all of Hayes and Hillingdon. We regularly lost by double digits, the other teams putting in goals against us like rebounding a ball off a brick wall. But, despite the embarrassment, as the season wore on it was the behavior off the field that became the real issue. Our hopeless, shameless players slashed the motorcycle tires of a referee who penalized them, in their view unfairly, drained the gas from his tank, and lay in wait for him to knock him down and kick him. It was always a nerve-wracking experience as to how they would react to officials after a match. In the end the ringleaders wanted to attack me and continued to challenge me to fight. "One punch," one of them kept repeating, "That's all it would take!"

In the end I felt in serious danger, and I took steps to escape. I dissolved the team, much to the frustration of the league and their fixtures; but I really could not continue. The night I phoned the league secretary and told him of my decision, Martin and I sat on the office floor of Botwell House and drained a half-liter of Johnny Walker together. I got sick drunk, but it seemed the only possible, truthful thing to do in the circumstances.

Drinking heavily was something socially approved in the general milieu of the Botwell parish. The men's club had a thousand-plus members and on a Friday or Saturday night it was bursting at the seams with the eponymous men, and their wives and children. Almost always there was an Irish or country 'n' western band cranking out an eclectic mix of favorites like "Black Velvet Band," "Knock Three Times," "The Croppy Boy," and "The Rocky Road to Dublin." The noise was deafening, a thick fug of cigarette smoke hung over everything, and to get to the bar and order a drink was like a scramble for a lifeboat on the *Titanic*. But it was all in the highest spirits and the whole raucous experience was the point of it all. I used to go up there some Saturday nights, because again we students were told that our mingling in the club could be for the good of the parish. By the time I had finished with the Guinness-and-cider Black and Tans and the occasional whiskey chaser, plus all the Rothmans and Benson and Hedges, primary and secondary, I'd be unsteady on my feet and my throat felt like excrement and sandpaper as I returned to my room. I'm not sure if it did the parish any good; it certainly was no good for me. Later I would wake up in the metal-tasting night feeling queasy and thickheaded and I'd hear the guttural calls and the car doors slamming as the after-hours crowd finally turned out. It was already Sunday, and in a few hours the first mass would be underway in the church not one hundred yards from the club. I'd wonder miserably what on earth I was doing in this place and what was the point of any of it.

The question then obviously springs to mind, what *was* the point? If this was the way of it, as intolerable as I am telling, why on earth did I not simply walk away? It is at the nub of this question that the real power of my cultural formation and family position becomes clear. That office space where I got drunk with Martin was the only area where I could make telephone calls with privacy. Almost every Sunday evening, after everyone disappeared, I would spend almost an hour there talking with my mother. I would go through my frustrations, the lack of prayer, the lack of order, the worldliness and materialism of our life as I saw it, and, worst of all, the negative leadership given by Dan, antithetical to everything I thought he should be doing. I would expend a great deal of emotional energy off-loading and asking for affirmation. Underneath was an unspoken undertow, a real desire and asking permission to go, to look for another way. On the surface, however, things went in the other direction: in the narrative I was the hero, the saint of faithfulness, while all those around me did not and would not keep faith. My mother would listen, agreeing at the appropriate moments, encouraging me at others, telling me how all the saints had to suffer in serving God. I would receive the positive strokes and feel good about myself and able to go on, thinking myself the righteous man surrounded by the wicked. All the same, underneath, there was always the dim hope that my mother would have mercy and suddenly tell me, son, it's enough, you've done all you can, it's high time to go!

Apart from my mother, and possibly my siblings, there was only one other theoretical source of emotional support for an exit, but the story of that is itself indicative of how unreal and metaphysical my mind was. Dan indulged himself and everyone around him in a suffocating relationship with his natural birth family. There were two or three rooms at the back of the new church, in the sacristy area, which he had furnished as a visitor's apartment, with bedroom and kitchenette. His style was shag carpet, deep upholstery, heavy floral fabrics. The area had its own special smell, which always signified for me a material attachment, as throat-catching as it was umbilical. Every Christmastide Dan's family would descend on Botwell House and take up residence in the sacristy apartment. Suddenly all the dynamics would shift, away from the religious life of the community, over to what I considered to be entombment in the private vault of Dan's family life. His mother would turn up, along with her two daughters, both nuns. What is it about a family where all the children take vows of celibacy, and then come back together as frequently as they can to breathe the same nursery air?

Dan's mother was treated as a queen. She would occupy the head of the table at the Christmas meal and all conversation would go through her like a valve. It was as if it was somehow a special treat for us all to be brought into the court of her presence, as if no one else had families of their own, and should share like orphans in the sinuous bonds of this one. The mother was in fact a hard-willed woman of hawkish opinions: I was in the TV room with her when news came on of the hijacked Lufthansa jet heading to Libya with surviving members of the Munich massacre perpetrators, together with eighteen hostages. She declared that the plane should be shot out from the sky, forthwith. At the Christmas meal we would pull the crackers and put on the party hats, and jokes would be flying, and I would feel like a rotten fish at the bottom of a barrel. Where was I to go? What was I to do? I decided to go for a walk. I would seek out the industrial part of town, the place where the working class gathered. There I would feel some true connection, solidarity, and comfort.

It was 1972 and it seemed the world still held a sense of class struggle that could be won. I walked by terraced houses with cheap stucco moldings over the doors and tiny front yards with box hedges and the rags of summer plants hanging on in the weak afternoon sun. These were the houses of workers and clerks in the transport and telecommunications industries, but I felt no solidarity; they were all as closed and inward-looking as any upper-class mansion. I made my way beyond the houses to the industrial estate, the huge EMI buildings, their metal processing units coated in a sickly rust-inhibiting yellow. The farther I walked, the more depressed I became, each step carrying me into an invisible pit. Far from bringing me to a feeling of identity and strength, my pilgrimage to the industrial working class served only to magnify my complete lack of human connection. I almost ran back to Botwell House, desperately conscious that my only relationship with life was with the dysfunctional religious community I had escaped barely an hour before. Dan was right, this group was my real and only family.

However, I still continued nurturing my rebellious politics; albeit in a less mythic-minded, more activist framework. In August 1971 the British government introduced internment in Northern Ireland, a policy of arresting and detaining without trial men suspected of being part of the IRA, or generally considered troublemakers. It was a standard British government response to the "Irish problem." When push came to shove the human rights of Catholic Irish could be abrogated by pen stroke of policy. I joined the London Anti-Internment League and became exposed to an intoxicating ragtag of Northern Irish lawyers, Sinn Feiners, anarchists, Trotskyists, socialists. There was something very refreshing at the meetings, hearing those Derry and Belfast accents telling of their long struggle, without obvious animosity, rather ingrained humor and courage. The London students and militants were entirely another breed. Almost invariably hairy and scruffy, they were riven by internal definitions and doctrinal disputes that it was very easy to fall foul of. It was like joining another religion, just like Christianity, with all its own history

112   UNBECOMING A PRIEST

of reformations and heresies. All the same (or perhaps for that reason) I felt quite at home among them, and occasionally I found myself truly impressed by an individual's conviction and passion in wanting to bring justice in the world and an end to war.

I started a Hayes branch of the league, recruiting members from the men's club and a young friend called Michael from the youth club. Michael and I rode around West London on a motorbike flyposting for upcoming demonstrations, feeling like members of the French Resistance. I even got myself some kind of soapbox and set it up on the corner of Botwell Lane and the High Street, haranguing the shoppers about the evils of the British Army occupying Ulster. Absolutely no one took any notice of me. Clearly my oratory was uncompelling. I wondered if anyone would complain—a student for the priesthood creating a public spectacle like that. But no one said anything. I think the principle was ignore him and he'll go away, which was basically what happened. Pretty soon I gave up. But not before I was involved in a riot.

It was the aftermath of Bloody Sunday, when emotions were running extremely high. A big demonstration was planned, converging on the Ministry of Defense in Whitehall. There was a sense of wanting to storm the place, of exacting some kind of real consequence for the wanton gunning down of civilians in the Bogside. But the police were ready, long practiced and prepared for just such occasions. It was dark and dank, a standard wintry London night. The demonstrators were in a thick press, hundreds deep. You could see very little ahead, but our sweat and breath hung in the air, and you could feel the passion of the bodies next to you, a mass of faceless young men and women, throwing themselves forward. I don't know what we were expecting, but suddenly the line in front of us evaporated and there they were—the police. In their helmets and heavy vulcanized rubber raincoats, they were lashing out uncompromisingly with their gloved fists and nightsticks. Some of the more militant students used placards to fight back, but these were quickly smashed to the ground and the protestor grabbed if they moved too slow. And then came the horses. A police horse up close is enormous, medieval, and they were reversing so that they could not be frightened, the vast rear end bearing down and their metaled hooves threatening to crush shins and feet left anywhere in their way. There was nothing for it but to retreat, ducking back under the arms of the wave behind.

I got behind the lines and out of sheer frustration started scooping up clods of dirt from some kind of grass patch and lobbing it over at the mounted coppers. This obviously accomplished nothing, and it did not last long. There was some kind of signal, and the police began pushing forward implacably. In a moment we were all retreating back up to Trafalgar Square. We streamed out into the open space and a car came toward us at speed, blaring its horn. In a trice the crowd turned on the car, screaming and yelling at it. Someone took off a shoe and threw it, bouncing it off the hood. The car applied the brakes to confront us, but this infuriated everyone even more. Twenty or so people immediately started to charge toward it. If we'd caught the car who knows what would have happened, but the driver saw the turn of events and had enough sense to hit the accelerator. The incident took a few seconds, but it was long enough to reveal within me the huge power of impunity conferred in and by a mob and the extreme danger and violence lodged within it.

And so, my unbecoming formation went between community, youth club, study, and my dalliance with Irish Republican politics. Despite their obvious chaos, my days continued to trickle steadily through the glass, growing into months and years down to a date with priesthood. I struggled to the end of my degree at Heythrop College, achieving an inferior grade, what they called a 2.2. In order to proceed to ordination, the Trinity had first to take final vows in the religious life—solemn, irrevocable vows rendering any other commitment (i.e., marriage) permanently invalid. The preparation for this enormous step consisted of Wacker calling us in and announcing brusquely, "If you're not ready now, you never will be." I felt the walls close in and terror grip my heart. I wanted to continue to delay, but I felt the implied threat in Wacker's words and my helpless bluff was called. I had to accept and solemnly vow my life away according to canon laws formulated in the thirteenth century.

I was approved by my superiors for ordination (with one voice dissenting, Dan's, as I subsequently found out). I did a solitary retreat at the Benedictine monastery in Ramsey, Kent. I read a spiritual book called *Listen, Pilgrim*, a kind of autobiography of a young man on a pilgrimage of faith, making mistakes along the way, but vindicated by the vibrant sense of his journey. I filled an exercise book with scribblings, trying to reproduce the same satisfying effect, but only creating an embarrassing pudding. Some French kid wrote in big chalk French words on the seafront esplanade *l'ennui est né ici* (boredom was born here), and that's the most real thing I remember from that retreat. Spiritually, the sheer blind decision to continue was the only thing that resulted, trusting that, like the pilgrim, the journey would ultimately count for truth.

My desperation spilled over into an emotional relationship with a married woman. Everything was so unreal by that point that neither was this relationship anywhere near practicable (nothing really happened), nor, at the same time, did I feel the entanglement to be in any way wrong. In many ways I was totally dissociated from actual human life. My ability to make a relationship with a single woman was severely stunted, both in practical life terms and the kind of spontaneous signals I was able to give out. I think most young single women would have run a mile from me. But when it came to unhappily married women with a spiritual bent, I had learned the physics of that connection, so to speak, at my mother's breast. It's something I am ashamed of, but in the circumstances almost inevitable. The closer I came to ordination, the closer I was, finally, to being my own man. Yet if this was to express itself in any way it could not be with a woman who was seeking a normal relationship. It almost had to be someone married.

The whole sorry business dragged on for about a year, with furtive colloquies during volunteer projects, and, once or twice, a brief, doomed, stolen kiss and hugging on group outings, all around the time of ordination. If anyone had maintained any real oversight in my life I would have been stopped in my tracks but everything by now was locked in toward the priesthood. Even Dan, who evidently disliked me—and, as I say, had formally not approved me—never once sought to intervene to persuade me against becoming a priest. The magic of ordination was too great to resist, its mystique already enfolding the Holy Trinity. We had gone through so much and been abandoned by so much, it was as if we had somehow earned our destiny and it would not be taken away. Outsiders too were under the same thrall. On another retreat, previous to the one in Ramsgate, I confessed my whole life to a Trappist monk. He was horrified and dropped a phrase that stuck in my mind like hot tar: "You're not fit to be a married man, let alone a priest." But not once did he try to dissuade me from the sacerdotal goal. If it came to a margin call between moral maturity and priestly identity, the latter would always win.

As the expression has it, clichéd but accurate, my date with destiny drew near. On the one hand, it was like some huge "coming out into society," a debutante event without par. On the other, it was an immensely serious spiritual commitment. The paradox tore at me inside, yet the surface machinery had entirely a life of its own. Knowing with an inner well of certainty that I was completely unprepared for priestly ministry, I asked permission to do an additional period of study in Rome, beginning that fall. To my surprise, permission was granted—it may have been that some hint of my romantic entanglement had gotten through and geographical displacement was a tried and trusted method of dealing with such situations. In any case I was temporarily in the clear and I was able to face the inevitable with something of a steady mind. The day arrived, a bright dawn in July. The parents of the three ordinands would shortly turn up, to share a breakfast with Bishop Gerald Mahon, auxiliary of the Diocese of Westminster. There was an immense buzz about the place, a deep self-congratulation. Getting three new priests was like three children being born to an old family who for too long had lacked any offspring. Someone told me that the local mayor of Hayes and Hillingdon had been invited and was being given a front-row seat at the event. I was outraged and, summoning my courage, went at once to find Dan to protest. I found him as he was going down the stairs to the sacristy and told him this was my ordination and I had not invited the mayor. He looked as if he were about to finish me on the spot and started to say something to the effect that this was *not* my ordination, and it could easily be called off at any moment. Then he stopped himself and turned away—there was nothing I could do about the invitation, and maybe he thought I would give everyone a break and pull out myself. But the wheels were in motion; neither of us was going to get off the train.

We shared the preordination breakfast with the bishop, and my mother, finding herself for the first (and last) time in her life at a banquet table with a member of the English hierarchy, took it on herself to castigate the institution and its representatives for being too distant from the people. The bishop received it all with good grace, while I was both painfully embarrassed and secretly proud of my mother.

I found the ritual itself almost meaningless, the prostration, the anointing, the sharing of the sacred vessels. The one thing that had true impact was the laying on of hands by the bishop. I felt the warmth and vitality of human hands laid on my head. I felt perhaps a kind of strength and authority passed on. By that time what is known as the "charismatic renewal" was becoming a new currency in the church—a practice of the "gifts of the Spirit" often imparted with a laying on of hands by a prayer group. The bishop's action merged with some of that practice and got some of its sense of authenticity from it. And it was that same action that I myself then repeated endlessly directly after the ceremony. As a fiery summer sun went down over the big copper-roofed glass-sided church, the Catholic devotion to the anointed hands of the new priest gave me unparalleled opportunity to pray over people, physically touching their heads, women and men, mothers and fathers, children and grandparents. On and on the line went, some people coming back more than once for a blessing (including a comrade or two from the men's club). It was a blind ecstasy, a sudden apocalyptic drowning in physical human contact after a hundred years of loneliness. But I already knew that I was completely unfit to minister in any regular way to these people; the blessings could be only the briefest of honeymoons. The more proximate I was to putting that supernatural "Father" in front of my name, the less and less equipped I felt to guide anyone. I had asked for permission to go to Rome, and that was where I was heading. I would find out what it all meant, there at the heart of it all. And, indeed, Rome would not fail me. It would measure up to my expectations in every way, but not in any way that I expected.

twelve

ROME: RUIN AND REVELATION

ROME, ROME, ETERNAL CITY, church of martyrs, master code of empire, and, at length, key to my personal liberation!

If you want to find out about the history of Europe and the story of Christianity entangled with it, Rome is the place. Rome is a giant holograph machine in which so many things take on an extraordinary clarity, their relations and meaning suddenly lucid like nowhere else. The nine months I spent there, at the ages of twenty-six to twenty-seven, gave me an unparalleled grasp of church history. The very physical presence of Rome is worth a hundred university courses, everything laid out for you materially without partiality, simply there to be appreciated, assessed, hated, despised, embraced, or loved, as you will. So much of my confusion, naïveté, and infantilism Rome dispelled by a single perspective from the Janiculum hill with its patriotic panorama and the Vatican nestled demurely below; or walking the market in Campo di Fiori under the lowering, reckoning glance of Giordano Bruno; or watching the prostitutes come into the espresso bars first thing in the bright dusty morning across from the Stazione Termini.

In many respects Rome is still a pagan city, and it is easy not to recognize that amid the splendor of basilicas and Christian art. This was now my third time to the holy city. I had, in fact, gone there on a vacation with my family and a group of friends directly after ordination, even at the time an embarrassing, misplaced celebration of my new achieved status in the eyes of my mother. But now I would spend continuous months there and little by little Rome would reveal its mysteries to me, at least the ones I needed to know. The light, the sounds, the smells, the food, the stones, the trees, the people, they all bring you back in a wound-around scarf of time to the first centuries and the birth of Christianity into an unwilling world. Unlike for Catholicism in England or Ireland where Rome appears in prismatic form as the embodiment of Catholic truth, the actual physical city is a living, breathing mass of contradictions and passions, of dirt and beauty, of violence and imperial calm. The statue of Augustus Caesar along the Via dei Fori Imperiali raises its arm in effortless salute over a place just as much in thrall to his kingdom as when Paul first arrived along the Appian Way. If the Holy Land is the Bible written in a landscape, then Rome is the scorch marks of the gospel as it is first fought and then was appropriated by worldly power.

I did not grasp this at first and it has taken me some more years to figure it out fully, but by the end of my stay this truth was written in my soul. Walking into my room for the very first time I breathed a physical, lung-liberating sigh of relief. The faintly sweet smell of coffee and floor soap mingled together was perfume to my senses. I was overwhelmed by the light pouring in through the huge double casement windows, a light at once abrupt and sensuous. It was such a shock to have this light, heady space all to myself and to feel somehow that the outside and inside were not as brutally demarcated as in England. In fact, the outside seemed almost as cognizant of what was going on inside as the inside, and then vice versa.

I was living in the international college of the order, an impressive five-story pink plaster and stone building with a tall iron fence and a *cancello* (gate), with an intercom for callers. There were pine and oleander and feathery reed grass and a thousand fireflies at night along the deep gully that ran at the back of the property. The college housed a large community of priests and brothers. On the third floor were the teachers and administrators, and the fourth floor was a collection of priest-students drawn mostly from Spain and South America with a sprinkling of other Europeans. Everyone there seemed to be a serious student and the routine of rising, prayer, and study was obeyed in a businesslike fashion. Here suddenly there seemed to be an ordered community, and at the same time it contained a rich palette of cultures from which to learn. I liked many of the Latin Americans. We would discuss the coup in Chile, the truck drivers' strike and the protest of the middle-class women banging their cooking pots, then the guerilla movement in Colombia and the civil war before that. We would also discuss other members of the order and their doings, especially figures of power. One of these was our very own cardinal, recently deceased, and his princely apartment all to himself on the fifth floor. We went there on a furtive visit, and saw his redundant succession of rooms, his brocaded furniture, his desk, and his scarlet cardinal's robe strewn and abandoned across an ottoman in a scene straight out of Fellini's *8 1/2*.

But it was the city and its life that had the biggest impact on me.

I would turn on the radio in the morning and listen to the songs, Edoardo Bennato, Celentano, Mina, and to the lilt of the women's voices giving the news or the weather. There was immediately something more poetic about the spoken culture that encouraged the soul to expand. I remember one of the first broadcasts I heard, and vaguely understood; it was a female voice discussing the word *farfalla* (butterfly) and connecting its meaning to the word for "soul"; how she did it I'm not certain, but it sounded beautiful. Each day I would attend lectures at the Lateran university. I would exit the gate and take the dusty track to the main road, the Via Aurelia, and walk down to a main intersection. There I'd catch a bus that would take me to the Piazza Cavour and from there another one to the Lateran. The buses were terribly noisy and crammed with people. They would groan and shudder as the driver crunched the gears along city streets designed in the sixteenth century and now jammed with Alfa Romeos and Fiats. Inside, the people would all tip together in unison with the bus and there was always palpable sexual tension among them. The men were much more on display than the women, wearing skintight pants and short leather jackets, and carrying little purses for their change and cigarettes. The women wore long woolen coats and scarves or, in the summer, slacks and blouses, but their glance, more than anything, spoke to me of how powerfully conscious they were of their erotic role and status—and how those things must always be kept in reserve, because that is the only way they could keep a hold on both. For the culture was meanwhile very familiar with another class of women. As mentioned, some of them were apparent in the bars in the more intense thoroughfares, but generally they were kept at a very precise distance. It was out beyond all the buildings and the family housing that exploitive prostitution really showed its face, surrounding the city like an army. The great ring road circling Rome, the *raccordo anulare*, looked as if an invisible sea had beached hundreds and hundreds of women all along its dusty edges. On worn grass patches and among clumps of tattered willows and reeds you could see them, each with a folding chair and sometimes picnic tables and parasols for comfort. Every so often the chair would be empty, and a car would be drawn up. The whole city seemed bathed in a surrounding sea of sensuality.

And that feeling merged via only the slightest spiritual gap with the architecture of Rome as the bus threaded its way through the sights: the monuments, fountains and churches, the ancient, the Romanesque, the baroque, appealing always and deeply to the senses. The human body on display surrounds St. Peter's square with 140 giant statues of saints, virgins, and martyrs above the colonnades, like its own ring around a city. St. Peter's and the Vatican were not on my bus route, standing over on the left of the Tiber. But they had a magnetic presence, and you could almost feel the bus swing against it as it turned east away from the river. The weight of its stones was physical, but its stones were also hardly distinguishable from the stones of ancient Rome, which lay scattered all around (and were often, in fact, the very same). Everywhere were timeworn remains, solemn and silent, yet haunted by ghosts of immense crowds under their enormous span of power: the Forum, the Colosseum, Trajan's arch, the Circus Maximus, the baths of Diocletian. I passed most of these every day and their arrogance and indifference still spoke with a completely modern accent. It was as if a huge time-blasting bomb had gone off and had left two and a half millennia of history cemented into a single simultaneous crust. As if everything had changed and yet nothing had changed. Every day I traveled through this exotic landscape and let it drift over me and through me, barely conscious of its effect. Because, meanwhile, the Roman Catholic Church still claimed to be essentially different and separate from it all, no matter what the architecture seemed to say. Thus, there was still a clear disconnect between me and what I was seeing with my eyes.

My classes were in Italian. I had begun studying Italian only on the boat across from England so most of the lectures were going over my head. In order to get up to speed, I enrolled in the Berlitz school of languages. My professor was a certain Piero, a man with a slightly hysterical laugh, no chin, and a great delight in the classical derivation of Italian words. He took an immediate liking to me, probably because I was an ecclesiastic and showed interest in his word analysis. It turned out that Piero was something of an aristocrat fallen on hard times, forced into teaching to make ends meet. He owned a town apartment in the toney, fascist-era Piazza Bologna where he lived with his mother. He invited me to visit and in a musty room with great elegant doors and dark burgundy drapes he brought out some of his own wine with a local cheese he wanted to share with me. He invited me to go with him and his mother to his country house somewhere in south Tuscany from where the wine came. It was a long drive, but I was rewarded with his commentary on the countryside. He pointed out the favorite places for Franciscans to build their friaries: at the end of low gentle ridges or spurs shielded by a stand of cypress. Here was a different art from Rome, kinder and molded to the earth, the buildings dreaming peacefully within their timeless moment of time. On the way we passed the medieval city of Orvieto, impregnable on its sheer cliffs, fortress of popes and site of the school where Thomas Aquinas first taught before transferring to Rome. Passing beneath it on a modern highway it was as if two eras had come up against each other in a lurching warp of space and time. It would not have been shocking to see a papal procession with soldiers in plumed helmets and gleaming breast-plates coming down the hill as we sped by in our automobile. When we got to Piero's property it was at the end of an unpaved track and looked like a large, deserted farmhouse. The rooms were tall and retained a sense of light and substance, but everything was covered in dust and smelled of mouse droppings. Piero and his mother were picking up wine from the cellar, and other bits and pieces. We brought out a big bulb-shaped *fiasco*, in its straw basket, a manner of keeping wine going back to Boccaccio. It had a three-inch cork stopper and contained at least a half-dozen liters of Chianti. It almost seemed like we were stealing it, as if the house had been surrendered to someone else and we shouldn't have been taking anything. Piero's mother was driving him on in an irritable tone, and I suppose my presence gave him some kind of comfort. Piero ended up loaning me a car, a dilapidated Lancia. Even though the passenger door half fell off, in full traffic, the car proved very useful.

 I used it to visit a community of the Missionaries of Charity, the order founded by Mother Teresa. She was just then growing in fame and acceptance as a living icon of the church, mainly through Malcolm Muggeridge's documentary and book, *Something Beautiful for God*. Her commitment to the poorest of the poor attracted me immensely, and when I heard that the novitiate of her order was situated in one of the shanty towns or *barrache* that dotted the outskirts of Rome, I resolved at once to visit them. Here was a religious community that took the vow of poverty seriously! In my struggles with my own community, it had been the poverty element of the religious life that I had always insisted on, to the point of obsession. Poverty did not consist of a set of rules about holding money, but rather a spiritual principle and one easily translated into sociological terms. The poor were always with us, but did we identify with their life condition? Not a chance. Apart from perhaps a handful of individuals, the dominant concern was to have a nice life. But now, here in Rome, was a group of women for whom the condition of the poorest was their specific goal in life, their preferred place to be. In this case it was the area of shacks and rough structures under and by the ancient Claudia aqueduct not far from the Via Appia Nuova. One Saturday I took a couple of buses to the stop where I'd been told to get off, and by dint of asking I found my way to the house of the *monache*. Like everyone else they lived along the unpaved road in the shadow of the aqueduct, in a single story house of cinder block walls and corrugated iron roofs. The only difference was their floor area was bigger because it had to contain two dozen persons. I presented myself to them and told them I would like to be of assistance. They invited me back to say mass for them and to visit some of the people in the area.

I returned regularly in Piero's car and got to know the community. The nuns were astonishing. As I say, there were about two dozen of them, and the average age had to be early twenties. They were an epiphany to me of youth, vitality, and chosen purpose to serve the world's most deprived. They seemed preternaturally beautiful and joyful. Their living area was less than the ground plan of a four-bedroom American house, they slept head-to-head on rolled-out mats, dined on the simplest food, and prayed three or four hours a day. They wore the tea cloth saris typical of Mother Teresa, which must have left them freezing in winter. I met them in the spring, and it was like a cherry orchard had burst into blossom here in the dust and stench beneath the aqueduct. Most of them were Indian, a few were European. Among the latter was Sister Gregory who was, I believe, the superior, although she never behaved as having status over the rest. She had left another order to join the Missionaries, and was slightly older than the others, with a keen, intelligent face. She encouraged me to visit and told me that Mother herself was coming soon and I would be sure to meet her. In fact, none of the sisters seemed able to talk about anything else but the forthcoming visit of their famous leader. It was the highlight of the year, the visit of a rock star. In the meantime, they gave me my pastoral connection to the area, asking me to call on one of the locals. It was Vicente, a wizened little man living in a one-room dwelling in the shadow of the arches. I called on him quite often and sat beside him in his narrow shack cluttered with books and papers and a few clothes. He would clear a space and brew coffee on a tiny espresso maker. It was black and thick as treacle, but it felt like hospitality. After coffee he would get out a guitar and sing in a sentimental Neapolitan style. He really had only one song, which was his own personal composition. It was a lament about the day of his first communion, how innocent he had been, and how he could never get that innocence back.

The attraction of this kind of poverty is also a sensuality. There are other kinds of poverty that are wholly repellent, and I was going to encounter them later in my life. But this kind, as exemplified by Vicente, is filled with pathos and, yes, even perhaps blessedness. People who have very little, and yet retain some kind of humanity and humility, bring a great peace and truth to the world. This is what Mother Teresa and her women wanted to plug into, or that's how I understood it. Vicente, of course, had made his life into a great big pity party, as it's called, but at least he felt pity about good things, and with the sisters up the road guaranteeing his currency, so to speak, my visits to him were rewarding, and still are. In Matthew's Gospel Jesus says, "Blessed are the poor in spirit," and this refers not so much to Vicente, but to those who voluntarily surrender everything for the sake of love. This was the meaning I was seeking among the Missionaries, but the cost was immensely high and the spiritual bomb-crater that my alienation in the world created for me was still going to be a problem.

Mother came and I said mass for her and her sisters. No doubt about it, Mother Teresa was an incredible human being. As one of her sisters said about her, "What you see is what you get." What you saw was a little shriveled lady, almost a female equivalent to Vicente, but what you felt was the gravity of an entire planet, and that's what you got. After the mass the sisters introduced me, and she sat down with me in a little room that served as a public area and spoke with me for a long time. I am conscious now of the drama of that moment given the enormous prestige Mother Teresa has since gained. At that point her ascent to stardom was only just beginning, and I don't mean that in a nasty way. I am sure she never changed from the person I met in 1974, but, really, she's now a canonized saint officially enjoying the full splendor of God! We talked into the late evening and then it was time for night prayer and one of the sisters came to tell her the whole community was waiting for her to join them. She told them to wait a while longer as what she was doing was important. "This is what we should be doing," she said.

We talked about the church, about religious life, about how it was so easy for orders to lose their original fervor and become wealthy and corrupt. She said there was no guarantee against this, even her own order could lose its fresh spirit, and the only thing was for each person to stay close to Christ and believe he would continue to guide his church. I protested this was very difficult in an environment where standards had lapsed, there was little prayer, and, in contrast, an accretion of material comforts. She was sympathetic and heard me out, nodding sometimes in agreement, but always affirming that Christ was in the church and to have faith in him. At one point I looked down below the table beside which we were seated, and I saw her foot in her sandal. My attention became riveted on it. I saw its bones, its veins, and its semitransparent skin and there was something about it that was intensely beautiful. She saw me looking and quickly withdrew her foot under her sari, but she did not stop talking. Finally, the novice mistress came in and said the novices really had to go to bed, and so at last Mother Teresa relented and our conversation ended. If there is any sort of karma, surely, I should be repaid harshly for keeping those novices kneeling on a hard cement floor, while I rehearsed my well-worn complaints and stared at their Mother's foot! But that is not the way grace works. She gave that time to me, and they did too. Its freedom would flow around me, and finally, in my last days in Rome, through me and into me.

Mother Teresa had mentioned she was staying in Rome a couple more days as she needed to visit another of her communities, out on the coast at Ostia. I remarked that I had use of a car and offered to drive her. She accepted and I arranged to return the following day. My relationship with Mother Teresa waxed and waned over the space of twenty-four hours. I did not use Piero's car as it was unreliable and somewhat unsafe. Instead, a Mexican friend at the student house loaned me his VW Beetle, which was much more trustworthy, and I picked her up with two of her nuns and drove us all to the ancient port of Ostia. At one point I briefly lost my way on the highway, and she became more than a little irritated. She asked did I know where we were, and I told her I thought we were on the right road but going in the wrong direction. She turned to her companions and said, without humor, "Ha! Did you hear that? On the right road but in the wrong direction!"

I managed to turn around, and we got to Ostia without further incident. It was a seaside town on Sunday and the sun was hot. The beach was packed with Italian girls and boys in skimpy bathing suits. Mother Teresa looked at them through the Beetle windows and said, "These girls, they are lacking something. What is the word?"

"Modesty," I suggested helpfully.

"No," she replied, "that's not it. They lack shame..."

This struck me as at once more accurate than what I had said and terrifically old-fashioned in viewpoint. What kind of conversation could you have with Western youth beginning with the proposition they should feel shame for their bodies? But my real rift with the future saint had taken place earlier that morning. Before we set out, I had said mass for the sisters one more time. We used Canon One, which is the translation of the old Roman canon. It contained phrases about angels carrying the gifts of the earthly altar to an altar in heaven. They seemed strange to me, a weird angel theology mixed in with Platonism, which instilled a gap between earthly matters and heaven above where the real stuff was. I made some remark to that effect, hoping Mother Teresa would agree, preferring to root the meaning of the mass much more in Jesus and this earth. But she replied tartly, "Is that a problem for you, Father Bartlett?"

I felt immediately the iron strength of this great planet pull against me. "No, no," I said. "No problem."

After the brief encounter of those days, I never met Mother Teresa again. I don't think either of us was too interested in renewing the connection. But I was not finished with the gravity effect I experienced around her. For me she was a highly personal form of a general phenomenon experienced in proximity to various modes of Catholicism. As noted, I also felt it in relation to the basilica of St. Peter's and the Vatican, and as an effect of attraction that at some point also turned to repulsion.

The "greatest church of Christendom" continued to be a presence and have a huge fascination for me. I felt it would be there, if anywhere, I'd attain the revelation I desperately needed, the one that would tell me how I fitted with this whole thing. Very early in my time in Rome the place had been given a huge boost in significance when I was taken with a party of priests on a special archeological tour. A few decades earlier during repairs to the floor, workmen had discovered a deeper level of remains, which turned out to be a Roman necropolis, or city of the dead, right under the piazza and body of the church. Further excavated by archeologists, it was possible to go down there and, following a string of electric lamps, view the mausoleums and urns of ancient Romans.

In the stark pools of light and receding into thick gloom, the class system of Hades was revealed: the more modest plinths for the less well-off contrasted with house-sized monuments for powerful families. According to our guide the archeologists had tunneled onward to the edge of the necropolis where there were no markers, only scattered bones, animal and human. It was clearly the place where paupers were dumped as well as the detritus and deceased from the Circus of Nero only 150 meters to the south and west. The spot also happened to be directly under the main altar of St. Peter's. By tradition, Pater was martyred in the Circus of Nero in the year 64 CE, and our guide in Hades argued that putting these factors together amounted to a strong archeological probability that it was indeed the burial site of Simon Peter, the Galilean fisherman. And that is what it felt like. (It seems that the actual bones of Peter were transferred in the first centuries into a niche in a wall adjoining the site.) It was like traveling back in time, or rather a powerful case of the warp in time produced by the story of the gospel. We were down there in a pit of Roman history and what was going on above seemed to be a single fused moment with an executed man amid the monuments of those who executed him.

Up above I used to pray in the Sacrament Chapel regularly, feeling an intensity there I did not feel elsewhere. I also used to go to confession, to the priests always available in one of the arms of the transept. This was never a pleasant experience, getting a load off my chest to stern-faced clergy, but I felt that if I was doing it here at the heart of the church, then I was bound to be given the formula to redemption eventually. The basilica became for me the critical location in which to seek my spiritual life. There was, however, one other key place to seek it, one that acted as a kind of counterbalance to the weight of St. Peter's—except not quite.

I had begun attending "charismatic" prayer groups in England, first invited by an old school friend with whom I'd recently got back in touch. He was a Roman Catholic but had discovered what is called "baptism in the Spirit," meaning a sudden sense of infilling by the Spirit, often marked by the gift of tongues, i.e., the ability to pray using sounds that sounded like but were not any known syntax. The movement had emerged in the Roman Catholic Church in the late '60s and was spreading rapidly, mostly in big cities where it was possible to gather numbers of people thirsting for a new, more direct experience of God. I had gone to a few of these meetings in London and my reaction had been contempt and hostility. They seemed dominated by over-pious women, the sentiments were trite, and the manifestation of "gifts" seemed artificial and fake. All the same I had met a couple of young people who had impressed me. One in particular was Joanna, a young Irish nurse. Her story was gripping and there was definitely something different about her in mind and spirit.

She seemed to have a spiritual light in her that made others, including me, dull in comparison. Her younger sister had joined the Children of God, a shadowy group originating out of the late '60s Jesus-movement and which would later be recognized as a cult. The group recruited young people with a mixture of evangelical fervor, youthful allure, and the promise of tight-knit group identity. Joanna pretended to join the COG herself in order to be able to sleep next to her sister and whisper in her ear at night how much her family missed her, how dangerous this situation was, how she was breaking everyone's heart. Eventually she sprang her sister loose, but she remained unimpressed with much of traditional Catholicism. She said to me, "Tony, you think you know everything, but you don't. There are some things you don't know."

Her words stuck with me and rankled. When I found out there was a charismatic prayer group meeting every week in the Jesuit university, the Gregorian, I was astonished and immediately wanted to go. It was bound to be a much more serious and authentic representation of the movement, demonstrating if in fact there was any truth to it. And I was not disappointed. Upwards of three hundred people gathered in one of the lecture salons early every Sunday evening. I used to climb on my bicycle and speed down the Via Gregorio VII, pass the Vatican, and make my way to the university building just east of the Vittorio Emanuele monument. I heard nuns and seminarians get up to speak and their sincerity and conviction struck a chord. I was amazed at the fluency with which they prayed and the immediacy and power of their relationship with Jesus. People prayed or sang in tongues and then someone gave an interpretation, which is the way the apostle Paul wanted it. These interpretations, although generic in content, were comforting and personal. And the same could be said of the "prophecies," which were not a matter of foretelling the future but a direct address by the Spirit to the community. The formal teaching was also persuasive: one of the Jesuit theologians gave a satisfying intellectual account, saying that many, if not all, of the manifestations of the gifts could be found replicated in other cultures and religions; the only thing that was different here was the Spirit of Jesus' love. Little by little, however, the old alienation reasserted itself. I tried to speak in tongues in the privacy of my room and it sounded just ridiculous. I wanted to give testimony, but I was terrified to speak. And so, the old suspicions returned. How was it that these people had such ease and fluency and I remained tongue tied? How was it that they seemed to have a hotline to God while I was filled with pain and confusion? Wasn't it all mumbo-jumbo? Weren't they just successful exhibitionists and this was all another form of self-promotion?

One Sunday evening I plunked myself down in the outer ring of the prayer circle and after ten minutes or so a young priest sat down beside me. He had obviously just come from a good Italian dinner and wine fumes clung richly about him. He sang but did not say anything and just seemed to sit there basking in the happy glow of the prayer group. "That's it," I said to myself as I breathed in the vintage, "These people are basically loaded. A *grand cru*, the Holy Spirit, it's all the same thing. It's all the after-dinner liqueur of the over indulged." I spent the rest of the evening in an orgy of resentment, but later when I got home and lay in bed I sank in despair. Who was I to judge that man? What did I know about his life, or anyone's there? It was evident that these meetings were now doing me more harm than good, awakening jealousy and hatred on top of my chronic failure. I decided that night I could not go to the prayer group again. It had proved a spiritual dead end and a trap.

My possibilities for achieving the crucial goal of my time in Rome were now narrowing fast. Peter (Wacker), my superior in England, phoned me and insisted I had to come home in June, at the end of the second semester. In principle, the theology degree I was doing should have taken two years, but from the slightly irritated tone of his voice, it was plain that opinion in the province had swung. From giving me extra time for sorting myself out it was now a question of getting me down to work as the best cure. Literally it was now a matter of weeks. Spring had come to Rome and the days were growing warm. The swallows that had massed over the Tiber in a red October sky for passage to Africa were now filtering back in a haze of sunshine. The radio played its passionate Italian balladry, the young women appeared in their figure-tight clothes, and I went back to confession.

Looking at women and subsequently going to confession was for me a kind of closed loop. Women were external, perceived objects of desire, but at the same time my flirtatious attempts at eye contact were doomed gestures of relationship. Women for me were not just forbidden fruit. They were closed doors along an endless corridor of closed doors leading relentlessly to my otherworldly destiny. Looking at them was a way to push briefly against the door and open the fleeting possibility of a different existence. Then, going to confession subsequently was a way of cleansing myself from my indulgent practice, and so reassert my celibate destiny. And so on, indefinitely.

I was kneeling at the open side of one of the boxes in St. Peter's, as was the custom for men. The priest faced me through the velvet curtains, a man in his late sixties with spars of shipwrecked hair across his pale scalp and the profile of a judge. I told him I was a priest and that I had been guilty of staring at girls on the buses and of nighttime masturbation. He exploded. He asked me what I was doing in Rome and did my superiors even know I was here. He said I should leave Rome at once and return to my community in England. I told him I was due to go soon, and he said not soon enough, and gave me a rapid and angry absolution.

As he was finishing, he tapped me on the shoulder with a little black rod (a privilege, I am told, of the penitentiaries of St. Peter's). It was the rod that did it. Not only did he turn my hope into further disgrace, he beat me for my pains. I walked out of the transept or, should I say, I crawled? Groups of laughing tourists passed me and I felt like I wasn't there, not present in their world. They had been made to don long plastic gowns distributed at the door for modesty's sake while underneath they were wearing standard shorts and T-shirts. The gowns were semitransparent and simply added to the effect. They were entirely recognizable Western youth but now in fancy dress, with walk-on parts in a medieval pantomime. Me, I did not have arms or legs to bare, I had no recognizable human form. I stepped out into the Saturday morning sunshine and there was a gap between me and the air. I was breathing but its taste was negative, as if it were fleeing from me.

I knew I could not continue like this, and not only that. Something profoundly wrong, unfair had just occurred. The very space I had looked for healing had wounded me. In its place, the worldly city of Rome and all its cultural history, stretching off in the distance, seemed much more congenial and affirming.

My very life was at stake, and my feeling was no dried-up monsignor with his stick should take it from me. In truth, a vast orchestral chord should have been playing. This was the turning point of my life. Although I did not know it then clearly, all that was good in the Renaissance masterpiece behind me—the compassion of Christ, the vivid signs of his teaching, his irrepressible impact on the world—all of this was detaching itself from the marble and gold and clinging to my own back like a very coat of Joseph. I was walking out of that ornate tomb, never to look back, with my inheritance now part of my bones, rather than painfully in escrow to bankers from whom I continually had to plead for funds. And the stick with which I had been beaten? It was in truth the flail that Jesus had fashioned to drive his sheep out of the temple. Reading these episodes later in John's Gospel—much later—I recognized the authentic action of Christ in what happened. These days I thank the good monsignor for taking the whip to me!

As part of my studies, I had been researching psychoanalysis, Freud, Melanie Klein, etc., and browsing among the library shelves I had come across a book by Erich Fromm, titled *Psychoanalysis and Religion*. Something drew me to that book. It was slender with a black hardcover and it communicated an impression of both rigor and compassion. The next morning I grabbed it and took it with me on my bike, on my standard route past the Vittorio Emanuele monument and along the bumpy cobbled road to the Colosseum. Halfway up I stopped and found a spot on the grass bank overlooking the Forum. I don't know why I chose that spot. I think I had always felt it would be a great place to read a book, especially when the sun was pouring down like today. It was, in fact, a very short book, a series of three or four lectures. And I think it took very little time to come to the nub of the matter. Fromm drew a distinction between what he called humanistic and authoritarian religion. The former stressed the self-becoming and autonomy of the individual, the latter obedience and control. He told many stories about humanistic religion and said the religion of Jesus had begun that way but had changed when it had become the religion of the Roman Empire. He even said something about the practice of confession, about how in one respect it was positive because it was able to relieve an individual from a sense of guilt, but at the same time it took away his selfhood and made him prone to a continued dependence. The words hit me like a shot between the eyes. It was not like the author was even making an argument. What he said was evident, as if an oracle had spoken and no possible question remained. I set the book down and gazed at the broken pillars of the Forum, the ruined temples, the ruptured pavement of the Sacred Way. I could feel the power of religion wherever it came from. And I could also vaguely sense the eruptive power of the gospel arriving in ancient Rome without any support or leverage beyond itself, beyond its insane faith in Jesus. All at once I no longer needed to pay deference to an authoritarian form that beat me with a stick and put my life in a place without air. Something settled in my soul, and I decided, for my health as a person, I would never go to confession again. I stood up and the ground was different under me. In a certain sense I was free for the first time in my life. I got on my bike and cycled back past the Vatican, back up the hill to the Via Aurelia and my college.

All the same, I was still in Rome, the Vatican just down the road, and I was still a newly ordained priest. I had gone through a negative revolution, freeing me from confession and its sense of condemnation, but my actual life was that of a servant of the church. In a way I was in a worse position than ever. It did not cross my mind to leave the priesthood, and yet I had just renounced one of its key functions. I had done so for the sake of my own life, my own integrity, and, in a weird but real way, I had done it in order to be an effective priest. It made no sense, and, what's more, together with leaving the prayer group, my refusal of confession left me without spiritual resources or relationship. I prayed, yes, but my prayer had basically been a matter of saying sorry or asking for help, and now I hardly knew what to say anymore.

A new feeling came on me, one of dullness and unimportance. The sun blazed, the trees came into blossom, and I walked around in a state of disconnection and inner numbness. About this time one of the priest students who had been ministering in a working-class parish in Rome had made friends with a couple of young women. He brought them to the student house and introduced me. He felt that with my left-leaning opinions I would be an okay person for them to talk to. I think his relationship with them was honestly pastoral, but it didn't do any harm that both of them were actually quite pretty. They were Silvia and Andrea, and Silvia was easily the dominant one. She had a ready tongue and whatever way she had bumped into my colleague she had no good word to say about the clergy. Silvia, in fact, belonged to the rooted proletarian tradition in Rome, one of fierce antipathy toward the church. This class used the term *bagarozzi* for priests, the name for a roach with the appearance of sporting a clerical collar. Workmen would yell it out if clergy happened to pass them by. Probably my colleague was trying to show Silvia another face of the church, but she was having none of it.

As we all walked around the path that skirted the dirt playing field behind the college, she asked which of the rooms was mine. I counted along the windows and when we got to mine, just at that moment, the light suddenly went on. Most of the students locked their doors but I never did—partly because the bolts made the clang of a jail cell as they sprang backward and forward, and I hated it. Anyway, I wondered aloud why someone should be in my room, but then I gave a shrug, thinking I was showing an example of splendid detachment. Quick as a flash she commented, "*Nella casa dei ladroni chi se ne frega?*"—In the home of robbers who *gives* a damn? (and, actually, less polite than that). Silvia and her friend probably lived in some concrete apartment block on the *periferia*, as it was called, with unfinished roads and erratic services, rumored to be the work of the Mafia at every turn. The sight of the spacious amenity of my life made her furious, and her words were stinging, so much so that they remain with me to this day.

At the same time Silvia was not going to leave it like that. On a subsequent visit she brought pictures of herself in a bathing suit, and I think perhaps she actually wanted to seduce me. She was slim and tanned, but in my present state of mind her body scared me. Sex was the last thing I needed or wanted. She invited me to a party in some leafy spot at a friend of a friend's in the hills outside of Rome. We drove in Piero's car and she and Andrea kept up an excited chatter on the way. When we arrived, there was a big crowd of young people and they all turned to look at me as a curiosity. Many were slow dancing and Silvia invited me to dance with her, but it seemed she had a dangerous gleam in her eye. I excused myself and said I would take a walk. She laughed in my face and those who had overheard looked at me as if I had two heads. I went out and walked for a couple of miles on a country road. If this was anywhere else but Italy it would be corny, but at the end of those two miles I found a thirteenth-century Franciscan church perched on the side of a ravine. I went in to pray, thinking this was the kind of story that happened to a saint, but even as it passed through my mind the thought felt dead and hollow. I stepped inside and the atmosphere was brittle grey. I turned and left at once. Back at the house I made some excuse, got into the car, and returned to Rome.

It was roughly at this time that I also got the task of helping with "Easter duties" in a parish somewhere in a country area outside of Rome. This meant assisting the parish priest in the onerous job of giving confession to all those who wished to fulfill their canon-law obligation of receiving communion at least once a year and preparing to do so by confessing their sins. The practice happened in the Easter period and offered the opportunity for anyone encumbered by sin to cleanse themselves, receive the sacrament, and so be good for the year. It did not strictly matter that my Italian was book learned, and almost completely unpracticed in the popular and conversational. What mattered was the power of absolution and dispensing it liberally, which I was perfectly prepared to do. It was almost all women who came to me and for the most part I had no idea what they were telling me. I found myself literally saying okay to everything, pretty audibly, and in a strong Anglo accent, and so I think a healthy line built up outside my door.

Afterwards there was some kind of patronal festivity at a local co-operative *cantina*, or winery, attended by the workers, this time mostly men. The parish priest went along to show his face and bless the occasion, and he brought me with him. The atmosphere was festive and happy and well lubricated, and immediately after we got there a table of the workers invited me to sit down and take a glass. Remembering my pastoral practice at Hayes men's club I sat straight down with a bunch of robust, dark-haired, olive-skinned men who seemed to appreciate my presence. Before I knew it one glass turned to a second large one—the wine took away the embarrassed feeling of the confessions—and I was a really popular guy at the table. The parish priest returned and had to prize me loose. And, truth to tell, I was a little unsteady on my feet getting to the door. The priest was fuming. On our way back to the car he hissed, "Remember the dignity of the priesthood?" If he only knew, it was exactly that commodity I sorely lacked.

From the chasms of memory rises a painful example. One time when I was about ten, I took the bus from the bottom of the road in front of the prison, to Newport and the church there, to serve at the altar in the rite of benediction. In the rush to arrive and pull on my cassock and cotta I failed to empty my bladder and as the service got underway the pressure built up unbearably while I knelt before the altar. I should have just exited and gone to the bathroom, but this was benediction, and I was terrified of the holiness of it all. I managed to hold out until the actual ceremonial blessing, but as the parish priest was safely stowing the consecrated host back in the tabernacle my unholy urine burst forth in an unstoppable stream providing both immediate relief and unspeakable disgrace. I watched in horror as a steaming flood slowly expanded on the Carrara marble step. The priest descended from the altar platform and his priestly eyes noticed my puddle and in an unforgettable gesture of avoidance twitched up the braided hem of his cope. We got back inside the sacristy and the other altar boys burst out into helpless sniggers, but the parish priest said nothing. I am not sure who cleaned up the mess. A couple of days later the parish curate came around to console me. He even said he had done the same thing when he was a kid. (His name was Murphy O'Connor, and he was a kind man. His brother later became cardinal archbishop of Westminster.) But it seemed the damage had been done: somehow in my soul and story I would always carry the hint of something unbecoming for a priest.

Another burden I carried from childhood was asthma, and it would not be possible to experience spring in the foreign climate of Rome without undergoing an episode, and a quite dramatic one. As those April days arrived, something in the blossom and the warming air—and perhaps the overall stresses of my situation—detonated a reaction in my lungs. I did my best to carry on, but it was getting worse, and alone in my room I became frightened. I struggled out into the corridor and told one of the students to inform the prefect of students. He came to see me and at once transferred me to a hospital not far away on the Via Aurelia. It was a private clinic staffed by nuns, clean, spacious, and upscale, apparently devoted to the care of sick cardinals and other high-ranking church officials. The nuns treated me like a lord, gave me oxygen and little vials of amber-colored vitamins every day, and in the cool air of the room my lungs soon began to recover. The crisis was passing but I was not allowed to go before the supervising doctor came to see me to pronounce judgment. His name was Professore Spezzaferri (which literally translates as "iron breaker"), and he swept into my room, white coated, stethoscoped, and surrounded by a posse of totally deferential nuns. He gave a perfunctory listen to my chest and told me at once that I should never ride a bicycle again. He then proceeded to prod my stomach, hard, somehow fulfilling his name with the action. When I flinched, he seemed satisfied and declared that I was "in the antechamber of an ulcer" (*nello vestibulo di una ulcera*) and would inevitably develop one. I have continued to ride bicycles all my life, and have never suffered from an ulcer. I don't know where this Spezzaferri got his mythologizing manner from, but it has crossed my mind that if he was used to treating cardinals, those princes of dogmatic authority, he may have felt entitled to outdo them, seeking, with his words, to bend the destiny of others in any shape he thought fit. I left the clinic the next day and returned to my room in the Claretianum. I spent another week convalescing, with my fellow students bringing me meals in my room. I read the whole of *War and Peace* and it was pure pleasure to be in Tolstoy's all-encompassing world without the need to fulfill any kind of timetable of my own. Time did not stand still so much as fill itself up, with story, with human feeling, with life.

All the same, it was now just over a month before I was due back in England. I myself was like a doctor who'd failed pathology and was scheduled to begin practice in four weeks. But it was already too late for desperation. In fact, I was more like a condemned man in the last few mornings before the date of execution. A profound numbness took over, a distance and apathy toward everything. I forced myself to keep a routine, working on research for a long paper I had to complete and getting up for meditation in the morning. The other students always had classes first thing and long ago they had told me not to bother getting up with them for morning prayers: they prayed in Spanish and didn't want me slowing them down. So, I would time my arrival to just as they were leaving, so at least we got to see each other. This particular morning, they had exams and were all gone before I got there. Loneliness crowded in on me. But in a way it didn't affect me, because nothing did. I had no relationship to anything, so seeing them or not seeing them did not matter. They had their lives, or what they took for life, and I had an ocean of nothing. There was an inert space in me and around me where no meaningful thing could enter. I prayed to God because that was the routine, the thing I always did. But this morning I tried and could not. Nothing, absolutely nothing came from my soul. It was dead within me, just like the space around me. With my mind I forced my mouth to say words and it seemed to hurt my head and jaw to do so. For what was there to say? To ask forgiveness? There was no one to ask forgiveness of. To plead for help? All avenues were exhausted and there was nothing left to beg. The thought went through my mind that this was it. This really was it. I was on the edge of a precipice and about to fall headlong in the abyss. I balanced on the edge and a last instinct of survival, a primeval fear, made me force a last verbal prayer: "Here I am." To say I said this is also perhaps to say too much, for "Here I am" or "Here" suggests some sense of person or selfhood to declare. It was much more the grunt of an animal, the empty bleat of a doomed lost sheep in the wilderness. I trembled on the edge of my extinction, and I was falling, falling, in a long dying arc of momentary time.

My gaze was on the altar at the end of the church, in a dull passive way. It is the place where the sacrament is reserved, the normal point of convergence and symbolic core of any Catholic place of worship. Behind it, on the wall, was a painting, a piece of iconography representing the Virgin Mary and fiery tongues of Spirit around her, as at the first Pentecost. I always tuned that out as it seemed to me a distorted emphasis on the role of the Virgin. Then in the moment of falling, in that long, lifeless arc of time, and somehow without noticing the instant it began, or the astonishing contrast with what came just before, there suddenly issued what seemed like dense, rolling rivers of fire. They came at me, surrounded me, and went by me. It was like the air was filled with red, riotous, devouring tongues of flame, as if the building was consumed and the roof was about to collapse, yet the fire was entirely not dangerous or fearful, but primordial, essential, joyful, infinitely generous, deep with love. Fire that raw and strong should burn up the world like stubble, but instead it was able to leave everything untouched, even to pass by invisibly, unnoticed for itself, unless perhaps some exceptional fracture of sight should reveal it. I felt my heart leap, just a little, and I said to myself, "What is happening here? Is this real? Or, is it some kind of mental breakdown?" And then quickly, "Yet, isn't this exactly what everyone talks about? Isn't this fire the authentic sign of God, the flame of divine being itself?" And then following directly, "But I have to say yes to it, I know, I have to believe it." And, once more, immediately, "You have nothing to lose and everything to gain. Go on, just say yes!" And I did. I said yes. The warmth, joy, and strength stopped moving and fixed itself inside me and about me. I stood up, looked around me, and then back to the middle distance. The phantasm of fire had disappeared, but the feeling remained. Where the moment before my legs and body had been dull and dust filled, now they felt alive and full of light. "Thank you, thank you, thank you," I said, and I almost ran from the church, unable to contain the energy I felt.

I spent the rest of the day wandering around, thanking God, thanking Jesus, soaking up the sun and just looking at the world and the light pouring into it and through it. All the feelings, or rather non-feelings, of yesterday had been replaced by an irrepressible joy and generosity of life. I would stay in my room for ten minutes and then walk outside again, incapable of sitting still. The day ended and I was still overflowing. Somehow, I found my way to the roof and stood looking toward the west where I soon would be heading, a horizon streaked with aqua and red. I raised my hands to the cornflower blue above and for the first time a Roman sky neither seduced nor sneered. I reached out to it in praise and love.

Many years later, describing my experience to an atheist PhD student in psychology, he suggested that what happened was simply a matter of the ego restoring or confirming itself, after some kind of collapse. I tried to make him understand that the actual experience was of the complete impossibility of the ego doing anything, let alone restoring itself. But should, impossibly, he somehow be right, he had simply chosen another metaphysical principle in place of God, and one which, with its will-to-power logic, has not a particularly good track record in recent history. In contrast, this principle—if that is at all the right thing to call it—was a pouring out of self, a giving without limit, a surrender without compass points in which to draw it. It was the "matter" of God in and for itself. In my religious life I had been trying to ascend to the height of God, to scale the pinnacles of his might. But the nature of God is infinite lowliness, so beneath and below being that it is invisible to any eye that does not come close to its intrinsic lowness and givingness. It is what the philosophers call *nihilation*, a function that allows everything else to be, but not in any sense of nihilism or of nothing. It is the only infinite function behind being that makes any sense—an incomprehensible self-exhaustion that keeps on going and never stops, and so is the only sense-making ground for the fact of being that is so baffling in its brute factuality. An infinite contingency of love explaining a factual contingency without explanation!

But this understanding does not depend on its own (abstract) reasoning. Instead, what happened to me was guided by a history of biblically inspired signs (the role of semiotics) and their inner relationships of love and self-giving, stretching back through centuries of human pilgrimage, including, no doubt, the image painted on the wall. There had to be a key to release the stream of fire and I knew what it must be.

The resources that reconstituted my mind were the person of Jesus Christ and his reinvention of all human meaning around his cross and resurrection. The love was both gentle and strong, strong and gentle, nothing and everything, everything and nothing, and I know of no other story in history where I sense that kind of love. I think I can honestly say that I met the living person of Christ that day. Not perhaps for the first time, but at a level that day where it could justly claim to be the core structuring of my life. From that point on I did not need to deal in dreams or phantasms, but in the power of existence, one that went by the name of Jesus. And I remain endlessly grateful for the revelation of that day, one that gives a song to my life and bears me up whatever the changing conditions of the years may bring. If I am ever in need of spiritual strength or surety I cast my mind back to that day, and specifically to the space around the back of the church where it seemed the fire came from and remained. It is, in fact, the outside of the church I remember, not the inside. I am under a small gold-colored colonnade there, next to a fishpond with lilies and red carp. The feeling is indescribably peaceful and blessed. It is like a gateway to heaven.

I was now ready to return to England. At this point I did not reflect on the actual circumstances that produced that readiness, i.e., the failure of hierarchical priesthood and the intervention of something from below or beyond the levels of legal, institutional form. After all, I had abandoned confession, looked to early Christian reality prior to episcopal structure for inspiration, and derived crucial truth from a personal revelation rather than doctrine and ideology. But I was simply too thrilled to be able to face my future with confidence, to return to my order in some kind of spiritual good shape, to worry about these things. Now at last I would be able to demonstrate in positive form all the things I had been arguing about. To prove that I was not just an angry young man but a trustworthy disciple. Those last few weeks were filled with happiness. All the students went on a trip together before we left to take our separate paths, for many would likely never see each other again. We went first to Tivoli and its gardens, and then south to Gaeta. I was astounded at the play of the fountains, descending across the terraces and down through the ornamental gardens. The genius of human design combined with a panoramic view had created a place of endless joyous fancy. In Gaeta we hiked up to the Montagna Spaccata and looked through the natural cleft in the mountain out at the dazzling Med. Local legend had it that the mountain split when Christ died and it was another sweet fancy: so much beauty seen through the prism of love. The afternoon sky above the mountain was a heaped-up silk and there was a sense of companionship that had something everlasting to it. There was one student whom I respected a lot. His name was José and he kept himself somewhat aloof from the others, spending most of his time writing. His room was opposite mine and he would hammer away at his typewriter at all hours of day and night, smoking packs of *Ducados negros* to keep himself going. In one of our last conversations he quoted a Spanish saying: *Vista, suerte y al toro!*, meaning "Look sharp, good luck, and go get the bull!" It seemed a handy motto to have. José went to Latin America to work and continued writing (I trust he's given up the cigarettes). I saw recently on the internet that he has been found guilty of "serious errors" by the Commission for the Doctrine of Faith of the Spanish hierarchy. Apparently, the commission felt some of his conclusions were incompatible with the faith of the Catholic Church. *Suerte*, José!

The day I left Rome the citrus trees around the Stazione Termini were shedding blossoms and a gale of white greenish petals swept along the platform next to the train. I was going first to Barcelona, using the chance to visit Spain and some of the sites associated with the founder of the order. I happened on a bunch of young Spanish nuns traveling together and I greeted them as I made my way along the corridor. They at once invited me into their compartment, made space for me and shared their food—chorizo and bread and grapes and cheese. They did not have the ethereal beauty of Mother Teresa's bunch, but they had a vigor and a fire that was completely captivating. They were educators, full of progressive opinions about the church and their upcoming work in schools. It was a second send-off from Rome, this one in female form. All of us in that compartment felt we were facing a future where we could make a real difference for the cause of Christ, and we felt bound together as splendid *compañeros* in that struggle.

When I got to Barcelona I stayed at what is called the Mother House. It was in a stifling small room, no more than a box, overlooking a courtyard with a nonfunctioning fountain. In the midday sun it became an oven with a tower of broiled air breaking in waves into the little room and making it almost impossible to breathe. I wondered how anybody could have spiritual thoughts in that house; it spoke rather of the iron discipline of men for whom a church militant was almost entirely that and nothing else. But because of that same heat, Catalonia had the tastiest peaches and on a couple of occasions when I was served a local vintage of their sparkling white wine it held all the warmth of that generous sunshine. Barcelona is a classic city and there were the standard places to see, Las Ramblas, the Sagrada Familia, and a bus ride away, the airy monastery of Montserrat on top of its mountain. Orwell hated Gaudi's masterpiece and that's because Orwell was a modernist, and he could not see Gaudi's biomimetic cathedral as a postmodern vision of the earth fully alive and without oppression. In Barcelona there are also beautiful women, of course, and I brought with me my habit of looking at them. On impulse I went to confession one very last time—I was, after all, in the home territory of the order. After I had stumbled through my sins in the Spanish tongue I asked the priest did he understand, *entiendes?*, and he looked me in the eye and answered one word, *entiendo*, "I understand." That seemed really to draw a line under it. In complete contrast to the manic diatribe of the monsignor in St. Peter's, here was a simple human meaning. I really never did go to confession again after that, and that single first-person verb joined the stream of fire as a direct address from the Spirit of Christ poured out in the world and standing at my side.

I visited the Catalonian hometown of the founder and walked the bleached-white country tracks he would have taken, hoping to discover a little of his soul. I hiked out to a little country chapel he used to visit and where he had experienced an important spiritual moment praying before a statue of the Virgin. I tried hard to embrace what had happened to him and merge it with my own senses, but in the end it was contrived. I could never really identify with his sentimental relationship with the mother of Jesus, and even less with his intense Catholic conservatism. It's strange but I only had the most formal of relationships with the founder, and the "liberals" and "communists" he considered the spawn of Satan I would have found quite sympathetic. I took the train to Madrid and stood in its packed corridor and observed the patience with which the working people traveled long distances in hard conditions but without complaint. In Madrid the crowds on the underground seemed less cynical than in Rome, but there was also the Guardia Civil on the streets with their three-beaked hats and submachine guns, all still under the command of General Franco.

I remembered Angel, my novice master, and how he had been run out of town because of his anti-Franco politics. Spain was the kind of place where it could be dangerous to fall in love. When I got back to Barcelona, I bought a train ticket to London from a student travel shop. The following evening, I gathered my things and headed to the Estació de França for the overnight to Paris and London. At the station the ticket collector looked at my small, numbered train ticket and told me this was valid only to the border. From there on there had to be a separate document. Where was it? I was floored. I had no other document and if I went back to the shop, I would miss the train. The likelihood anyway was they had scammed me and would admit to nothing. And I had no money left to buy a second ticket. I waited until the inspector wasn't looking and then hopped the train. I stowed my bags in the area next to a toilet closet and chose a seat where I'd have a good view of the carriage in either direction. My nerves were on edge until we crossed the Pyrenees but then I settled down. At least I'd made it to France. During the whole journey in the high-speed train the inspector came by only once, sometime about midday, and then I hid out in the toilet until I felt sure he'd moved to the next carriage. Somehow, I made it all the way to the boat and across the channel. On the boat train to London, I did the same thing, avoiding an inspector by hiding in the bathroom. I arrived once more in London, worn out from my vigilance but with a sense of righteous triumph. I'd paid someone for my trip and had gotten what I paid for!

I arrived in England a little shy of ten years from the day I set out from Portsmouth to join the religious order. I was energized but on a completely different basis from the outlook I had first embraced. All during my time of preparation I had sought a true land of religion, my island of belonging, a hermetically sealed bubble of life within the world. Meanwhile everything around me had conspired to blow it to pieces. Rome had completed the work of explosion, but now, at the last gasp, it had also filled me with my own personal source of life. It had given me a new set of lungs that enabled me to breathe for the first time in the world, capable of recycling its toxic gasses through a personal filter of belief and love.

At the end of those ten years, I had severed important ties with my institutional lifeworld, but I had not lost practical connection to it. Quite the contrary: any external frame of life for me still sat entirely within the Roman Catholic Church. I simply believed I had found the secret for living my ordained destiny in a tolerable, practicable way. I had a message to share, one that would carry me forward through the rituals I was given to conduct and the sermons I had to preach. Amid the wreckage of my chosen organization, I would express from within myself an altogether personal life through which I could continue to exist. And I would invite into it anyone who wished to be there with me. I had no thought at all of how ultimately dysfunctional this might prove. I was simply happy that I could go forward publicly with the role that I had been given and which was expected of me. I had been extended, quite literally, a lifeline; yet I did not understand that I was still at sea without a ground to stand on, and perhaps even more than ever. My imagination had been set free to shape theologically and meaningfully the immediate space around me—to live, in fact, my own kind of fiction of Catholic priesthood. But, by definition, it was a fiction, and I was still outside an actual, real world. That tension would not rest. I still needed a way to relate to the human history I was in fact part of. Only after almost a further ten years would I arrive at last at the point where I would find real physical territory beneath my feet.

thirteen

BUCKDEN *ADOLESCENS*

AT THE HEIGHT OF our activity at the Buckden youth retreat center we had groups almost every weekend of the year. There was a permanent community of young lay volunteers, male and female, attached to the center, organizing and leading the retreats. And over the summer there were five weeks of continuous events running through July and August involving more than three hundred young people ages ten through thirty. This I had achieved in the space of three years, beginning from a baseline of nil activity, from point zero. The reason I had been called back from Rome was to take on the development of this ministry in the setting of Buckden Towers, the place of sad repute to which Michael had been exiled, and which in the minds of many in the order was equated with rain, cold, and failure. The cloud from the collapse of the junior seminary still drifted across the battlements there and no one wanted to have any part in it. For me, however, there was something quite perfect about the location and my appointment to work there. A reputation as a place of exile together with a tangible sense of somewhere time had forgotten made it immensely attractive. Here, if anywhere, I could begin to write a new story, one that corresponded both to my general distance from society and to the strange new fire that had erupted in my life. It was, for all intents and purposes, a blank canvas. Again, I didn't reflectively consider these things but nourished an immediate instinct of how they might work.

As you drove up the A1, the old Roman road from London running straight as an arrow all the way to York and the Scottish borders, you would crest a low hill and catch a first glimpse of the red turrets of the Towers lit by watery sunlight. They quickly disappeared from view until you came over a second hill and then they would stay in sight just above the line of the trees. There really was something quite special about it. The Towers would have been a powerful landmark in the late Middle Ages, a kind of Hampton Court in the flatlands of the fens, or, in modern terms, a Trump Tower exalted high above a feudal village. Today, however, the worldly status had shifted almost entirely into something otherworldly and actually a sense of prayer and spirituality. Built for the bishops of Lincoln and situated halfway on the journey between Lincoln and London, the estate had a full display of battlements, moat, gatehouse, and fifteen-foot curtain wall. But being literally intended as a lodging on the way to somewhere else, and disconnected from any centers or issues of political importance, it slipped through the centuries into a drowse of historical irrelevance. Its one notable resident carried with her a feeling of weakness and suffering, contributing to an atmosphere of loss and of hope through prayer alone. Catherine of Aragon was imprisoned there by Henry VIII as punishment for her refusal to agree to his divorce. After a while when it seemed the villagers were becoming too sympathetic, she was removed to an even less frequented great house and died there shortly after. Her stay at the Towers was always a matter of great pride, the site of the chapel where she practiced her devotions always pointed out. She was our resident saint, a lonely but brave and faithful soul.

Many times I made that journey and the glimpse of the Towers almost always filled me with hope and delight. Here was yet another noble pile occupied by priests and brothers, yet this time it had a hint of political, even theological, resistance about it, and best of all a good bit of it was mine! The main entrance and its high wall lay to the west, close to the Great North Road. Eastward, facing it across a broad lawn, lay the gatehouse. Beyond this and to its south an inner wall, continuing to run east, connected it to the turreted keep, the towers from which the whole place was named. At one time a moat had protected the outside of the gatehouse and its wall, but it had been filled in and the space south of the inner wall and the keep was now the property of the local Anglican church. Its grey spire nestling beneath the red of the turrets continued to emphasize the ecclesiastic air of the place. Crossing through the arch of the gatehouse you came suddenly into a space quieted from the modern world. You had passed the dole seat under the arch where the poor of the neighborhood had sat waiting for charity from the bishop's table. Emerging now from the time-rusted shadows, the great three-story building rose straight up to your right.

The battlements of the inner wall connected to it could be reached by steps, and you could peer through the gaps to see the parish cemetery below. An elegant sycamore stood on a grassy mound between the gatehouse and the Towers. Over to the left was the community house, the large Victorian mansion built by a brewing family occupying the site a century before. Directly opposite, between the house and the Towers, was a church constructed a few years before to serve the seminary and the Roman Catholics of the area. A covered way linked all three buildings, creating a loggia and merging them into one. Together with the gatehouse they formed a kind of quad or close. After that, out behind the house and the church and to the north of the Towers lay fourteen acres of parkland, including a playing field, trees, and a fishpond. For some it was a dank wilderness; for me it was a little Eden.

For the next six years it would be my domain. Already I felt a kind of conquest, returning to the scene of my encounter with the '60s-era Catholics. I was now in charge of the Towers, and I carried with me a spiritual fire that would displace the shadowy soirees of the King's Room. I would be the one leading the way and it would not be in the direction simply of liberated sexuality. In this special place it would be possible to drink in a spirit that was two millennia old and yet completely new. More than likely my attitude would seem very holier-than-thou to those who were not part of my Jerusalem in the fens, but that was to be ignorant of the journey I had undergone, seeing things only from the outside. From the inside it is hard to exaggerate the moments of joy and sense of love that would be found in some of the events at the Towers in those years.

The task given me was to open up the Towers as a retreat center, so a certain distance from the world was already implied. In addition, the general condition of the buildings—bare floors, public dormitories, few toilets, no showers—made them suitable only for young people, and a particular class of youth at that. Adolescence is its own type of eternity, when the world can appear with a terrible clarity and bleakness. And this was the era of the '70s, the beginning of punk rock, of the Sex Pistols, of "Glad to Be Gay," the end of Vietnam, pre-Thatcher and pre-Reagan. It was still very much possible to dream of human liberation uncomplicated by polarizing politics. It was only a matter of gathering young people of a certain sensibility, and of then living with them the story of a world out of time, for the sake of another time.

While I was in Rome I had already observed the potent results if you mixed alienated middle-class youth with religion. I had seen the Children of God at work, the very group with which my friend Joanna had to contend to prize her sister free from their grasp. But when I went to an event of theirs in the Villa Borghese Park one sunny Sunday all that was visible was towheaded young men and willowy girls doing skits about the way the world controlled us and singing songs to Jesus. They easily gathered a crowd, and it would be no surprise if, when the sun was sinking, they had left with one or two new devotees. Back in England I was invited to attend a diocesan retreat up in the Lake District. This time it was the Roman Catholic Church seeking young people's loyalty, but many of the same techniques were in use. A lot of young people together, contemporary music, games, role play, talk about Jesus, and a fair bit of teenage sexuality. I didn't approve of the late-night room hopping, but I also saw clearly how in the heightened atmosphere one or two of the young people could have real personal experiences of Christ. This was the very thing I now specialized in. I had waited long years for my own encounter but what had happened to me provided a gold standard, and when I saw that teenagers' hearts could be touched I thought, "I can speak to that!"

Not long after, I was asked to direct my first youth day, at the Westminster diocesan pastoral center, at London Colney. I used art slides of Christ with a backing track of pop songs, including "Your Love Keeps Liftin' Me (Higher and Higher)." I didn't make any converts, but a couple of young people there invited me to come to their weekly prayer group. I thought, "Oh no, not that again," but I saw an opportunity. I said yes, I'd come, on condition that they came to see my place. The deal was struck, and it was one of the best deals I ever made. The girl whose name was Judith soon visited Buckden and saw at once it would be a great place for youth. She said she would get her brother involved too, because he had already helped in chaplaincy work at his college and was really good at organizing spiritual events for young people. She set up a planning weekend for early spring, and true to her word she got her brother to agree to come, bringing some of his college friends into the bargain. We were up and running.

Her brother was Brian, towheaded and energetic just like the boys in the Villa Borghese, but that's where the similarities ended. He was completing a social work degree and stood out as sincere, levelheaded, and dependable. He and his group took to the Towers like ducks to water. We decided to run a two-week program in the summer: the first week would be basically for Brian's group, consisting of prayer, meditation, and community living, plus time for preparation for the following week. This second experience would be the real beginning of Buckden outreach, a time for teenagers with little or no direct exposure to a spiritual message before. Some younger siblings of the group would come to the second week, plus anyone else I could pick up on the way.

In the meantime, I took an Easter trip to Taizé in France. Judith and her boyfriend came and my sister Christine did too. She and I rode up front, and the other two spent much of the time making out in the back of the van. Really there was not much option for them as there were no seats to the rear and to be comfortable they had to lie flat. The monastery, founded by Brother Roger, was famous for its intervention in the student disturbances in Paris in 1968. Brothers from the monastery had appeared on the riot-torn streets of the French capital and invited some of the young people they met there to come to their monastery and share with the monks their frustrations and longings in an environment of prayer. This was the birth of the so-called "Council of Youth," an open-ended series of meetings and conversations of young people focused on the anxieties of the contemporary world and held in an overall context of silence and prayer. The motto given them was "struggle and contemplation" and I knew that here was a vital reference point if I was going to be ministering with youth. Our small band in my little white Ford van wandered halfway around central France looking for the place and it was really only by dint of asking (no Google maps back then) that we finally got to our destination. The van labored perilously through snow-covered hills until we made it to an area once made famous by the eleventh-century Cluny abbey but now newly a draw because of Taizé. What was astonishing was the rudimentary nature of the accommodations: they made Buckden look comfortable. The monastery itself was set on a ridge, at the edge of the massif central, with a cold sun declining behind the tableland. The slopes below the monastery were covered with ranks of army surplus field tents. Layered with a foot of straw, they slept about thirty persons each. The standard joke was it looked like the Italian army in retreat, but generally it smelled more like a rock festival with hints of marijuana drifting tantalizingly among the tents. The nights we slept there the frost was thick on the ground, but the straw kept us surprisingly warm. I thought of the Buckden dormitories with their eighteen-inch walls, rows of iron bedsteads, and tick mattresses. I decided that, given the romance of a medieval building, their primitive conditions inside needed absolutely no improvement.

Where Taizé really set the bar, however, was in its quality of prayer. It was deeply impressive. When I first heard Brother Roger pray it was like a gentle light switched on at the heart of thick darkness. In order to accommodate the huge crowds of youth, the monks had taken out a whole end of their church and extended it under a circus tent. In this way they created a vast carpeted atrium opening on the sanctuary, in which thousands of persons could be seated together on the floor in dense fellowship. At night there was little illumination apart from the clusters of candles in their glass shields around the icons. The effect was enormous intimacy and solidarity. Brother Roger's microphoned voice in its hushed tone of love encompassed the whole setting and sank it in worship. We attended the Easter Vigil service that evening but even before the formal liturgy, when I had walked into the church that afternoon, I was bowled over. There were scatterings of young people throughout the space, all engaged in the most profound prayer. They were in a state of contemplation, unmoving and full of peace. Some of them were prone on the floor, arms outstretched before them. Others were wrapped in stillness seated cross-legged before the icons. I understood with a sudden shock of recognition that the revolution in human existence that had been taking place all during my own youth extended into the world of Christian religious tradition. These young people did not make a distinction between the body and the soul. They did not make a distinction between bodies engaged in politics, sex, or marijuana, and bodies engaged in prayer. It was all the same arena, the same medium, the same inescapable human space of nerves, and bones, and struggle.

Taizé had taught me the possibility of contemplative prayer for young people but that was not the last spiritual learning I gained in those marvelous times. My end of the bargain with Judith was something I'd been holding up consistently. It was good for me to go to the prayer group at her parents' house because I could keep contact with her and other young people there; but this motive was quickly displaced in importance by another. I actually began to enjoy the meetings; to my surprise they gave me the greatest of pleasure. I used to drive sixty miles down the A1 in the little Ford van and arrive at a house in Kenton Gardens in a sun-strewn cul-de-sac. Inside were twenty or so people sitting around on the living room floor in an atmosphere of kindness and joyous prayer. The moment I walked in all my old resentments and suspicions evaporated. I don't know whether it was something in me or just the character of the group had changed. The leader was a man called David and, definitely, he communicated a tone of humility and genuineness to everything. He was outstanding, a truly spiritual person. There was also the presence of young people and one or two of these were not Catholics but Evangelicals. In consequence there was a bracing dose of nonconformist freedom in the air, which may have dispelled lingering traces of stuffiness and heaviness from more Catholic devotion. But finally, I'm sure, it was the openness and care of Judith's parents that made the difference. Lorna and Bernard unfailingly welcomed and accepted all who came, and it was their open-armed love that made me immediately and literally at home. I thought nothing of making the 120-mile round trip every week and little by little these meetings had a huge impact on me.

After some months David announced that the group would be running what was called a Life-in-the-Spirit Seminar. It was a seven-week course teaching people about the Holy Spirit and leading them toward a receiving of the gifts of the Spirit. These gifts were the external manifestations of an infilling with the Spirit, phenomena I had dismissed before as illusion and narcissism. I was still skeptical, but the atmosphere of warmth and love in the meetings had made me more prepared to accept there possibly was something to the whole thing. When someone, for example, announced a "word of prophecy," a direct address by the Spirit to the group, the general expressions of love and encouragement did not seem so improbable. But as always it was the "gift of tongues" that produced the most anxiety. At once showy and absurd, out of control and open to faking, this so-called gift was seen as a sure mark of anointing by the Spirit, but to me it was designed for self-deception. As the final week drew close, when the group was to pray over the participants for receipt of the gifts, I felt the strongest urge not to be there. A situation where half a dozen or more people were laying hands on you was ripe with possibilities for collective suggestion. And that was not taking into account the added expectations on a spiritual leader—priests were the ones who needed all the gifts they could get but they were notorious for "not being open."

In view of all this I had set a general condition on the Holy Spirit: if I was ever going to get the gift of tongues it would have to be entirely on my own, without any possibility of group pressure. And as things turned out that's more or less how it happened. It was around that period of time I was due for my annual private retreat, and when I inquired at the monastery where I normally went for spiritual R&R I found that the most convenient dates coincided nicely with the final week of the seminar.

Thank you, Lord! I was in the clear. I could not attend the prayer group, because I would be fulfilling the yearly retreat required of me as a dutiful member of a religious order.

The monastery was Mount St. Bernard Abbey, the sole Trappist foundation in England and host over the years to many famous visitors and spiritual seekers. Its setting is dotted by dramatic outcrops of ancient igneous rock, as if the earth itself is struggling to give birth. During my first full day there I was suddenly overwhelmed by a desire to find out everything I could about the Holy Spirit. My experience with charismatic prayer groups—stretching back now two years—had always prompted a wish to find out more but mostly from simple curiosity or even a kind of jealousy. Now there was a thirst, a hunger inside my throat, for a substance it had a taste of but needed more, much more of, to satisfy. The intellectual caveats were replaced by something close to raw desire.

I went down to the small bookstore at the entrance of the monastery church and bought all the books on the Holy Spirit I could find. Returning to my room I began devouring the text on the page. It didn't take long. I came to a part where it said if a Christian believes it possible to hand over the heart and will to God, why not hand over the tongue too? This seemed incontrovertible. I thought to myself, well, I've tried this on a number of occasions before and it always came out feeling horribly fake, how can I know it won't be the same now? But the need to try was imperative and I gave in, releasing my voice to the empty room.

A "language" issued forth that had much greater appearance of form and fluency than anything I had attempted before. But it was not the sound so much as what occurred to my attention and sense of meaning that convinced me. Immediately as I began to make sounds my eyes were turned somehow automatically to the crucifix hanging on the wall of the monastic cell. And it seemed at once that what I was speaking was a hymn of love directed by God the Father toward his crucified Son. Simply that. And the feeling of love and the intimate spaces of God led in turn to the greatest freedom and joy, an upwelling of the heart that wants spontaneously to express itself as thanks and praise. I had heard before, and subsequently, that the gift of tongues is learned behavior and can be taught successfully by any skilled practitioner. There is little doubt about that, and it wasn't a coincidence that this experience occurred on the very evening the group was praying with people for baptism in the Spirit: I had learned from them, and this night completed the acquiring of a behavior. But just as evidently, these "tongues" were a vehicle for something more than sounds, they also taught a living sense of communication in the mystery of God. This latter is no different from all New Testament theology, but the new element was its immediate sense of experience, rather than simply abstract doctrine. Unable to contain myself, I left my room and went clambering up and around the stations of the cross, which traversed the ledges of the huge granite mass close to the guesthouse. I shouted my thanks and joy to the dark heavens and to the pain and strangeness of Christ's passion represented in stone and plaster.

And so, the way ahead was made for me. On the strength of all these crucial experiences I planned the summer weeks at the Towers. They were to follow a set of themes, one for each day, Monday through Friday: trust, freedom, love, hope, joy. The topics all proposed a content of spiritual and emotional experience to be communicated directly among the participants, things I had myself encountered or understood on reflection. Because they had become real and tangible to me, I was fully confident they could become real for the young people who attended. And that is what happened. We used the grounds and their natural features as a kind of spiritual landscape, trooping out in the sunshine to do morning prayer around three huge trees framing the park, a plane, an oak, a hornbeam. We treated them as a living inspirational semiotics, gathering around them, singing songs, and reading prayers. In the afternoon there was always some building project, transforming the space further into collective theater. We built a huge Noah's ark, camps made out of brush mimicking the sukkah of the Israelites in the wilderness, an ashram, a third world favela. After morning prayer and breakfast there was a presentation by one of the young people on the theme and then the big group would break into smaller groups to share and discuss. Sometimes they would prepare artwork or a drama skit to respond to the theme, always a physical engagement with the topics and their significance. In the late afternoon there would be sports or a walk, and in the evening always some kind of party with games, more skits, music, and dancing. At the end of the week, we would have a disco out in the field with big speakers set on a platform and the latest dance tunes and songs ricocheting around the park, and the kids dancing until they dropped.

The year 1975 was a first run for all of this. When 1976 came the formula was established. After attending the first summer weeks, two young men had volunteered their full-time services, Peter and Simon, and with their help we were able to run weekend gatherings almost continually, plus plan for a full five-week summer program. All the activity provided a recruiting ground for further volunteers. One of them was Michelle, a striking personality with a cascade of red hair, who went on to join our resident community and proved a charismatic force in her own right. But, oh, 1976 and its summer! Everything we turned our hands to seemed to work and to confirm the Holy Spirit was with us. The weather was the best on record. The grass dried out and the young people swam in a haze of sunlight. A young man came to visit us, Bernard by name, attracted by an ad I had placed in a Catholic newspaper. He'd experimented with alternative lifestyle, sharing a house with a member of the British punk band the Clash. He was now seeking, in his own phrase, a life of "total communion" with God. Bernard had amazing natural talent—a brilliant guitarist, pleasing songwriter, and gripping performer. His presence in the summer weeks lifted the sense of Buckden's connection to rock 'n' roll youth culture several significant notches. At the same time the place was saturated in prayer. It was by no means just a hip youth scene.

We developed the custom of offering a prayer ministry to the teenagers at the end of the week and almost everyone responded. We gathered in a little chapel in the gatehouse, situated right over the entrance arch, and by the end of a three-hour session it was as if the walls themselves were leaking light. Just to walk into that space where so many bodies had gathered in openness to the Spirit was to feel a shock, a tingle of communication with something amazing, different, and real. I have concluded since that for those years the Buckden experience was not really in the world. It was apocalyptic. It belonged to another time that is sometimes called the time of the end, but that end can be experienced in many ways that are not an actual end, but more of a breakthrough. Buckden made apocalyptic time its own. It plugged in directly to the time of the fire that I had sensed in Rome, the time the church spent so much energy trying to freeze in its eternal metaphysics. What I put forward at Buckden never invoked those mechanisms the church used to produce that frozen product—heaven, church authority, its rule-bound sacraments, the caste of priesthood—but did everything possible to release the movement of fire itself within a defined space of relationship called Buckden Towers. It's possible to say that in my position I likely had undue influence with the youth, and even to some degree what I created approached the nature of a cult. But I was always under religious superiors who were right there on-site. They saw everything I did. Moreover, I was always conscious that ultimately all this had to translate into sustainable human community of some sort. At the beginning, however, I did not let that worry me. I was too thrilled to be fulfilling the destiny that had been given to me, the one that had caused me so much suffering and yet I had stayed committed to—for something precisely like this!

One of the key reasons for the success and the halcyon level of comfort of those early years was the support and affection I was given by Michael, the then parish priest and religious superior. As I explained before, Michael had been through his own battles and had taken lumps from the students at Highcliffe and then from the salon of progressive Catholics that sometimes gathered in the King's Room. Much of the steam had gone out of this group and when I arrived in 1974 Michael was being left largely in peace. He had devoted a lot of his energy to building up the rents from the three or four apartments that had been created around the property, improving the overall finances. He also got government help for the preservation of the Towers as a historic building and little by little battlements and brick facing were restored to pristine strength. In contrast I gave little or no thought to the material upkeep of my gospel castle. Michael did not resent the fact, rather he was always most welcoming to the youth, and in fact began to appreciate my direct approach to God's action in the world. Later he would say that I had taught him what it meant to evangelize. In the meantime, he was constantly open to all the activities we planned and the uses to which we put the Towers and the surrounding park.

After witnessing the first success of the work, he put money and resources our way. He allowed Simon and Peter to stay free of charge, and as the community of volunteers grew, he maintained this policy. He bought us a full-size minibus with which we took our show on the road, visiting schools and long-distance local groups formed after retreats at Buckden. Soon after the 1976 summer weeks ended Michelle came to join us and Michael accepted a mixed community. The only condition was that Michelle had accommodation off campus, something he duly found for her in the neighboring town of Huntingdon. Not long after this he contracted a local builder and began work on equipping the basement of the Towers with a modern kitchen and male and female bathrooms with multiple shower cubicles. Up until then all cooking had been done on a camping stove in one of the corner turret rooms, in cramped and dangerous conditions. Nobody minded much, but that's because they didn't know that rats had established a way in and were continually stealing bread and other supplies. The tiling and equipping of the kitchen went quickly and the finished product proved both sanitary and a huge plus in catering for the ever-increasing numbers in the summer weeks.

In the meantime, Simon had finished his year of volunteering, Bernard joined, and about the same time one more young man named Malcolm became part of the live-in team. Tall and sporting a rock-star shock of hair, he too was an excellent guitarist and a vivid personality. He was evangelical, not Roman Catholic, and yet found himself almost completely at home with the Buckden message and outreach. The four volunteers now comprised a highly effective group of communicators and leaders, known as the "core community." Their presence at the Towers tokened the nucleus of a wider community of young people spread out across England, returning on frequent occasions to be together at Buckden—for not a few of them these occasions added up to well over a score of times.

A powerful identification had been conjured into being, a romance of place and of repetitive moments associated with it. This was its human impact. The theological meaning went far beyond this, as I have suggested, but it would have needed long years of journeying for this meaning to settle maturely in people's minds and hearts, years that nobody could realistically expect to give (including spectacularly, as it turned out, myself). As young people they were all seeking their way in the world and practically speaking the Towers could help only marginally in that. In the meantime, therefore, what existed was a dream, a story, a myth, accompanied by powerful emotions of teenage fervor and longing. Sometimes parents would phone me complaining about some average teenage behavior in their offspring, while adding that visiting Buckden Towers had not helped but even seemed to offer an excuse or pretext. Really only one or two parents ever did this, but I believe generally these parents were right in their assessment. In contrast, for some parents Buckden offered the possibility for troubled youth to find a glimmer of identity and hope, and that was valid too. Because Buckden did, in fact, occupy a marginal position in the world, somewhere at the edge of standard society. In these circumstances, my own energy at the heart of it all would sooner or later have to seek some way of relating it to the actual world. I had created a story out of time, as a result of my own story, and then the discovery of a workable formula for a temporary, "adolescent" acting out. But it was highly fragile, and perhaps one of the first places it was likely to break down was with me.

Because Michelle lived five miles away she needed a ride to the Towers in the morning and then back to her lodgings every evening. Often, I had the job, and our constant closeness had a progressive impact on me. One early winter night dropping her off I surrendered to a dizzy sensation of attraction and reached in to hug her a moment too long. The meaning was unmistakable, and she froze. The very first time I had spoken to Michelle was about six months prior when she had been one of the nearly two hundred gathered at Buckden for a big national youth event. She had caught my attention, sitting on a low wall. It looked to me like there was something about being with all these kids she very much wanted and yet there was also something very sorely missing. I had sat down next to her to talk, giving her all good gospel reasons why her life could and would be good. She didn't need a second announcement. At the end of the summer, after she had turned eighteen, she asked to become a volunteer and then quickly proved herself an effective organizer and spiritual leader at the center of the Buckden activities. To seek to hold her was forbidden, not only by my vows but by rules that I myself had drawn up for the volunteers—no romantic relationships during the time spent in community! The very thing I wanted to keep at bay I had stretched out to take. I let go at once, but it was too late, the intention could not be taken back.

Next day she didn't show up for work and the lay community was thrown into crisis. Various messages got passed back and forth, to the effect that Michelle had no reciprocal feelings for me. Malcolm and a recent addition to the volunteer group, Gabrielle, prayed with me, providing a community rite of penance. I was very remorseful and cried public tears of pain and regret, and the cloud began to lift. In the meantime, Michelle connected with Peter, the longest-standing member of the community and a gentle, immensely trustworthy young man (and again a great guitar player and songwriter). Maybe things had already been growing between them, but now an open relationship quickly formed. I was devastated, and hypocritically (albeit, in general, consistently) told them they had broken a key rule and would have to leave the physical community. The two of them showed a lot of maturity and found accommodation close to the Towers while agreeing to work through until the summer. The rest of the community—plus a couple of friends Michelle was in touch with—decided I was human, and that the whole thing should be kept more or less confidential. The crisis passed.

Human life is inherently a broken program. But the Spirit of God rises like a sun over the undergrowth, teasing tendrils upward to form a final life-filled canopy. Michelle and Peter went on to become very well-known and highly respected lay leaders in the Catholic Church. They founded the Sion Catholic Community for Evangelism, a long-running training and leadership organization in England and overseas. Michelle has been a representative at numerous international meetings, including high-powered events convened by the Vatican itself. She is a valued speaker, her evident wisdom and passion delivered in her characteristic Yorkshire inflection. As for me, looking back, my feelings for her were my first real attempt to open a door of relationship with someone who was both free and a recognizable possibility as life companion. It was a signal that my time in Rome really had changed things. But at the same time, I was still committed to my work at the Towers and from then until the end of my time there I adhered to my own rules.

I was also to discover there are other means of relating to the world than romance, ones that actually should come first in the order of human meaning. There was, in fact, an existential encounter waiting just around the corner, one that would change the whole way in which I stood in the world.

Our core community had got back into a routine and even seemed stronger with Michelle and Peter developing their experience as a couple, and Malcolm, Gabrielle, and Bernard maintaining the community and its work at the Towers. It was now 1977 and there were a few weeks to go before the start of the summer weeks. I came down to breakfast one bright morning in June, opening the door into the big kitchen that served the group of religious in the main house. Normally there were just one or two of the brothers there, and it was always a quiet and somewhat glum routine. Entering the room, I saw something I could hardly believe. As if for an instant I'd been transported into someone else's story, and should I go back out, close the door, and reopen it, the temporary wrinkle in space and time would be gone. But no, standing at the big, white-marble preparation table, as large as life and fixing himself coffee in a pan, was a tall, athletic man dressed in a canary-yellow jumpsuit and crimson top, with glistening black hair and beard, olive-brown skin, and eyes sparkling like stars on a southern sea. Beside this exotic creature the brothers clad in their faded black cassocks looked barely real, as if this other story had, in fact, displaced theirs and they were already merged with the dust of a departing world. I registered the shock, and a message arose from the river of memory in my blood, that this, *this* is the person I've always truly wanted to meet. And with it came at once amazed self-questions:

Can it really be possible for someone's most cherished dreams one day to take flesh? Was this not, in fact, a physical echo somehow of that wonderful visionary figure descending the stairs in my childhood home in Gloucester?

We introduced ourselves. His name was Eloy, a priest in the order studying for a doctorate in Rome who had come to Buckden for the summer to learn English. His country of origin was Ecuador, South America, but he belonged to the province of the neighboring country, Colombia. I welcomed him, cranking up my hard-won Italian, telling him what a thrill and surprise it was that anyone would come to our forgotten house in the English fenlands. He laughed—a joyful infectious laugh that I would hear many times again over the next several weeks—and said it was a good place for him to be, peaceful and calm, and yet not far from a great cultural center like Cambridge. I explained my job at the Towers, and he showed an immediate interest, saying he would love to get to know the work I was doing. And that was so typical of Eloy as I would find out: an inexhaustible interest in everything around him, as if he were an anthropologist specially funded by a university to investigate every detail of a strange new land to which he'd been posted.

The next two months were spent in a nonstop barrage of conversation between the two of us, even as the summer weeks began, and I was continually caught up in leading them. The whole thing was exhausting but amazing, joyful fun. Eloy asked about everything and engaged everybody. He made friends with the young people and joined in the meetings, prayer times, and sports. He loved the intensity of the relationships and commented on people's personalities with genuine respect and love, and yet a constant sense of mischief and humor. I told him my stories, my upbringing and endless search for connection, my spiritual turning point in Rome, and the subsequent experience of the Spirit in England. He told me of his own background and about Latin America, particularly the contemporary situation of political struggle. This was particularly acute in his adopted country of education, Colombia, the land of the '60s guerilla priest and academic, Camilo Torres, and the impact he had left behind. These geographically and culturally different narratives poured themselves one on top of the other like a layered cocktail, each liquid slowly melding into the other in the glass. Because, compared to surface differences, what they had in common was much more powerful: passion, intellect, human struggle, and in each case hugely significant mother figures.

Eloy had a spectacular bond with his mother, sealed in a birth narrative of biblical intensity. She was on an air flight crossing the Amazonas when the engines began to fail. There just happened to be a bishop aboard and as the plane sputtered downward toward the dense jungle, he went up and down the aisle comforting the people. When he came to Eloy's mother, he saw that she was pregnant and commented, "Don't worry, we will survive and the boy inside you will become a priest!" Evidently the bishop's words in respect of the plane proved true, and whatever the story's exaggerated elements, it had provided the frame for Eloy's personal epic. What child or boy could resist a prophecy like that? It seemed the passengers' lives depended on it!

Eloy's umbilical relationship with his mother paralleled mine. But alongside this stood his adventures both political and romantic, and it was here more than anywhere else he was ahead of me and would become a lifetime mentor. He had been involved with an activist group and had received political training. He had thrown in his lot with the peasants and working class but then he had fallen madly in love with what he described as a daughter of the elite bourgeoisie. She was from the other side of the tracks, the opposite end from everything he had worked for, but he had been totally captivated by her. It had come to nothing, but I think Eloy's presence in Europe was something to do with how it had all played out. What was, of course, clear was that being an ordained priest provided no kind of barrier for him in regard to emotional relationships with women.

On the contrary, Eloy considered it essential that one have these relationships in order to develop as a human being. They were part of the "journey" by which one came to oneself—the discovery of one's "other." Here was something totally new for me. Any emotional entanglement I'd experienced had been gotten on the run, held in one part of the mind while in the other I respected the rules and ideology of the priesthood. The obvious tension between the two halves had been something I had learned to live with despite its dysfunction. It might even have presented as a way of existence in its own right, a kind of habitual, if not sanctioned, double life. At all events, there just did not seem to be an alternative. But here, on the contrary, and for the first time, I received the thought that a man with a vow of celibacy might as a matter of principle and truth engage in a relationship with a woman. Eloy in fact had a whole theory of human development he had learned under the heading of "cybernetics," and it involved the primary recognition that all of us had been subjected to a "mental regime," a mental filling up or programming that had shaped our existence for us. To become a true individual, it was necessary freely to reject that programming and enter a desert of the self, the empty space where it was possible to become an autonomous and fruitful person. The goal of human life was to be a *yo fuente*, an "I fountain," a source of life for others arising in and from the desert of a free self.

I am sure I got only a secondhand and incomplete notion of these ideas and no doubt things that in one context may sound like an epiphany may in another seem banal or self-indulgent. Yet at that point in time and in that situation my conversations with Eloy struck a hugely resonant chord in me. "When the student is ready, the teacher will appear"; everything he told me had the taste of morning and liberation to it. I drank it in, and my soul began to gather its strength in a way it had never done before. I felt myself uncurling like a fern stalk in a wood, seeking its own special niche of light. However, at the same time, I remained entirely committed to the work of the Towers. Indeed, it all seemed to be the same thing. This new vision was simply a logical extension of everything I was already doing: creating a deeper self in the pattern of Christ, the liberator to all creation.

But, definitely, a fresh, unfulfilled energy like this would need some outlet. And true to form Eloy was there before I was, answering a question I hadn't yet clearly posed. So often he would come running up to me saying, "I have an idea," and I had learned to run in the opposite direction, for these ideas frequently involved some change in the programming or group dynamics that the youth leaders didn't always relish. However, this last time he told me his idea and it was music to my ears. He said I needed to take a journey, *un viaggio*. I needed to leave behind the world I had known and enter a new and strange one where I could discover myself in a new way. I had, in fact, already been doing this, seeking new spaces since the age of thirteen, with my first visit to Rome, but this time I was given the impetus by another, not myself, and the subtext was I should go to a truly different place, not one offered by traditional horizons. Eloy himself proposed I should go to the Holy Land, but I said emphatically no. Really, I wanted to journey to his own land, to the place all his stories had come from. I wanted to go to South America, to the world of human suffering and dreams of revolution. I wanted to learn about liberation theology, to meet people involved in this new way of thinking and living the Christian faith. And without hesitation he agreed. More than that, he said he would arrange everything. He would plan an itinerary and organize contacts for me all along the way. There would be nothing to worry about. It would be the journey of a lifetime.

But to put together something like that takes time and I would also need to get permission and find sources of funding. Nothing was going to happen at once, and in the meantime other things could come up, some of which would continue to reinforce my need for radical change of situation. In October I returned once more to Italy. I'd been invited by the head of the order to form part of a study group tasked with writing an inspirational letter or manifesto in preparation for a general council of representatives from all the provinces. It was to be a kind of road map for the future, providing the basis of discussion for the priests who would assemble in Rome for the regular six-yearly chapter. Other members of the group included professors, young theologians, and seasoned missionaries. I had been invited, I think, because I'd garnered a reputation as a restless spirit, and it was thought that a meeting with forward-looking minds would help me find my path. We met in an airy retreat center high above Lake Como. Looking down over the garden parapet the surface of the water looked like tiny tooled designs on a great dark animal hide. With a young German priest I climbed three hours to a neighboring high ridge where we could see the Swiss Alps spread before us. On the way back down, we sang charismatic choruses together, each in our own language. Later, I overheard one of the older professors speaking of my contributions. He remarked my comments were earnest but lacked intellectual rigor or weight. At the end of the meeting, I left feeling that I had not yet discovered my voice and that my presence was a concession to youthful fire much more than serious content. I took a train to Venice across the northern Italian plain. We rattled along, passing twinkling farmhouses in the glaucous night and their private signs of life remained foreign to me. It was nearing eleven p.m. when the train came to a halt in Venice's main terminus, and I set out looking for a cheap hotel. I made my way along the dreamlike canals and bridges, eerily deserted by Venetians at that hour. I passed only one other human being, a woman standing motionless under a lamp at the center of a bridge. She may have been a prostitute; back then she seemed just a young woman, a student with a backpack, waiting for a person whom she didn't expect to show. It was as if she'd always been there, waiting.

I found a small *pensione* close to the waterfront and slept on sheets so soft and fresh they seemed edible. In the morning I took a *vaporetto* across the lagoon to the island of Torcello and its ancient Romanesque abbey. The sunlight filtering through the upper windows was thick with dust motes like centuries-old prayers, but it was the massive cobalt blue mosaic of the Virgin Mary in the apse that captivated me. I fell in love, but what with? Tens of thousands of enameled stones as vivid as the day they were minted created an image of a woman transcending time. But to what end? What had summoned her into being and why in this moment did she seem to rule my heart? I traveled back across the sea like blue silk, the *serenissima*, and took a local train to a road on the outskirts of the city. I stuck out my thumb and hitchhiked to Ravenna. There I saw the same Byzantine style in the stunning sixth-century mosaics of San Vitale. But now it was Christ in the apse, enthroned on the sphere of the world, and on the wall to his right is the emperor Justinian, with a sacred halo around his head, arriving in procession with his robed generals and priests, and to his left the emperor's wife, Theodora, surrounded by her maids. In one magnificent cameo the whole of imperial Christianity is captured, hardly more than two centuries old at the point of depiction. I saw the sacred alliance of church and emperor burned on Europe's retina and although its permutations would vary, here was the core relationship shaping Christianity's role in the world. But what was more deeply disturbing—although I could not bring it clearly to words at that time—was how close was Theodora's majesty and allure to that of the Virgin. Who then was the woman whom I was seeking, or, more correctly perhaps, was seeking me? One standing crowned at the top of the hierarchical order, or in half-light on a bridge?

I continued my hitchhiking to Rome, crossing the Apennines, sleeping in a vineyard beneath a black sky weeping with stars. In Rome I reconnected briefly with Eloy and the community of students, and then I caught the train home to England. I was going around in the same endless circle I had traversed on so many occasions before. It was high time to move on. When I got back, I applied for permission to take the trip to Latin America, presenting the request as a sabbatical and study tour researching liberation theology. I would visit priests and bishops engaged in this development of Christian thought and practice that had generated such buzz over recent years. I waited to hear and at the same time I was adjusting to a new local superior of the community at Buckden Towers. In the standard three-yearly turnaround of appointments Michael had been replaced by my nemesis, Dan. However, flush with my expanded horizons and my actual responsibilities at the Towers, I thought I was in a different situation and could meet Dan now as a peer, somewhat on equal footing. So I was not unduly concerned. However, I did not understand how deeply divergent were our worldviews, and that this would become more pointed than ever. And, more crucially, regardless of the brotherhood of priesthood and religious life, he still held all the power.

It would always be a marriage made in hell and I can only assume that no one was paying attention, or, conversely, someone thought it was time we worked out our differences, i.e., that Dan would finally knock me into shape and make a priest of me. I was immediately offended at the high-handed manner in which he took up his duties, or rather did not take them up. I checked off forty days and still counting from the date when Michael left and Dan was officially in charge, and still he had not appeared. And neither did he communicate with us or send any word to explain his absence. He was, I'm sure, taking a long and, probably in his view, well-deserved vacation. But in my view the role of a religious superior was both to command and serve his community, and with an accent on the latter. Failing to communicate said bluntly this was not how he understood his job. Then, when he finally did show up, he at once removed the builder whom Michael had set to work on the Towers basement. Instead, Dan put him to remodeling a big room in the main house, fitting out his trademark plush accommodation for guests. I was left with a gaping hole in the basement wall where windows had been taken out, and a great pile of rubble blocking the corridor to the toilets and showers. In the three years during which Dan was my superior at Buckden and I continued the retreat work, the improvements to the Towers never were completed. We put plastic sheeting where the windows had been and removed the rubble ourselves, but the girls' showers remained rough concrete and the facility for the boys was never built. It was only a few months after he first arrived that Dan would tell me to my face that he did these things deliberately. It seemed he really had no desire at all for the success of the youth work, and I suffered paroxysms of frustration and resentment. Nevertheless, permission for the Latin America trip had come through quickly—the provincial council signed off on it without comment, much to my surprise. So, it was there I was able to focus my hopes. After all, everything that Eloy had told me was about some kind of new life, and that's where my thoughts flew, helping me ignore the pettiness that "plays so rough."

For funding I had applied to a province of the order in the United States. Reviewing their flourishing bank balances they decided it was time to share with less fortunate parts of the order, and they had just then begun to offer grants for support of new ministries and in-service training. I pitched the trip under this heading, and again the response was speedy, and now also generous. They gave me a substantial sum to cover airfare and expenses, and all the doors were opened for me. Eloy had by now created a detailed itinerary leading me through six countries, with a schedule of dates and a list of essential contacts and support to which he recommended me. It was a one-of-a-kind outline, a kind of continental safe-conduct making use of a few relationships I already had and adding people known personally to Eloy, including family members, who would be bound to give me first-class assistance. My expenses would be minimal and my experience optimal. I took the schedule to a travel agent and the air tickets were booked, carrying me in a great circle through North America, down to Peru, across to Brazil, and back again to England. All that remained was to write to the contacts, confirming my plans, and then to make arrangements for a few retreats that were to be run by the youth leaders in my absence. I went to Dan giving him the dates of these events and letting him know that one group had requested mass. I told him as he was the only available priest it would be necessary that he celebrate for them. I was completely oblivious at the time but later he declared my tone showed contempt for him, and I would never get anything out of him after that. I do remember at that initial moment an element of satisfaction, that he would now, whether he liked it or not, be part of my more progressive ministry, because of the solidarity of the priesthood. I suppose I saw myself to be at last on the same level with him, with equal if different pastoral approaches. He took it as an insult.

But, as I say, I was oblivious in the moment.

I waited for the day of my departure with a sense of incredulity that this was really going to happen. It seemed as if the whole of my past life clung to me like a cobweb and was unwilling to let me go. However, it was simply a matter of getting to the airport for the trip to become reality, and when the day came, I was there.

fourteen

EIGHT MILES HIGH FALLING FAST

The trip to Latin America is an episode in my life that stands in its own right. Even though it lasted just a month and a half it occupies a huge space in my imagination. So many of its incidents remain vivid in memory. But even more than that, the deeply changed mood it left me in—a shift in my whole basic positioning in life—makes it equivalent almost to the experience of childhood itself, and certainly to the years I spent in seminary. It went on generating an effect in me long after its actual time, and it continues to do so up to the present. The only comparable period is the eight months I spent in a small community in the hills of Umbria during which I took the final effective decision to leave the priesthood. This other period happened over five years later, and the years in between are bracketed by these two hugely important moments. The five years constitute the irreversible withering of my life in the priesthood and a religious order. The reasons why it took so long will show themselves in the next chapter, but the point here is that essentially and really, I crossed a Rubicon on the trip to Latin America. Before, I had never seriously considered leaving; after, I would never be able to look back, no matter the endgames. In this way the trip fulfilled all the promise Eloy had attached to it, and for this reason Eloy himself must be counted the single major influence in my life, humanly speaking. His intervention tipped me into a new world, one I had been looking for, but without him it would never have appeared. With the story of the trip, therefore, I find the turning point of my life, the moment toward which it had been working, and from which everything would flow. The story has itself a natural movement, building toward its own climax. I could tell it just for its own sake, although it belongs most properly here.

The plane took off from Heathrow airport at 3:15 p.m. on Monday, January 23, 1978, when I was thirty-two years old. It was a TWA jumbo and the stewardesses (as they were called then) were American and upbeat. They smiled and laughed and flirted a lot. It seemed that it was mostly businessmen on the flight, and it was like we were all going off to summer camp together—Camp USA. We were served a constant stream of nibbles, drinks, and full meals: nuts and pretzels, 7 Up, scotch and ginger, bean salad, beef stroganoff, chicken breast, vegetables, pineapple pastry, cheese and biscuits, After Eights, beer, champagne, coffee. I'd never breathed this air of wealth and success before and I was sternly aware that I was making my way to the "third world," a place whose relentless exploitation underpinned this effortless sense of privilege. All the same, I accepted everything they had to offer. When I got to Chicago, night had fallen and as we drove by downtown, I was astonished at the huge skyscrapers with electric lights blazing on every floor. I remarked on how much energy this must have been using and the priest who was driving the car said it was necessary for the sake of security. My general attitude to North America had been conditioned by the struggles against the Vietnam War and by Hollywood movies. While offering images of conspicuous wealth, the movies left an abiding impression of restless freedom and sudden explosive violence. To critical assumptions about the USA, I also added a positive embrace of liberation theology, something I had become progressively aware of as it became widely known after the meeting of the Latin American bishops at Medellín in 1968. The Latin American hierarchy had declared their famous "option for the poor," and if I was now traveling to the headquarters of global capitalism, everything I saw I would surely see from the perspective of the earth's oppressed. But that meant I felt uneasy and reactive. I found myself slipping into a critical mode when asked to preach a short homily on my second day, and then I got into an argument about the vow of poverty with the community of students when I had dinner with them. I was being a fractious guest and it could not be soon enough that I headed south toward the actual territory of the oppressed.

I got one of the last planes out of O'Hare as a sudden blizzard hit. It was like the last flight out of Stalingrad with snow ploughs fighting a losing battle to keep the runways clear and stranded planes looking forlorn and beaten. Then suddenly we were at thirty-five thousand feet, and the sun was blazing in a cerulean blue. Later on, the weather cleared, and I could see the great plains, the desert, and the Rockies. Making notes,

I penned tragic lines about the fate of the so-called American Indian. Finally, we banked right across a spur in the mountain chain to begin our approach over the fifty miles of houses, highways, and strip malls that are the city called Los Angeles. After we'd landed and I'd exited the airport, I caught it, the smell of California. It is a warmth and sweetness of air beneath the palm trees—perhaps already the scent of orange blossom—mixed with an acrid hint of car exhaust. It was sensuality and the freeway together, the American dream. But neither did it take long to get disillusioned. On the shuttle into town we passed one of the ubiquitous yellow school buses, testimony to desegregation, in which young people are taken to public schools outside of their neighborhood. It was filled with black youth, and I stared at them dumbly, playing out in my mind all the sad history this bus represented. Almost as if he could tell what I was thinking, one of the boys suddenly erupted in fury, giving me the finger. And then the whole bus exploded, yelling curses at me through the windows. Here was a white man, riding above them in an elite air-conditioned coach, and they were not going to be looked on as specimens in a jar. I immediately glanced away, shocked at the level of hostility. Good afternoon, America!

But the bubble of privilege folded back around me. In California the religious order was wealthy. It had been given property by the descendants of an old Spanish "Indian fighter" granted thousands of acres back in the colonial era. After the US took possession of California the family survived with most of their estate intact. Eventually they became pious—perhaps they always were. Anyway, they went on to endow the order generously. I stayed in a white-arched, galleried ranch house just south of Wilshire Boulevard. It had carpets and wall hangings and was paneled in what seemed a black mahogany. Its scent was heady, like musk. It was used as a retreat center but just sleeping in the room there I felt I had an uncle who was dangerously rich. Nevertheless, I was more at home with the seminary students in California. There was a greater Latino element, which seemed to give them a less entitled perspective, and I talked with them more easily. They took me to visit the old Spanish churches, and of course to the Hollywood Hills where I looked down at the sea of lights made famous in so many movies.

During these experiences I tried to maintain an internal spiritual framework, to give it overall meaning. I played out a spiritual dialogue in my notes as each new event occurred. It was like, "Here God, this is happening, and what is the meaning of this for my life?" But then I also wrote this: "Woke up wanting to hear my body think and the earth move under me. Just to listen, and be one with the world in what it is living, to be in concert with life and birth and hope—to make love with life and not to approach it with any imposed method or seek to give it any significance that I might wish it to have—even by formal or ritual prayer. Rather to let prayer come up always within me with life itself—to be empty of all exterior structure or category."

On a round trip to San Francisco I sat next to a young American woman called Vicky. She had a nursing infant and fed the child during the flight. It was the closest I'd ever been as a grown man to a woman's naked breast. Vicky was returning from Mexico, and she told me about US power in its "back yard" and the profits made by the big US companies there. A natural gas pipeline from Mexico into Texas had been installed but the rate for the raw material was minimal and Mexico had sought a higher price. In retaliation the US had canceled an IMF loan and threatened to pull out of other trade agreements. Mexico had no choice but go ahead with the dirt-cheap sale of its assets. The complaint of unfair returns for raw material within a relationship of dependence and oppression would become a constant refrain during the entire journey through Latin America. To hear about it firsthand was different from an abstract concept of capitalism and the poor, and especially to hear it from a woman breastfeeding her child. Here was human actuality and a real potential for resistance. I was stepping into a stream of human truth, out of the sterile world of ideology. Building a story of these encounters would, I believed, bring a series of anchor points by which my tendency to abstraction might, in some measure at least, be overcome. I think, in fact, this is what happened.

I left Los Angeles after a farewell meal with the students the previous evening and a communal trip to see *Close Encounters of the Third Kind*. My flight took me over the Sonoran Desert, dazzling white next to the blue of the Pacific. It was in the Sonoran that the opening frames of Spielberg's movie took place, with the discovery of the lost World War II aircraft. Spielberg was thinking about an impossibly advanced civilization coming from outer space to spirit away individuals like the pilots. I was on my way to an impossibly difficult city on our actual planet, one teeming with very real, present-tense people. It was Mexico City, and I was met there by Fernando, a priest friend from my days in Rome (the same priest who had lent me his car to ferry Mother Teresa). He at once took me on a tour of the city barrios or shantytowns. At the time there were fourteen million people in the metropolitan area of Mexico City and they were predicting forty million. A relentless tide of internal immigrants from the countryside continually expanded the borders of the city, establishing new *colonias* on the dusty volcanic hillsides surrounding the ancient Aztec center. They set up their packing-case and tin-roof shacks without roads or running water or sanitation. It was a pattern I would see all over Latin America and it at once produced a hallucinatory impression of sheer human number. A countless multitude, without basic necessities or a built human environment, created a sense of pure mass, of a simple enormity of humanity on earth. The sheer weight of this fact would progressively and powerfully shift my senses from heaven to earth. My intellect had often moved in this direction, but it was time now for the senses to catch up.

The next day I visited the wonderful Museo de Antropologia. The guides were women, personable and assured, and I was impressed by their highly articulate sense of cultural heritage. They took great pride in the original peoples, the Toltecs, Aztecs, and Mayans. They spoke of the profound religious feeling of these people, of how giving the heart of a victim to the god was to give life and vitality to the god, and how it was an honor to be so sacrificed. This, they said, was the roots of the deep religiosity of the Mexican people. Their passion, although attractive, somehow seemed to gloss the evidence—after all, who really wants to be sacrificed? That evening we drove to Huajuapan in the state of Oaxaca and spent the night there, prior to decamping at five thirty the next morning for a remote location. There was no fear of not waking up. At first light, bells clanged furiously and powerful loudspeakers blared popular hymns: I went from sound sleep to a raucous public meeting in a heartbeat. The rude wake-up provided the context for this reflection, written later that day: "Again a feeling of indifference to all *a priori* norms and standards. Lack of desire to fulfill any preconceived image of who or what I might be or do. All would be inapplicable in this utterly new world. Anyway I wish to be free. The moment is the sacrament. A deep desire just to be."

Our destination was a place called Tlacoapa, an isolated mission post of the order lost in the southwest territory of Mexico. To get there we took a Cessna, flying in across the rugged sierra, a journey that would have taken seventeen hours on muleback beginning from the nearest paved road. We skimmed between the hills, coming to land on a narrow airstrip in a world almost completely cut off from the outside. Poverty in the slums of Mexico City was life and hope compared to existence in this spot. The mission was a notorious eater of priests. Few resisted there beyond a year. The present incumbent, a friend of Fernando named Makarios, held something of a record, having lasted for over two years. He was a big, handsome man, exuding a painful, tightly bound energy. He was private, even taciturn, answering questions in short abrupt sentences. He devoted much of his energy to beekeeping, which he thought would provide an economic uplift to the area. All the same it seemed a mystery why he was there. He seemed to have powerful personal reasons that were no one else's business. He took us on a tour of the area.

Tlacoapa could be called a town only in the loosest of senses. It was a scattering of cane-walled huts roofed with leaves, a handful of adobe buildings, and all the spaces in between overgrown with brush and trees. I actually saw only two solid structures, one the priest's house built of cinder bricks, and the other an unpainted adobe cabin called the post office where the town mayor held court. As we walked along the track to the patch of beaten mud that was the municipal plaza in front of the post office, Makarios explained in an undertone the system of taxation imposed by the local law. Everything sold or traded in town was subjected to a sales tax payable directly to the mayor. The ridiculously meager goods available in town were purchased by the inhabitants with a surcharge that went straight to the boss. We stopped in at the baker's, a mud floor shack with a few dirty crates spread with trays holding perhaps three or four dozen freshly baked rolls. The bread itself looked inviting but the baker spoke desperately about the extra price levied, which limited the custom he could get. Just before the baker's we had turned off the path to visit a family living in a small space of poles roofed over with freshly cut banana leaves. The mother was up in the hills tending a patch of maize, the only thing that stood between her children and starvation. No father was to be seen but a girl of about eight years was preparing a tortilla on an open fire in the middle of the dirt floor. Huddled together and watching the pan greedily were three younger siblings, their limbs and faces streaked with mud. As we stood there, almost as if it had been scripted by a film director, a chicken raced in, grabbed the tortilla and dashed away, with the pancake flapping in the dirt and the eight-year-old taking off in hot pursuit. Makarios shrugged savagely (he didn't even help apprehend the chicken), and we left. I'd never seen anything like it. In the cinematic vividness of the scene the creature with the most force, and the most promise of survival, seemed to be the chicken.

We arrived at the plaza and gazed at the municipal building as if it were an outstation of hell itself. All along a low wall or buttress at the bottom of the building was seated a string of about a dozen men. Their ages were indeterminate, anything between eighteen and forty-five. They were called "runners" and were supposed to deliver messages, but they appeared not far from starvation themselves and looked to me for all the world like spies and killers. I can't say I'd had much experience of these things, but they had a doomed, deadly feeling that seemed unmistakable. Here, I thought, was a bunch of "bad guys" straight out of every Western you've ever seen, terrorizing and living off the community. But there was no Clint Eastwood, only Makarios, and with their badge of civil authority there was very little he could do about them.

We retreated to the priest's house and the housekeeper served a light supper. Fernando got out a bottle of Aguardiente he had brought with him, and he and Makarios went off into a muttered conversation about the order and its Mexican province, which I could not follow. Finally, I excused myself. This was certainly the most terrifying place I'd ever been, and it seemed to have a sucking power that threatened to pull me in. It was irrational but I feared I would be stranded here. It was something to do with the crucial role of poverty in my complaints about the religious life. I was always saying that we avoided actual poverty, but now here it was in all its brutal power and I found it horrific. As night fell the darkness took on a bitter taste and I felt a tectonic weight pressing in on the town. I went to sleep praying desperately that the plane would return. The sensation was still with me the next day, but in the early morning the air was bright and fresh and Makarios took us for a walk up in the hills. The terrain ran along dusty, steep-sided slopes with pockets of plantain and tangles of tropical plants. On the path, a party of indigenous people passed us, coming from town, some with colored, rolled-up serapes. Makarios said they were the original Tlacoapan people, and they were returning from spending the night in the church praying, something they did often. He said they were descendants of the priestly caste of the Aztecs and possessed formidable powers of contemplation, able to pray for hours on end. I felt this was a genuine wisdom; in the absence of an actual plane, six hours of prayer was the only feasible ticket out of there. But it was also in its own way as troubling as everything else. Were these original peoples of the Americas the only ones who had any closeness to God, and was it some kind of a secret that all the immigrant Latinos and their great Christian religion had missed? As for Makarios, he did not try to resolve the contradictions. If using his church made these people happy—regardless of what they were actually doing there—that was fine by him.

We were speaking with one of the workers from Makarios's beehive project when suddenly there was a commotion down the track. A group of men and women were talking excitedly and beckoning to Makarios to come over. When the babble of voices had subsided, he explained that the people had found a demon, evidenced by a putrid smell on one side of a straight line and totally absent on the other. I sniffed vigorously but could detect nothing either way. I did imagine, however, there were plenty of rotten things lying around those paths, and there were certainly demons in abundance—of poverty, violence, fear, oppression. As usual with human beings they associate disconnected things and so get some measure of control on their fraught world. Later, back at the priest's house, I took a walk on my own, trying to get my bearings. I looked up at the sky and saw the glinting cylinder of a jet passing high overhead, without making a sound. It was a thin pencil of light, and I could imagine the people aboard in their air-conditioned comfort scrunching nuts and sipping scotch. Just a couple of days before I was one of them, but now I was a billion miles away and my voice and the voices of all the people around me were completely absent to them. I felt a sense of pure panic and understood what it meant to be bypassed by history, by humanity. To be worth nothing. For that moment, for as long as it took for the silver ghost to pass across the sky, I was an invisible man dwelling in an invisible land.

I continued having to fight a sense of panic. By late afternoon the weather turned overcast, and when, finally, we went out to the airstrip and saw the Cessna come teetering in against a pile of grey cloud I had the crazy feeling that it would not be able to take off again. It would not overcome the gravity-well that Tlacoapa had become. Only when we'd boarded and the plane at last swept down the airstrip and lifted off did I begin to relax. As it zoomed above the priest's house, I noticed with a shock that Makarios's little yard was the only place in town where there were any flowers. A bushy vine of magenta blossom trailed along the top of a wall and winked phosphorescent in the twilight. It seemed at that last moment to be telling me I was wrong, saying all was not lost and hope remained behind with the people of Tlacoapa, even if I could not.

fifteen

EVER UPRIVER

OVER THE NEXT MONTH and a half, I would visit five other countries, and each left me with a dominant impression. I have to say my experiences got steadily better, and that probably had as much to do with me as with the actual places. But the truth of the matter is Mexico produced in me an overall sense of harshness and cruelty, and the next country on the list, Guatemala, was little different. In this case my dominant impression there was one of fear: not for myself, as had been the case in Tlacoapa, but a sense of the palpable fear afflicting so many of the people of Guatemala themselves. In 1944, the fascist-leaning president was overthrown by a wave of protests and a national strike. A military junta took control but carried through a free election in which a liberal leader won, beginning a period of social and agrarian reform, including the redistribution of a percentage of uncultivated land to landless peasants. The Guatemalan landowning elite saw all reform as communism, and anti-communist paranoia in the US and determination to block anything resembling a left-wing movement in Central America ensured direct steps to crush the initiative of change. In 1954, the CIA trained and supplied an armed coup, including a misinformation campaign, that toppled the liberal government. There followed the long years of the infamous repression carried out by the Guatemalan army. Military advisers from the United States Army trained its troops and transformed the role of the army to a politically driven counterinsurgency. In 1978, the military's focus was shifting from dealing with workers and students to countering small guerilla bands looking to mobilize support in the rural highlands. The indigenous Mayan people were relatively numerous, and their occupation of traditional territories and their non-Western lifestyle put them directly in the crosshairs of the army. They were seen progressively as collaborators with the guerillas and over the years became by far the majority victims of military atrocities. A long time after, when through the efforts of the international community the civil war had come to an end, a "Commission for Historical Clarification" was set up as part of the peace agreement. Its report concluded that the ethnic peoples had been the subject of a policy of genocide. It was into the early phases of this oppression that I wandered, without understanding very much of what was actually going on.

I saw the army frequently and with their combat fatigues, automatic weapons, and automaton faces they always inspired a rush of apprehension. I picked this up from the people I was around, including members of the order with whom I was staying. It was largely unspoken, but the implication always was to avoid these guys, if at all possible. In other countries commentary was less reticent. Eloy's contacts in Colombia—the next country on my agenda—were explicit about the army as an enemy of the campesinos and indigenous peoples, although the actual soldiery were made up of sons exactly of the same people. In Bogotá in the religious house where I stayed, I was awakened at five thirty in the morning by the barked orders, beating drums, and running boots of the Guardia Nacional drilling outside the Presidential Palace. My guide, who was named Miguel, assured me this was deliberately meant as a form of repression, keeping everyone's nerves on edge with the constant display of military force. He also pointed out to me the place in town where notorious special forces trained to carry out their assassination operations against the left. Colombia also had a background history of violence, one even more bloody than that of Guatemala. Its civil war between "the reds" and "the blues" was as arbitrary as it sounds. The colors represented two political parties, liberals and conservatives, and violent clashes between the two produced hundreds of thousands of deaths. As the liberation priests and sisters I met pointed out, fifty families in Colombia controlled the great majority of its land and resources, and as both "reds" and "blues" were led in the conflict from the same cohort of families, they continued to work together to maintain class interests even while the violence raged. Thus, while the communal killings were going on, these families "ate at the same table, from the same plate."

Meanwhile Bogotá was full of the poor. Every night homeless people would seek shelter at the Claretian church or in the porchway of its parish house. According to Miguel, there were fifty thousand prostitutes in Bogotá. And these prostitutes produced a small army of semi-feral children, the *gamines* who roamed the city streets in gangs begging and stealing to survive. The statistics just kept piling up, including later in Ecuador and Peru. Dr. Sanchez—Eloy's father—took me to his dispensary in Quito and told me of a 20-percent infant mortality rate, the result of infant diseases exacerbated by malnutrition and parasites. Just the sheer volume and scale of the poverty were a shock to a mind and body brought up in the expectations of the British welfare system, allied to an abstract, disembodied notion of the world. I was drowning in reality, a great dark river of human injustice and pain. The need for revolution seemed evident, but revolution called into being a monster of repressive violence that seemed to become an end in itself and impossible to overthrow. The more you fought against it, the more it grew.

The dilemma became intensely personal and real in another of the self-contained dramas or vignettes that make up so much of the character of this journey. It was recommended to me to take a trip to a mysterious mountain lake called Guatavita, about fifty miles from Bogotá. The flooded mountain crater was thought to be the original basis of the mythic Eldorado of the Spanish conquistadores; it was certainly worth a visit. A bus would take me out there and I would be back by nightfall. Unfortunately, I missed the early afternoon bus. I decided to hang on for a later one, hoping that I would still make it back by evening. While I waited ninety minutes for the bus, a spontaneous theater broke around me, with a woman and a man involved in a furious walking altercation surrounded by a crowd of spectators. The man would say something as he walked away, and the woman would follow directly behind him screaming bitter protest and insult, until, satisfied, she too would turn and walk away. Then the man would feel obliged to regain his honor and so he would about face and yell things at the woman until one of his barbs stuck. Then, of course, she had to turn once more and repeat the whole formula, and so on, interminably. The crowd kept pace, creating a manic procession up and down the dirt patch along the sides of which the buses were drawn up. The effect was dizzying and exhausting.

And piteous. Because all the while there was a woman of indeterminate age sat on the ground in the middle of the open space, among its scattered weeds and damaged trees. She propped herself on her hands, naked from the waist up, every bit of her as nut-brown as the ground on which she sat. Her head and hair hung down from her shoulder in an attitude of abject resignation. No one took any notice of her, and she showed no response to the drama going on around her, almost as if she were merely some kind of tragic icon painted on the scene by a virtual artist passing through. By the time the bus arrived my nerves were shredded, and the endless oscillation of anger still continued to play as the bus pulled away from the square.

The legend of Guatavita told of a princess of the Chibcha people who had become the lover of a great water beast or dragon who lived at the bottom of the lake. On moonlit nights it was possible sometimes to see them walking together on the surface of the waters. At least that was the version I heard, no doubt romanced for the benefit of tourists like me. "Becoming a lover of a beast at the bottom of a pool" is standard myth-speak for an unpleasant sacrificial end for a beautiful daughter of a chief, source, or scapegoat of mimetic crisis. And in this instance, there were well-documented sacred associations of the lake. It was the site of a splendid ritual in which a high chief of the people would cover himself in gold and ornaments and, riding to the center of the lake on a raft, would divest himself of the precious metal as offerings to the goddess below. There is an exquisite Chibcha gold filigree of the actual ceremony, on display in the Gold Museum in Bogotá. Several engineering projects were undertaken from the sixteenth century onward to recover the gold from the lake, yielding a small but tantalizing return from an impossible sea of mud. At all events, by the time I got to the town of Guatavita it was nearly dusk, and I had no wish to encounter another desolate woman, even if she were a goddess. I set out to find the parish church.

The town itself was very pretty, recently constructed in classy Spanish colonial—white walls; colonnades; blood-red, curving roof tiles; and pots of flowers everywhere. It was set next to another lake, very large, and as I later found out, an artificial reservoir created by flooding the valley of the original town of Guatavita, now stylishly rebuilt higher up the hillside. Sometimes when the water level drops, the top of the original church can be seen breaking the surface. I knocked at the door of the house next to the new parish church. The priest did not bat an eyelid but received me as if this kind of thing was normal, someone claiming identity as a fellow priest and showing up at nightfall for a meal and a bed. All of this was happily supplied together with good conversation. The priest's house already had a guest—a young doctor doing a residency in town. The doctor spoke excellent English and was especially glad to chat: maybe that was the reason the priest welcomed me so readily—to give himself a break. Anyway, we quickly got talking politics. The necessity of revolution again seemed a given, and this well-educated young man who himself belonged to the upper echelons (he said he was a friend of the governor of Bogotá) seemed to fit the Che Guevara profile. He took me outside and showed me red fire in the hills. He said this was the campesinos practicing what they have always done—slash and burn. An area of montane forest is set on fire and the ash provides fertilizer for a maize crop over a few years. But quickly the soil is exhausted, and the family moves on, leaving an ecological scar that takes a century to heal. It is poverty and lack of social security that force the people to do this. Things have to change.

We go back inside, and he pours himself and me the standard aguardiente for a nightcap. I say I feel great solidarity with the struggle of South America. He sighs and says, "People are ready to support us on an emotional level, but not with arms and money."

A cold sweat breaks through me, and not long after I make my excuses, saying I am exhausted. I go to bed, his words ringing in my head, and imagination running riot. What if he should ask me straight out tomorrow to supply some kind of material support for the guerillas? How could I refuse? I thought of the constellation of Orion, visible when we were outside. The Japanese Red Army used to say that guerillas killed in action joined one of the stars on the hunter's belt. But the next morning at breakfast the enigmatic doctor said nothing, and it was a huge reprieve when I was able to say goodbye and finally get a bus back to Bogotá. Any thought of driving up into the hills for a vision of the legendary princess had long ago been extinguished.

It was an important moment, a coming to consciousness of how a thought of liberation could not be simply and emotionally identified with revolution. I attended a conference of priests and nuns in the Colombian city of Cali, and liberation was in the air. The sense of youth and its energy was enormous. It was as if the world could never withstand the power of this hope and truth shared among so many bright, ardent faces. And yet the final mass was a celebration of the martyrs of Latin America, and that meant modern martyrs. Accounts of torture and death were read—vivid, actual, painful. At the offertory a list of names, ages, and dates was announced and placed on the altar. The final item was "Jesus Christ, AD 30, Jerusalem, aged thirty-three." Many, many priests, nuns, catechists, and church lay leaders were killed in those years. The figures of Óscar Romero, the four Maryknoll sisters of El Salvador, and the six Jesuits of the Central American University, San Salvador, are only the most well known (to US audiences) in the roster of martyrs, or witnesses, for human liberation. So, what from one side can emerge as a highly charged public engagement for the downtrodden, on the other can end up a very personal, helpless surrender and suffering. A group of us went for a walk in the Cali city center. As we paused at a bridge over the Cali River a young man, badly deformed, crawled up to us to beg, his stumps like the appendages of a stick insect—a person without social welfare or public dignity. At the same time a young Afro-Colombian started a conversation and boasted how easily he could make money carrying drugs into the US. I had an overwhelming sense that so many of the issues started there, in North America, and ultimately one day a message of real liberation must bring me to that place.

I was learning a lot and changing perhaps in a deeper way than I knew. If the experiences in Mexico, Guatemala, and Colombia were an encounter with brute faces of violence, then Ecuador and Brazil shared much more the beauty and tendernesses of the continent. Ecuador was Eloy's homeland and his family received me with great affection and hospitality. Quito is almost a mystical city, the second-highest capital city in the world, and the one nearest the equator. It rests on the eastern slopes of an active volcano, Pichincha, and is ringed by at least half a dozen other active volcanoes in the central cordillera. Sitting on a roadside within sight of the snow-covered crests I wrote my postcards. The air was thin and clean as if creation were new there, and writing to Buckden friends back in England it seemed the newness would rub off on the paper and help transform even a tired old world on the other side of the ocean. I took a trip to *la mitad del mundo*, the monument marking the approximate location of the geographic equator. It was little more than a rock-strewn field with an inscribed stone. A blind man was there begging, and it seemed horribly appropriate, like a job he'd been given by some puckish genie to depict the human condition. Pitched on the edge of the planet, without bread or sight, imploring some power—God or tourists?—for a miracle.

At the equator you weigh less than elsewhere on the planet. The equatorial bulge of the earth makes the distance to the center of the mass greater. Despite the gravity of my experiences to this point, from then on my journey did get lighter. It seemed less crucifixion and more resurrection. Humanly speaking, you could say I began to learn to fall in love. The Claretians in Ecuador had a vacation and retreat house not far from the tourist and surfing destination of Salinas, a Miami-style resort with multistory hotels and kilometers of palm-fringed beaches. I was taken there by a really kind and generous priest, Father Ospina, who put himself at my disposal the whole day. The actual house was at Bellenita, a tiny cluster of dwellings on the edge of the ocean, silent, white in the sun, against the clear warm blue of the sea. Inside it was a light fragrant space alive with tropical plants, all maintained by a solitary brother, Bonifacio. I went out to the ocean and swam for two hours just beyond the breakers, feeling the mighty Pacific hold me up on its warm swell. I went nearer the shore and allowed one of the breakers to flip me, like matchwood, headfirst. Its force was immense, uncompromising. But I felt an embrace, too. A baptism, into the earth; into earthborn humanity.

That night we returned to the city of Guayaquil, a coastal city of a million people (at that time), a sequence of potholed, dirt-piled streets, bordered by a limitless jumble of cane-and-board dwellings, stretching out into tidal flats on stilts and jetties, without services of fresh water or sewage, but with snaking electrical cords powering lights and televisions, a human tide hanging on to life by their imagination and fingernails. These were the *invasiones* or informal settlements, built day by day, without planning or support, literally the invasion of the cities by the rural poor: an immense visual drama of humanity living without security but nevertheless living. I attended a charismatic prayer group in the air-conditioned house of a company director perched high on a hill above the huddled masses below, their twinkling electric lights lining out the chasms of darkness between. He prayed, thanking God for all his gifts, clothes, house, food, body, health. His well-coiffed daughter played the guitar and fielded telephone calls.

By the time I arrived in Peru I was unable to take in any of the ancient Incan culture for which their land is famous. I was not interested in visiting Cusco, although I regretted it later. I had been mainlining on poverty and class, and together with two episodes of severe diarrhea (from locally made ice-cream and a similar soda) I was, literally, running on empty. Lima perhaps made an even more desperate impression than any city before. Maybe this is because I did not meet anyone there who seemed to be struggling for change. I am sure that progressive ministries and individuals did exist, but I did not encounter them. One of the priests of the community took me on a tour of the city. From a safe distance he pointed out the huge slum known as San Augustin, a vast hill of dirt and dust and shanties, again without any kind of services. He told me no one goes there; if you do, they'll cut off your fingers and ears, for any ring you might have on them. In contrast, his interest lay with a basilica dedicated to the Virgin Mary, under forty of her various titles, which he pointed out to me from a neighboring vantage point. It rose, in true medieval fashion, like a great spaceship somehow set down in a sea of single-story dwellings, clustered around without evident streets running between them. It seemed a visual parable of the mythic power of the church without social engagement. I was not impressed. So, the climax and richest focus of my journey must belong to Brazil, my next and final destination, the one for which I was saving as many energies as I could, and which makes a bridge of life with Ecuador. On the plane across the Andes, I was enduring terrible stomach cramps from yet a third episode of poisoning. I kept one fervid eye on whenever the toilet at the back was free and glimpsed the blue of Lake Titicaca briefly from a window as I dashed down the aisle. But I made it somehow without collapsing to my destination in São Paolo, the furthest point south on my epic trip.

Arriving in Brazil on a Sunday there was an immediate lift. I felt an ebullience and vitality among the people that stood in sharp contrast to the generally oppressive sensations I experienced on the west coast. I could sense Pele and "the beautiful game" in the air. At that point, however, I was in no state to respond. Arriving at the Claretian house I was weak as a child. After making my explanations I headed straight to bed. I spent two days in my room, half-conscious and withdrawn in myself. But there was also something different. The house held the office of the provincial treasurer, and the office employed a secretary, Cristina. I don't remember when exactly I met her—perhaps when I arrived or coming down to get something to eat—but she at once showed me care and attention. On Tuesday, I think it was, she brought me coffee and biscotti in my room. The gesture of gentleness and concern awakened something in me. Suddenly, almost out of nowhere, it seemed here was the first uncomplicated personal feeling between myself and a woman. Was it possible, right at the end of my journey, I was to discover something that I had, more or less unconsciously, been seeking throughout?

When my stomach infection eased and I started to move around, Cristina volunteered to show me a little of São Paulo, and she drove me around the city in an open-top car giving a commentary on the place, and the politics of Brazil. The concluding goal of my trip was to visit the Brazilian interior, a province called Mato Grosso, and connect with a famous bishop there. This was going to be demanding physically, so I was really trying to husband my energies for this final leg. When I headed out on Wednesday afternoon, I took a plane to Goiania, and the following day to Mato Grosso. I returned to São Paulo the following Wednesday and all that week there was a continual faint glow inside me at the prospect of finding Cristina again. At the back of my mind, I could continually see her copper-toned southern skin, brimming intelligence, and what I felt was her growing attraction toward me.

Mato Grosso is a vast expanse of plateau savanna, escarpment, wide rivers, and gallery rainforest. Isolated in the interior, it represents a kind of Brazilian Wild West. In keeping, there is the classic explosive mix of indigenous peoples, settlers, fugitives, and cattle bosses. Bishop Pedro Casaldáliga was a member of my order, and already a giant of liberation theology. His defense of the indigenous people and poor of his diocese was internationally known, and Brazil's military wanted badly to get rid of him but could not. It was a privilege to meet this man and worth traveling four thousand kilometers round trip across the bush to get to him. I flew in on a fifteen-seater to São Felix, across miles and miles of flooded land, trees sticking out of the water like floating weed. Like Noah in the ark, I thought we'd never find a dry place to put down. But like Noah, eventually we did. It was just an airstrip next to a huge river and the town was on the other side! The pilot told me there was a boatman at the end of a descending track. I was terrified that I would find nothing, but had no choice. Following my nose I descended the track, and sure enough, like in a dream, there was a boatman. I paid him fifty cruzeiros and he rowed me across the river. He did it skillfully, with so few strokes of the oars, and in the gathering dusk above the deep, dark rolling stream, again it seemed like a dream. I had definitely crossed to life's other side!

The flooding had affected everything. In the town half, the dirt streets were under water and many people from the adobe and cane structures were being housed temporarily in the school. I was staying in the bishop's house and waited four days to meet with him, but there was an American priest there, Richard, doing a photo-story on Casaldáliga's ministry and I was able to tag along with him. He rented a boat, and when we finally managed to get gas on Sunday, we headed south, along the Rio das Mortes delivering a religious sister to her post upriver, a town called San Antonio. We traveled 150 kilometers each way, skimming across the water, and the experience was dazzling, unforgettable, like a day trip in paradise. A thousand species of birds were on the wing or on the banks: jacamars, flycatchers, collared swifts, curassow, hoazin, even huge harpy eagles, and so many, many herons, storks, and egrets, living on the waters. The great white heron held its wings half spread at the end of the day, extending them to the golden rays of a declining sun, motionless, catatonic, like an Incan priest. And, of course, the fish, mostly unseen, but more of them still than the birds of the air, every now and then breaking the surface in a mad dash to get away from predators—as many below as in the sky above. Then the animals, too, including the ones we saw: capuchin monkeys; capybara, the world's largest rodent; and turtles plopping off the rocks. The next day we traveled the river Araguaia north to Luciaria, the oldest town in the prelature, founded in 1934. It is the seat of government and center of taxes, and consists of four streets parallel to the river, and four perpendicular. The street furthest from the river is the poorest, and it's where the mission has its house. The priest's work consists of four street meetings per week, in which the people prepare the Sunday liturgy and then come together on Sunday for the collective celebration. The Sunday service was under constant police surveillance, so the priest said the real work was always done in the street meetings where people knew and trusted each other. Returning to São Felix, we passed an indigenous village on the river's edge. A young boy took a bow and arrow and ran after us, gesturing to shoot as we passed at speed.

There was a sense of raw human struggle in Mato Grosso, and within it, and in parallel, a persecuted church struggling to be faithful to a radical gospel. The priest at Luciaria was no rural guerilla with a Marxist ideology, rather someone engaged in direct concerns of the poor in outposts of human life largely ignored by the world, places where the rule of the powerful and violent goes unchallenged. My mind returned to Makarios and his lonely vigil in Tlacoapa. The difference here was the example and support of Bishop Casaldáliga, a man who lived in similar circumstances, surrounded by the same challenges. I finally met the man on Tuesday, my last day in Mato Grosso. I found him in a place called Porto Alegre, a town barely a decade old, primed into existence by the construction of a road that brought settlers and ranch workers into the territory. Pedro was a man with the girth of a kitchen broom but a fire within that came straight from the stars. He walked like a general in the field and when he hugged you it was like you were being imprinted on his heart forever. This man had made it his task to defend both the indigenous people and the smallholders settling in the area, families who often found themselves the targets of ranch owners if they got in the way of cattle, or simply of the desire to accumulate land. Casaldáliga gave testimony just a year earlier (June '77) to the Brazilian Parliamentary Commission investigating land use in Mato Grosso. He denounced three generals, accusing them by name of corrupting the mayor of Luciaria on behalf of a big landowning company, to force out twenty-nine families of smallholders. He testified that between 1960 and 1970 in the Amazons forty-four thousand smallholdings had disappeared, replaced by much larger properties.

This kind of thing did not go unnoticed and made Casaldáliga a man with a target on his back. Already in 1971 men had lain in ambush to kill him in Serra Nova, and throughout his ministry his life was continually under threat.[1] Two years before my visit one of his priests, Jesuit Father João Bosco, had been gunned down and killed as he stood right next to Pedro at a demonstration. On my return to Goiania in the plane there were two hard-looking men who seemed to me like enforcers, one of them with a holstered pistol. They asked me in a blunt kind of way what I was doing at São Felix. I told them I'd been visiting Bishop Pedro Casaldáliga. They looked at each other and I could see that name was at once highly significant. They tipped their heads respectfully just as you'd expect a professional enforcer to do, and one said he was a "fighter" and the other that he was "a brave man!"

Pedro's conversation with me was a primer in radical pastoral theology. He said there had to be a return to a sense of poverty among Christians, especially in Europe and North America. This was the only way to be authentic while placing yourself beside the worker and criticizing his capitalist mentality. It meant giving up the rewards of a professional career and going to work as a young married couple simply as teachers of literacy among the poor. It meant learning and living what he called "political charity," alongside personal charity, which included changes in the structure of society, in its laws and methods of work and ownership. Needless to say, this was viewed by many as communism, but Pedro saw it as arising from the gospel.

When I got back to São Paulo I went to the treasurer's office to repay a loan they had made me for the trip to Mato Grosso. I met Cristina and she invited me to go see Zeffirelli's *Jesus of Nazareth* with her. It was Holy Week, and the atmosphere was a heady mixture of gospel passion and personal romance. After the movie we had mulled wine together in a street café before we went our ways. The next day was Holy Thursday and we spent the day visiting the natural history museum and a first communion in a wealthy parish, Chocava Flora. The children were exquisitely dressed, with fifteen photographers around them at the moment

---

1. Teófilo Cabastrero, *Diaológos en Mato Grosso con Pedro Casaldáliga* (Salamanca, Spain: Sígueme, 1978).

of communion. Cristina invited me to delay my return to England and go with her to her grandmother's house somewhere on the coast, a bit further north. She said it was quiet, very beautiful, and we could spend a week there and enjoy it, oh so much. It was a simple matter of going to the airport to change my ticket. There was no doubt in my mind this was a gilt-edged romantic invitation. A private week with Cristina seemed to mean only one thing, and everything in me that was human yearned to say yes and go with her. But it meant I would not be back in Buckden for Easter, and as far as I was concerned, I had promised the young people that I would be. All the same, I weighed the choices, and I knew that this was one of life's palpable crossroads. Yet hesitating before crossroads is both mental and spiritual, and I was still hanging on to gospel radicalism: I needed to carry its message home to Buckden. The pastoral responsibility that I had declared so decisively to Dan (and which he took as an insult) was at stake. Being at the Towers for Easter, as promised, was critical to its program and my witness.

Good Friday and the day had double its usual freight of pain and sadness. Cristina and I went together to a liturgy, and I felt the attraction between us increasing by the hour. She brought me back to her apartment and we sat on her bed and talked. She took my Gatsby cap between her hands and smoothed it continually. It was a shared apartment and there were other people there, but in my eyes the meaning was unmistakable. However, it was too late. I had to return, and though I felt so close to doing so, I could not reach out to touch her. One more free day and I am sure we would have embraced, but that day was not granted. When the hour came she and a Claretian priest took me to the airport, and I took the red-eye back to England.

It was a ten-hour-plus flight with stopovers in Casablanca and Madrid, flying quickly into the coming day. I traveled with businessmen, and their conversation about the mining industry, China, and commerce was repugnant to me. I arrived in London at three p.m. on Holy Saturday, took a taxi to Hayes, got into my little van parked there, and drove straight up the A1 to Buckden. As I pulled in, it was already dark and drizzling rain. I went to my room, dropped my bags, and went to knock on the door of my superior, Dan. He was shaving, with his shirt off. I saw his face in the mirror, half covered in soap. He did not turn around or look at me. He had no wish to greet me. I went over to the King's Room where the youth event was in full swing. The leaders looked shocked that I had shown up. They felt, I think, that my return for the event demonstrated a certain doubt in their abilities. They even said that it hadn't been necessary for me to come back. Really, I was not welcome, but I felt I had to vent. I said a few words about my trip, about how everything got down to love in the end. I milked a weak round of applause and left. I headed to bed, utterly depressed. It was still Saturday afternoon in Brazil, and I could have been on a beach somewhere with Cristina, a breath from embracing her. Instead, I was in a dismal climate with people who didn't like or need me. If I'd crossed the river back in São Felix, I now found out conclusively there was nothing for me on the bank I left behind.

There now followed the final unraveling of my commitment to the priesthood, religious life, and my work at the Towers. Things can happen on the symbolic and emotional level, but it may take a long time for their consequences to work themselves out in practical terms. I still had dreams about how I could make the priesthood work. I also lacked practical ability and life-skill confidence to strike out differently. The ministry at the Towers went on for another year and a half. After that I would work in the parish at Hayes for three years, although by that time I really had made the emotional and personal break. At the present, immediately post-Latin America, I still felt strongly I had to try to translate the experience into some kind of pastoral program.

I shifted the work with the youth in a more politically conscious direction, making more overt criticism of capitalism and adopting some of the language of liberation theology. Overall, the young people did not like it, and splits developed in the community and at the level of leadership. A few adopted the perspective I'd brought with me, and this group became my loyal cohort or faction, something inevitably destructive to community. As far as the organization of religious life was concerned, I was completely disillusioned with the province's work (basically sacrament-dispensing parish machines) and proposed starting my own informal community. The idea was that I would establish a house in an urban neighborhood where I could live with some of the young people and promote the gospel as I understood it. The idea was fraught with peril, but it did have the merit of still being within the general scheme of the province's activity. Pretty soon I realized it would not be given permission anyway, and at the provincial assembly where it was due to be debated, I withdrew the plan. As I did, I saw Dan looking at me with what appeared to be barely disguised triumph and satisfaction. From that point on I really had no future within the order. In the late spring and summer of 1980, I wanted to leave, and many times came close to making a formal request, but something held me back. It wasn't just that I had no clear idea of what I would do, but I also had a strong feeling the time was not right. I used to watch the crows at the Towers launching into flight, and I thought I could leave just as easily as one of those crows hopping off its ledge. Yet still I waited. Meanwhile, Cristina and I briefly exchanged letters. Her messages carried the feelings of that last day in Brazil, and I did dream of a chance of getting back there and pursuing our relationship. But it seemed totally impractical—from where would I get the cost of the flight?—and also I still felt the tug of my responsibilities at the Towers. I advised her to pursue her emotional future in someone else, and she stopped writing.

During this time my brother Terry came to work as a volunteer. I think I invited him after the previous group's year was completed and they all went their separate ways. I reached out to him, and he agreed with a willingness to be with me and support me that I have never been able to repay. In many ways he filled the emotional gap that opened once I had determined to leave the Claretians, and, deeper down, the hollowness left by my intense encounter with Cristina. Terry became an established feature of the youth work, beloved for his generous spirit, ready humor, hard work, and prayerful practice, alongside constant smoking of untipped cigarettes. The truth is Terry sustained me for the year through 1979, and after he in turn moved on (invited by Michael Mahon to be a lay volunteer at the parish in Hayes) I was bereft. I kept going only with a mixture of militant spiritual activism and constant looking around for a way out. One of the things that sustained me was listening to Dylan, especially the recent album *Street Legal*. I did not know at the time but its songs reflected a harsh divorce he was going through. Unconsciously I identified with so many of the sentiments, often laced in typical Dylan manner with biblical allusion. Playing the tracks over and over helped keep my soul alive on its drawn-out chartless journey.

Together with the youth group I developed a plan to run a youth mission in Euston, London. The thought was to go out on the streets and talk directly to young people. But by the time we came to do it the tensions in the group were so great that the project was dead on arrival. Everything really was coming undone. People sensed that I was emotionally untethered, and there were fuzzy beginnings of a possible relationship with one of the young women in the group. I had, however, experienced the first moments of a genuine adult relationship in São Paulo, and my formal role and position at the Towers acted as a barrier to anything that could remotely compare to its naturalness and passion. Really, that whole connection felt painfully adolescent and going nowhere. Essentially, I was in no-man's land. In Euston I went through the motions of the outreach and gave the talks as scheduled. We made not one contact or convert from the parks and the streets. The only person who was listening to me and had not heard it all before was the girlfriend of one of the helpers.

sixteen

HAYES UNBOUND

EVERYTHING WAS COMING TO an end. A fractious city wind blew through the concrete walkways and forecourts where our failed mission was centered, and I was alone. The province decided what I needed was to do regular priestly work, and they sent me to Hayes. This was the last place I wanted to go, but I didn't care—because I didn't care. Inside I was completely disconnected and prepared simply to go through the motions, waiting for something different to happen. The one positive thing was that I would be again with my friend, Michael, who was superior and parish priest. I arrived in the flagship parish and began the standard priestly life of masses, confessions, baptisms, marriages, funerals. Because of its huge membership the volume of these functions was overwhelming, with two or three weddings every Saturday, and likewise a regular parade of funerals. There were three priests, Michael, myself, and Phil (the same Phil as I was in novitiate with). Each of us had days on duty, answering telephone calls and doorbells, and if you added in schools, societies, and groups needing chaplaincy we were always running to catch up. Trying to insert anything extra like education or spirituality was simply to add burdens to the point of breaking the proverbial camel's back. Of course, a machine like this was not designed to be tinkered with. You kept it running, oiling the gears, and counted the income each Sunday. I totally hated it. I hated Hayes from the first moment I set eyes on it in 1964 and it was no different now. The point of Hayes was sociological and predetermined, and my personal existence was more or less always in crisis and seeking. One of us had to give.

I had a semi-psychotic episode that scared me. We were coming back from a day's community retreat, and its lack of grounding in life already made me feel queasy. I got out of the car and looked at the wall of the parish office. It crumbled before my eyes, and I felt myself tumbling through the hole into an infinite fragmentary nothing. If I had put my hand out it would have gone straight through the brick. I hurried to my room, feeling physically sick. I knew I had to get out, but how? At another time, not long after, I knelt in my room praying. I lit a candle. In my mind's eye my life was a smoldering wick about to blink out. I prayed desperately that the Lord somehow kindle it into flame.

But my world was about to take a definitive turn, something for which everything else was just preparation. So many things were about to fall into place in a way that could not have been expected and which, in retrospect, have compelling symmetry—something that in my mind can be explained only as divinely wished and provided. The helper's girlfriend who listened to my talks at the ill-fated city mission had told me at the end of the event that she wanted to become a Catholic. Her name was Linda, and she was the only one who paid attention or showed any sign that what she was hearing was in any way exciting.

As it happened, Linda lived not far from Hayes, in South Harrow. I suggested that she come see me in September when I arrived in the parish. Sure enough, she turned up and renewed her request. I said I did not have experience in people converting to Catholicism, but I would give it a try. As far as I understood it, it was a matter of going through the Nicene Creed, ensuring assent to its propositions, and then the inquirer would be ready. At that time Matt—my one-time fellow student who had moved to Hayes rather than live in another order's house—had recently returned from a conference in the US. He was now a well-respected priest and in charge of a catechetical development project in the diocese of Westminster. The conference was, in fact, related to the process of joining the Catholic Church, and he gave me some of the material, suggesting I adopt it in the "instructions" I was offering to Linda. As I went through the description, I began to take to it like a trout to freshwater. It was based in what was called the practice of the "catechumenate," the early church pathway to membership in the context of societal rejection and persecution. It ran for anything between a year and three years, and was based around the telling of both personal and biblical stories, interweaving the two, at the same time as following the church liturgical journey with its high point at Easter. In fact, the whole period of Lent and Holy Week was constructed around the experience of the converts or "catechumens."

Lent was originally intended exactly as an intensified period in the pathway of initiation into the mysteries of Christianity.

If I ever had reason for any hostility toward Matt, I now have reason to be eternally grateful to him. Connecting me with the catechumenate simultaneously set me and Linda on a profound adventure together and taught me a human truth that I had been dimly aware of but that progressively changed my intellectual landscape out of recognition. Where before I broadly (and naïvely) accepted "class struggle" as the necessary engine of human change, now under the impact of the catechumenate (and other intellectual discoveries), I began to see the human activity of storytelling as the most seminal agency of human transformation. It is not for nothing that Christianity is "good news"!

When Linda came to me first, she was seventeen years old, that age when the world is pitched dazzlingly like a rainbow between bright story and storm-dark fact, and when so many, female or male, wish to stake their part in the first while triumphing over the second. Her age was the same as mine when I joined novitiate, and becoming part of Linda's journey at this moment was in a way a rewinding of my own life back to that point. I invited her to try this new approach, the catechumenate, and she readily agreed. She certainly did not understand what it meant, apart from a bigger commitment of time, and I understood not much more myself. But I gathered a small group, including another inquirer for reception into the Catholic Church, plus sponsors and catechists, and we all set out.

Linda's particular situation was really quite special, because in her case she was not primarily becoming a Catholic; she was actually getting baptized, becoming a Christian from nothing. Both her father and her grandfather on her mother's side were decisively, intellectually atheist, and they had a major impact on the family. Growing up, religious belief was generally a nonsubject, a matter of no interest. Her overall experience was that of a secure, liberal, middle-class family, the kind of people who would not be out of place in the standard social niche of an Agatha Christie movie. Yet there was nothing snobbish in their attitude and in many ways the tenor of family life was suffused with Christian values. Linda seemed to be fulfilling a deeply suppressed spiritual thirst, one that had lain dormant in the soil of her nonreligious upbringing. The family had moved from Oxford and Linda had been sent to a Catholic school in the Harrow area because it had a good reputation and was convenient—I think her parents simply did not think of the Catholic angle. That way she made Catholic friends and tagged along with them to Buckden, and then the city mission. It was the latter that had taken hold of her—the sole fruit of that Buckden outreach. Christian faith and life started to appear to her as something enormously exciting and attractive. In more contemporary parlance, she was offered the red pill and did not think twice about swallowing it down, helped by a large glass of water called the catechumenate.

We told stories from the Old Testament, especially Exodus. The role of that story I had learned very much from liberation theology and its centrality has stayed with me ever since. It taught me that the God of the Bible places a decisive footprint within the oppressive affairs of human empire, introducing a radical change, an overturning at root. I did not fully appreciate then the ultimate consequences, including the overturning of violence itself in the person of Christ, but I knew enough to teach the Exodus story as an act of redemption within the midst of human history, with a profound and joyful outcome. The members of the catechumenate, and their catechists, took to it like ducks to water. They were encouraged to tell stories from their own lives in parallel, teasing out the ways in which God desired to set them free or had already done so. The journey continued into Lent of the following year, steadily moving to its high point at the Easter Vigil. The purpose of the whole thing is to relive the "mystery" of Christ's own story, to enter the transformative path of Jesus' death and resurrection through its liturgical reenactments in Holy Week. Linda was a star, completely identifying with the teaching and pathway, and demonstrating to everyone watching the spiritual vibrancy of the tradition. My friend, Michael, the parish priest, baptized her, and the young people who were there as part of a singing group cheered her to the church rafters. If Holy Week three years prior had been a descent into the depths, in which the Saturday had endured without a Sunday, this was now emergence from the tomb, an Easter like it's meant to be. I now understood perhaps why I had not yet handed in my resignation.

In life terms Linda became my master key, my letter of safe conduct, my path in the world. Where before I floated like spiritual ash in a bombed-out postapocalyptic landscape, now my feet were solid flesh, and on firm fertile ground in the twentieth century. She put off her application to university, normally coming directly after "sixth form," deciding to take a year out to commit herself to work at the church. She was in fact a bit of a cultural phenomenon, one of the first people in the UK to undertake the Catholic catechumenate, and certainly the first to be baptized in an all-or-nothing, zero-to-one-hundred personal Christian conversion. She and I were invited to conferences to tell the catechumenate story and witness to its life-changing impact. She was eighteen years old, highly intelligent, clear skinned with compelling eyes, copper-brown hair, and all the intensity of a new convert. Together we organized various youth activities, and little by little I began to feel that she might have more of a role in my life than simply a valued disciple. I had been careful in my own mind to maintain what I saw as an appropriate distance between us, both because of her years and because I had responsibility for her as a neophyte Christian. But that did not stop me enjoying her company, a lot, and as we got to the year mark, I started to look at her in a different way. Because all during this time I had not reversed my decision to leave. On the contrary, I continued actively to seek the relationship that would help me make the break. But in many ways, the people I knew were "all the usual suspects." It seemed that I was always a rat in the same maze, going round and round between the intolerability of my situation and the Augustinian horror and hesitation that seemed to hang over any developing connection with a woman.

Linda was different. Augustine had no hold over her. In fact, her upbringing had positively immunized her against the baneful influence of the saintly Platonist. All she knew of Christianity was the Jesus she had once read about in the Gospel of Mark, and then the one I presented to her. This meant that she was as close as possible to the type of person Paul speaks of when he says he personally taught the gospel to them, to wit she shared my particular account fully and was open to all its possibilities. This meant, in the long run, she would share with me a gospel of God's nonviolence, an understanding that would lead us progressively to a life and eventually a ministry in the US. With never a backward glance Linda embraced this pathway.

But it is not enough just to say this. To make the point sufficiently, I have to step back briefly from the story to underline a larger perspective, one perhaps more recognized even as I write this. My personal situation was of serious rebellion against the role I was in, but that does not mean the long arm of Augustinian dualism did not still shape my view of the spirit separate from the flesh. I was used personally to understanding the celibate life as the highest calling, signaling the future kingdom of God here on earth. Meanwhile, for the great majority of average Catholics, it tokens rather an otherworldly nonmaterial destiny of heavenly perfection; and within the broad frame of this culture the second perspective easily overwhelms the first. Linda had none of this baggage. She was free, and more than free. It's only little by little that I have come to see that whatever language I might have used of this-worldly liberation, it was and is Linda who traces, thoroughly and holistically, the material gospel in the world. Through Linda something qualitatively new happens. With her I experienced a relationship with the incarnational Spirit in the real world that I had always missed. It was this that I connected with, fell into, almost without noticing, without my own backward glance such that I would ever need to second-guess a life of spiritual meaning with her. In the final analysis, the fact is I fell deeply in love with Linda, overwhelmed by her presence and truth more totally and irreversibly than all of the programing of my life to that point.

No doubt, of course, Linda came from a different world from mine. Her family were not strikingly rich; in day-to-day terms they had a style of simplicity, even frugality. But all the same they had a background of security and education, and carried an assurance that marked them off from the terraced-housing, capital-lacking classes that were my own tribal DNA. She had that natural assurance, and there was no fear in any of her responses to me. But, I insist, there was also something much more than mere class and social background. It was a springtime, unique of its kind, that God had found for me, and for which I previously had to wait, until it was ready. (There was a time, in fact, ten years or so earlier, when, all unknowing, I lived very close to Linda: I used to pass her road almost every week traveling into Oxford.) I was looking for a partner who would help integrate my life with a material world that had basically been damned to hell for me. But at the same time, and by the very same token, I was seeking a relationship within a spirituality of real-world human transformation. The world had not suddenly become hale and whole just because I needed to be part of it. On the contrary, my need to join it was conditioned by a Pedro Casaldáliga-style engagement for historical human change. Linda was totally at one with this, and more than I knew. Her commitment was proven categorically as life with her went on: whatever madcap scheme I came up with—from running a mission for the homeless, to leaving everything and coming to the US—she never blinked or ever thought twice. With her I was merging my life with the very radicalism I could not attain in the priesthood. I could not know this fully and reflectively at the time, it had to be instinctive and implicit. But it was as I vaguely guessed it to be. Linda was a day in May when all the trees are in blossom, after twenty years of winter.

So, it's not surprising that, from then on, life actually became a good deal of fun. Because of the generous welcome Linda's family gave me they opened a door to the land I never had. My childhood trauma could never be completely healed, but Linda and her family became, as much as conceivable, a pathway for me to enter England. Just next to their house in South Harrow there was a track that literally went back in years to the Domesday Book. I could go out there on my own and think of Shakespeare walking that path on his way through to London. I would wander down the hill and imagine possibly chatting with him as he passed. And I would sometimes walk over the hill to Harrow school and its church, seeking out the churchyard with its lookout, and the wood below. I imagined Lord Byron gazing out from the same spot, producing his immortal lines of poetry. With Linda's family I could feel free, assimilated, comfortable even, in the land of my birth.

We took a trip to Italy, along with Linda's sister and another friend, John. By this time Eloy himself had left the order, marrying a woman he met at Buckden in 1978. She was Paola, from Rome, and their relationship blossomed when they both returned to Italy. Paola had described to me a place in Italy that she compared to Buckden. It took its name from the nearest town, Spello, and was a retreat center guided by a spiritual leader named Carlo Carretto. She spoke highly of Carretto, and I very much wanted to meet him and experience his center. After visiting Rome and Naples our little group headed to the location, a picture-book walled town in Umbria, and beyond, in the hills, a number of small farmhouses that acted as "hermitages" for visitors. We caught up with Carretto when he was having his dinner along with a substantial community of visitors. At first, he was suspicious, but after demanding that we each give a spiritual account of ourselves, he was persuaded. He was impressed, I believe, especially by Linda. He allowed us the use of one of his lodgings. We followed the routine of the center for a few days, working in the fields in the mornings, resting and praying in the afternoons and early evenings, before the communal meal at night. We had a grand time and the heavens continued to smile on our adventures. We visited the town and, strolling the rosy-stone twelfth-century walls in the warm night, Linda and I held hands for the first time.

And it was right we did. My epic journey of emptiness and futility was about to come to an end, and its pain that clung like a toothache was about to ease. The place where the train would finally cross the frontier and enter truly fresh horizons would be Spello. And the engine that effectively brought me to that place and its blessing would be Linda. It was Linda who ultimately prompted rationality and freedom in my life, and the setting of Spello would eventually seal the meaning of the change for me.

It was not long after returning to England that we kissed for the first time. The day after I spent in agony, lest on reflection she might decide this was wrong to do. But she turned up that evening for mass, and got in readily beside me in the van to go pick up some other youth. I knew then everything was okay. Our relationship had begun, including physical intimacy, and from there on it never looked back. Linda gave me the gift of her freedom, her faith, and the vibrancy of her youth. Because of Linda everything became possible, including coming eventually to the US and making a life here. What did I give her? An exciting life? Perhaps. A place for her instinctive freedom to express itself? I think so. Most of all a way of life that responded to her deepest spirituality and heart's desire, a following of Jesus that expressed itself as the primary condition and character of her life. I have helped give her that, and she in return has given me the very same.

But before this could play out, a major twist had to happen. I now had the most enjoyable lifestyle: fulfilling my priestly duties without inner conflict while being in love and experiencing the continual companionship of the person I was in love with. I saw her almost every evening, and on my days off, Tuesdays, I spent the whole day at her house. By the following year it seemed simply the honest thing to tell Wacker, the provincial, that I wished to leave. I had no actual plan, but the happiness and solidity of our relationship gave a strong sense of security and I felt somehow or other I would find a way. Wacker's reaction surprised me a lot. He did not argue or attempt to dissuade me—he seemed to accept the situation as beyond recall. Instead, he pleaded with me to postpone the actual event, because my leaving would disrupt the province's appointments and make his life difficult. This was amazing, as he was asking me to make a gift of my time personally to him, and meanwhile he was simply not concerned with what was going for me. Still, part of me felt sorry for him—I think he was burned out. After all he had borne the burden of authority throughout most of the '60s and '70s. Moreover, his imposition made little difference, as I had all that I needed to make me happy. So, I decided simply to carry on. And there is the twist. Because of delaying my exit, I would end up being persuaded to spend a further nine months away in Spello, discerning my decision. And that turned out to be spiritually and professionally perhaps the most formative year of my life.

But for the next year and a half I continued with masses and confessions, with weddings and funerals, while at the same time promoting successive groups of the catechumenate. Linda helped with these. She also started a correspondence course in Scripture and then she applied for a three-year bachelor's degree course at Heythrop College, the Jesuit theological school in London where I'd also studied. She had taken A levels in science subjects, but her grades were poor because she sat the exams during her time of catechumenate when all her focus was on learning Christianity. Not for the last time in her life this spendthrift neglect of worldly priorities was reversed in the final frame. She took some of her correspondence course essays to her interview and these, along with her story, gained her entry to the prestigious Jesuit college, part of London University.

All this was the era of Margaret Thatcher, British prime minister, and her companion-in-arms on the other side of the Atlantic, Ronald Reagan. It was the endgame of the Cold War with the introduction of a new generation of US nuclear missiles on mainland Britain, wrestling down an increasingly failing Soviet Union. There were cruise missiles located on US air bases in England and trident missiles for British nuclear submarines based in Scotland. The policies provoked heightened anxiety and approaching despair, with the thought of a trigger-happy US unleashing "limited" nuclear war in Europe. Movies like *The Day After* and *Threads* played on TV, graphic depictions of nuclear apocalypse. The feeling grew that humanity's days on the planet were numbered.

Linda and I joined with a few other people in creating an activist group to protest as Christians the threat to creation and its human stewards from nuclear weapons. The leader of the group was an American, Dan Martin, and the name we gave ourselves was Catholic Peace Action. Dan taught us a lot about nonviolence, especially about not engaging or responding to aggression encountered in the course of any action. Dan's teaching and example became a key part of my personal change from elements of historical struggle to gospel-based nonviolence. All during the '70s and '80s the Provisional IRA carried out an intermittent bombing campaign in mainland Britain. I can't remember exactly when I began pulling away from default family acquiescence to the violence, but it was not long after my ordination that I had a heated disagreement with my mother when I condemned pub bombings—these, at least, could not be justified. She responded with her standard broadside on the centuries-long suffering and genocide of the Irish population, and it ended in a stalemate. It is not easy to let go of generational wounds—they become a reason for existence, in and of themselves. Being a priest for me was not emotionally separate from resentment at the English immiseration of the Irish, so the collapse of the former went step by step with a gradual abandonment of the spiritual identity of the latter. I was obviously already on the way, but Dan's teaching helped clarify and establish the gospel primacy of nonviolence.

We carried out an action at the British Ministry of Defense in Whitehall, chaining the doors shut and pouring vials of our own blood on the steps. Of course, it created a huge amount of disruption and, looking back, I have to say that my heart was not pure. There was still a measure of antagonism in both the action and the symbolism. At the same time, there was and is a huge truth there. The gaming out of war, especially nuclear, within the walls of that building remains an anti-gospel, and given that many who worked there would be self identified as Christians, it represented a legitimate call to conscience. We were tried at Bow Street Court but received conditional discharges—essentially the judge decided not to waste taxpayers' money on innocent fools. I was glad at the reprieve, as I knew I was very nearly out of the priesthood and that would have complicated the supposed witness I was giving when, inevitably, it became known.

But we were not quite done with our actions. The Falklands War between the United Kingdom and Argentina blew up in the spring of 1982, a dispute over ownership of a windswept archipelago and its two main islands three hundred miles off the South American coast. The British dispatched almost its entire naval force to the South Atlantic, regaining possession from the Argentine forces at the cost, in sum, of nine hundred plus lives. The city of London organized a victory parade, and we undertook to protest the occasion. The previous evening Linda and I delivered two large planks of wood to a church situated on the route of the march and hid them in the bushes outside. The next day we returned with Dan's wife, Carmel, their baby in a stroller, and one other person, bolted the planks together into a large cross, and fixed a written poster on the crosspiece, "Jesus Was Murdered by the Military." We erected the banner-cross at a corner, stood around it, and waited for the soldiers. They drove down Moorgate in their personnel carriers and we could see the eyes of the lead officers swivel away as they encountered the words. At first no one in the crowd on the road took any notice of us, but then they did. Two youngish men in pinstripes, carrying briefcases, came up, outraged. "You can't be here. This is our space. Get out!"

Something about their edge and attitude was actually frightening, much more than the Ministry of Defense. This was not about doctrine or meaning or law, it was about territory. We retreated with the cross to the church, dumped it back in the bushes, and headed to the nearest underground station, Bank, I think it was. As we helped Carmel down the stairs with the stroller, we were relieved to disappear into the crowd. Nonviolence does not entail deliberately provoking your own hurt.

Linda was now full time at Heythrop College, and I was playing out my final months at Hayes. I was looking to the September of 1983 when Wacker would step down as provincial and my deal with him would come to an end. The fact that I had actually made the deal confirmed the certainty of my leaving the order and the priesthood, and each passing day on the way to that moment increased its inevitability. One particular event that occurred forcefully underlined my decision.

My friend, Michael, had been engaged in a running battle with the men's club in the parish. This was a particularly noxious institution I had frequented often during my time as a student in the parish. My view of it had changed considerably and I generally stayed away. Michael, in contrast, regarded it as a feature of the parish that should really come into line with his general policy of parish renewal according to the teaching of the Second Vatican Council. He wanted the club to be more identified with the pastoral goals of the parish, contribute more financially, and allow their space to be used for parish meetings. The stage was set for an epic confrontation. Somehow Michael was ill advised in his battles, or, at least, he chose the ground for the fight poorly. He had insisted on placing a couple of gambling slot machines in the club lobby alongside the club's machines, indicating thereby that this was indeed church property. What he achieved was simply to stoke a rivalry, with the sympathy going easily to the club and its camaraderie.

The time came for the club's annual general meeting at which Michael's proposals would be discussed. The three priests all attended, but when Michael rose to address the gathering he was howled down by two hundred men with pints and shots in hand. A good half of these individuals attended mass on Sundays, and I had counted some of them friends. But none of this mattered when they were defending their territory, accusing Michael of "clergyism and landlordism." The clergy retired in disgrace, leaving the field to the bellicose voices of the drinkers and the club secretary hypocritically waving his hands for order. After the meeting none of us could sleep, wandering around the parish house like ghosts at our own funeral. My feeling was that the parish should immediately disassociate itself from the club and begin legal proceedings to wrest the property back. But that was never going to happen, given the revenue the club provided. Not only that, but in the subsequent appointments the following spring Michael was removed as parish priest, handing the club a political victory. Michael never returned to Hayes. All the same, the club had overreached and little by little its reputation and membership declined. Reports tell that two decades or so later legal proceedings were at length instituted and the club was finally removed from the parish.

But for me it was symbolic. So many horrible distortions converged that night, some of which I had been party to in my own backstory. I could not wait to get out. I refused to attend the provincial assembly and when the new provincial superior was appointed, I told him I was going to leave. The new superior was Matt, the man who had given me information about the catechumenate, but the man who also most represented the wreck of my early ideals and someone with whom I never had any commonality. Matt was always verbally manipulative, and neither was he going to fall short this time. He remonstrated, "You leave us in the situation of a jilted wife, trying any possible way to keep her husband." The choice of image is illuminating: When had I ever been treated as a beloved? However, he did manage to strike home on one point. He said that at least I should submit to a period of discernment, given that I had been nineteen years in the order, and I had always been approved going forward for vows or toward ordination. How could all that be wrong?

It might seem a major reversal at this point to reconsider my future one more time, given everything that had happened, and in a way it was. I was about to step through the door and now I drew back, yet again. But I was of course still deeply committed to things of the spirit, and the move like the one I was contemplating demanded an even greater spiritual truth within. I was about to jump but did I really have wings? Matt's language had a hold on me, and I agreed. I remembered that Carlo Carretto had invited me to come and spend what he called a "sabbatical year" with him in Spello. I offered this as a solution and if Matt didn't take the deal, then I would leave anyway. He accepted, thinking, I believe, that the physical distance to Italy would be enough to choke off the relationship with Linda. Perhaps, even, he thought I'd implicitly agreed not to see her for a year. Meanwhile, in my mind Linda had been to Spello and trusted the place, so the break was not total for her. She'd be there with me in some way. As for her own reaction, she supported it, in her typical, formidable way. Gentle, accepting, and full of assurance.

seventeen

SPELLO

On September 17, 1983, I arrived by rail through the heaped-up hills of Umbria, on tracks bedded in fragments of shining limestone. The walls of Spello and its houses were toned a honeyed rose, similar to Assisi, which lay just around the foot of the mountain. The mighty mountain, Subasio, reared its head into the blue, trailing gentle clouds like lambs on its summit. Everything seemed softly sculpted, and purpose built for prayer. I took a taxi to the central community house, San Girolamo, and found my way to the cool of the kitchen. I was welcomed by a priest, a Franciscan, physically slight with a high-strung feeling about him, like an overwound piano wire. But he seemed happy, and he treated me graciously as he showed me my room. The house was an old Franciscan convent and the rooms consisted of stone walls, wood partitions, bed frame, mattress, and a small desk. There was no ceiling except the terra-cotta roof and an occasional crack filled with luminous sky. Here was an artistry of the Spirit, a thousand years in the making, where I might finally trace the line of my own long-uncharted spiritual journey.

The whole project comprised thirty or so dwellings, one or two of which were also old convents, but most were the homes of former *contadini*, peasants who had worked the land for centuries. Since the Second World War many had progressively abandoned their tiny farms for better-paid jobs in the cities. But the families had not lost attachment to the old places with their vineyards and olives. The arrangement was ideal whereby the family would entrust the house to the center for the use of individuals or groups, in exchange for keeping an eye on things and some basic care and maintenance. Carlo Carreto belonged to a religious order called the Little Brothers of Jesus, and in principle he lived at Spello as a member of a community in that order. But it was his personality that dominated everything, and to him in particular the families confidently entrusted their dwellings. Carlo was basically a humble person, and he had learned his humility in the school of life's reversals. He was also, however, a deeply passionate man who attracted passionate devotion in return; he towered over the scattered dwellings, now renamed hermitages, like a feudal abbot over an abbey's domains. Because of him things ran well.

When I arrived toward the end of the summer there were still a number of groups staying in the houses. They consisted mostly of young people, visiting usually for a week at a time. There was plenty of work for the groups, harvesting crops, clearing fields of brush, repairing roads and ditches, preparing meals. Every morning was dedicated to manual work, until midday, then in the afternoon there was silence, for personal prayer and study. In the evening an intense, spontaneous community of late teens, twenty-somethings, and some older folk, would assemble in the chapel at Girolamo for evening worship. Buckden had some of the same intensity, but it lacked the contemplative depth that Carlo, together with the native territory of Francis, afforded. I fell into the rhythm without difficulty; it was a division of time and labor that focused the self inward, and really that was what I wanted to do. Within a short time of arriving, I was also given permission to spend a week by myself. I did not properly understand it, but this seemed to be something of a privilege. Later I understood why it was a privilege, but for the present I took it as perhaps a challenge, to see whether I could do serious time alone. I was given the hermitage of Sant' Elia, perched high on a hillside, facing east, and looking down on a narrow valley of woods and fields.

There was something about these times of solitude in an ancient landscape that now entered deeply in my soul. I experienced, I think for the first time in my life, the meaning of contemplation: to be in the presence of something beyond names and beyond words, known more by its absence than by its presence, but also paradoxically present because it was absent. I use the neuter participle for this presence not because it is not personal, but because it refuses to enter any of the modes by which we so easily shape and limit the personal. It is so much bigger, and then also so much more truly and deeply personal than the personal. To be in the presence of the unnamable is to construct a rhythm for your day that is simple and ordinary, a time to get up, a time to pray, a time to work, a time to rest, a time to study, a time to eat, a time to enjoy, and a time to sleep once more. It is to do all these things with a faithful regularity, like a watch or a clock, ticking away indifferently, but always with one eye cast beyond its sweep to where the unnamable may yet appear. And the eye that you cast is itself simple and undemanding, no more accented than the act of washing your face or preparing vegetables, merely one more part of the continuing round of hours and its unyielding hope. For that very reason, it is always there, always keeping vigil.

I spent one night watching in prayer, without going to bed. I waited for the sun to rise across the farther ridge, felt the cold night wind blow through my bones, trained my eyes helplessly on the few house lights glimmering in the valley. The dawn and the new day came, but nothing was revealed. There was no answer to my life's questions. And yet I still feel that huge dark cleft where the hillside ran away from me; I feel it in my soul. It has become a great dark eye within me, unfailingly watching the skyline.

Carlo at first kept me at a distance, although he was certainly glad of my presence in the community. He himself was not a priest, so he depended on having ordained men around him to celebrate the Eucharist. A traditional liturgical Catholic, the setting and liturgy of the mass were essential to him. However, I think few priests were prepared to work with him; because he was himself so clearly the one presiding, they had to take a backseat. Moreover, it turned out that he had very little patience with many priests, considering them little better than institutional drones, while he was always seeking a sense of someone's living spiritual story. Carlo had been a man of authentic political and personal charism. He had risen through the ranks of Catholic Action, the lay organization well known and established in Catholic cultures like France, Bavaria, Italy, dedicated to implementing Catholic social teaching in the political sphere. He had consistently been at odds with the Italian fascist regime, and then after the war he had been appointed the national president of the youth section of Catholic Action in Italy, organizing and traveling widely. However, his success was short lived. He quickly found himself on the wrong side of the anti-communist pope, Pius XII, and was deposed from his position as president. In response, Carlo gave up everything and joined a religious order, the Little Brothers of Jesus. He spent eleven years in the deserts of North Africa following in the footsteps of the inspiration of the order, Charles de Foucauld.

Foucauld himself pursued a unique pathway. Inspired by the hidden Jesus of Nazareth—the man predating his public gospel ministry—Foucauld tried to get as close as he could to the style of life of God's Son when he was indistinguishable from the rest of humanity. This was an invisible, noninstitutional Jesus, committed only to being close to his neighbor, to men and women, as the unconditional presence of divine love. Foucauld began as a Cistercian monk in France and then Syria, moving on to live as a hermit in Nazareth itself, and finally plunging deep into North Africa in southern Algeria to live among the Tuareg tribespeople. There at Tamanrasset in completely Muslim territory Foucauld sought to witness simply by his life to the unfathomable depths of divine compassion, willing to receive as much as give. Carretto brought with him to Spello this radical experience of prayer, solitude, contemplation, and solidarity with all creation. But he also gave it a twist that was linked uniquely to his spirit and gifts as a man, and it was this that I learned from most especially.

He would sit to the side of the chapel, at right angles to the altar, and merely by his presence in that spot he would shift the center of gravity from the presiding priest. When I first arrived, two or three other priests were available, and so I did not say mass every day. But, as the year drew to its close, first one and then another disappeared, until I was the only one left. At this point my stock rose considerably. Carlo used to introduce me to his visitors as *"guarda che bel prete che abbiamo!"* Which, roughly translated, I took to mean, "Look at this fine private chaplain who says mass for me!"

But the context of the mass provided a deeper reason why Carlo began to appreciate me. It wasn't sufficient just to celebrate the Eucharist; part of the deal was I had to preach. Carlo insisted on it. So my few halting sentences in Italian, commenting on the Scripture, became the occasion for Carlo to grab an idea and run with it. The fact that I couldn't say much allowed him to supplement me, and more and more he began to appreciate the few things I did say. He would place his brick-like peasant frame on the edge of the bench, grasping his cane with a double fist, his face bright and gleaming, waiting for something to spark his interest. Normally, when he gave the address from start to finish, it would take him ten or fifteen minutes to warm up. He would chunter on, not saying anything exceptional, while everybody waited patiently for him to become inspired. Then, finally, his motor would ignite and he would be off. He would tell a story, or he would grasp a phrase or an idea and be transported into an unquenchable eloquence, about God, the immense beauty of God, the need to wait on God, the mystery and wonder of such waiting, and, through it all, the poetry of divinity and humanity intertwined through space and time like lovers. When I spoke, however, he did not need his initial labor. He would look to find his theme and his passion in something I said, and he would basically say, "Okay, okay, that's enough, Anthony, zip it. I'll take it from here."

Later he would say about me, "*Antonio non corre molto, ma tiene la zampa di leone*" (Anthony does not run far, but he has the paw of a lion), testimony both of his power with words and the esteem in which he held me. He also took me aside to explain to me his view on my situation. He understood that I wanted to leave the priesthood; that was taken for granted. But the fact was I couldn't. It was impossible. And placing himself in the first person of my life he would say from deep down in his belly, "*Non posso, non posso*" (I cannot, I cannot). What he meant was certain individuals were chosen by God for certain tasks, and it was more than humanly possible for them to back out. God had put his mark on them and their destiny was sealed. He pointed out other priests in the group and said, "It doesn't matter if that one leaves. Or, this other one. He can leave too. But you, you, it's impossible." He told me I should join the Little Brothers of Jesus, and as an inducement he promised he would personally ensure I got to go to Tamanrasset, to the heartland of their identity and spirit.

It was flattering that Carlo tried to persuade me this way, but I felt inside there was something wrong with it. I would have to abandon Linda, of course, but, even apart from that, would I not just be exchanging one religious order for another? How could I be sure I would not carry my old problems into this new one, or, put another way, meet the old familiar ones there? To travel eight hundred miles into the North African desert, would that not simply reinstate, and with a vengeance, all the alienation I had been struggling with? My struggle had already been inscribed on a certain southern landscape—Latin America, and the compelling sign and significance of concrete human relationships had been provided by it. Would this not set up one southern continent against another, creating another impossible divide in my soul? This last thought has come to me only lately, but I feel I sensed it deep down in the invitation. Carlo's offer really was a kind of spiritual antidote to everything before, but was it truly life giving and healthy? Would I not find myself at some point screaming out to an African desert that it had stolen from me the river of life I had plunged so fully into in South America?

And, yes, of course, there was Linda to consider. When I told Carlo about her, he swatted her away like a page of a book already read. "Yes, of course, there is the woman, but that will sort itself out in time. Maybe eventually there will be some kind of *sanatio in radice*. The important thing is you are a priest and stay as a priest." What he meant by all that exactly I was not sure, but the outcome of me remaining a priest was definite. What I heard here a little was the traditional attitude to clergy's dalliances with women; a blind eye could be turned but no legal status should be changed unless somehow one day officially by the church. But it was not just a matter of "a woman." With Linda I had made a huge life-turn, away from the sacrificial and otherworldly, toward the human, earthly, and ordinary. I could not and did not expect Carlo to understand that.

I missed Linda painfully. I was very much in love with her. We had spent all our time together and it had been sheer joy to be in each other's company. She had herself visited Spello with me in October of 1981, before we began a relationship, and I had memories of her there. Now when I was back for my extended stay, and not long from its start, this happened: I was at the main house, San Girolamo, and a whole crowd of youth were filing up the steps from the courtyard below, toward the refectory for the evening meal. I was stood at the top of the steps watching them and suddenly a giant locust flew out from one of the small juniper trees in the central cloister, over the heads of the youth, straight at me. I had to duck to avoid its direct, unerring flight. That night in my dreams Linda was in the crowd coming up the steps and now the great imago flew out from her eye, not a tree. This time there was no ducking. Her soul flew straight into my own eye and lodged deep in my own soul. I woke up stunned at the swiftness and totality of the union.

But Linda had also had been left hanging, and I knew she was suffering. As winter closed in and the community routine settled to the seemingly endless task of harvesting olives, I made a decision. I would bring things rapidly to close. On November 20, my birthday, I made the mile-and-a-half trek I did every Saturday, from Girolamo down to the bottom of town where there was a bar with a telephone. I phoned Linda as usual, pushing in a constant stream of the metallic *gettoni* until she picked up and accepted the collect call. But this time was different because I proposed that she be my wife. The conversation was joyful and hopeful, even if the situation was unnatural. The very next week, however, I received a letter from Matt, the provincial, reminding me that I had committed myself to a year's discernment—I think he had picked up something of my intentions from a letter I'd written to him, and was very much holding me to my word. At any rate I felt at once that what he said was true. Not that my decision was wrong in itself, but that I had to suspend it, as per my promise to let the Spirit have time to work. I think it was the very next Saturday I went back down to the bar and told Linda I had to retract my proposal. I was negotiating a very narrow and unnatural track, between the mountain on one side of institutional Catholicism, and the precipice on the other which was a possible loss of spiritual truth. Linda took it in her stride, showing incomparable trust while going along with such stomach-churning shifts. She accepted the suspended proposal and we continued.

So it was that my true experience at Spello began: a time of waiting without any horizon beyond waiting. It seemed again a putting off of life, but this time it had a consistency and depth, different from the mere emptiness before. Much of this came from Carlo and his teaching, but a lot was due also to the company of other men and women who were spending a similar "sabbatical year" at Spello. They came from diverse backgrounds and nations, with different journeys, geographical and spiritual, and had ended up in this place because they really had no clear spiritual idea of how to take their lives forward. There was a gay Milanese medical student interrupting his course of studies; a German hippie who had lived rough, surviving on snails in the woods; a young Italian woman recovering from a disastrous relationship; a small-town youth struggling with faith and alcoholism; a Croatian priest with a story of persecution by Yugoslav secret police; a young man from Bergamo thinking of becoming a Little Brother; and many others like them, probably a couple of dozen in all, some staying for periods of a few weeks, others for the whole year. They all had one thing in common: they were seeking to find their way, and the general ambience of attentive waiting and hoping seeped through and became a condition of spirit shared by the group as such, a mode of contemplative being belonging to the whole.

I was impressed by Lelio, an educated man in his forties, who had walked the length of Italy, a true pilgrim, praying every step. There was Elisabetta, a woman of gentle, vibrant spirit. Frustrated with the barrenness of Western religion, she had spent time in an ashram in India. There was Franco who became my friend. The son of a communist father, Franco had been a Capuchin friar, but he too was in the process of leaving his order, disillusioned at these followers of Francis with their institutional wealth and power. But, undoubtedly, the most important figure was Pierangelo, poet, musician, peasant farmer, previous postulant with the Little Brothers, now also separating himself from his order. Pierangelo's songs, his guitar and his voice, gave artistic counterpoint to Carlo's words. He added beauty and memorability to the words of the gospel and provided an essential dimension of the Spello experience. It was also he who organized the manual work for all the visitors, and for us *sabbatici*. He was a fountain of passion and energy, a genuine Renaissance man of the gospel. Finally, there was Giuseppe, a priest in the order of Little Brothers, an aloof, aristocratic person who traveled a lot and was only rarely in community. But he remained a presence, reinforced every time he returned, by his brilliant gifts in expounding the Scripture. Together with Carlo and Pierangelo he completed the "triumvirate" at the heart of the project. These three provided order and teaching to the motley gathering that came from all over Europe just to be there.

At Christmas Linda came to visit, an eagerly awaited break from the routine labor and the imposed separation between us. In my mind I still maintained the ritual of discernment, but my relationship with Linda seemed necessarily part of the process. Rather than a penitential seclusion in a remote monastery, my time at Spello was something somehow always shared with her, and no one had authority to embargo her visit. I went to Fiumicino to meet her, and we lodged there at a community that had close ties to Spello. From there we went to visit another contact with an apartment near to Lake Albano, the famous site of the pope's summer residence. We got the loan of a car and took a trip down to Anzio, a south-facing bay with a temperature still in the '60s, and the still-echoing location of the Allied landing in 1944. We spent the night in the car, with bread, tomatoes, and pepperoni for dinner and breakfast. Those days were spacious and unforgettable, a time out of time filled with rumors of war, yet much more with peace and happiness. Two more friends joined us from England, and we all visited Rome and then Spello together. But the moment was fleeting and before I knew it Linda and the others had left and the gelid clock of winter once more closed around my days. Nothing had yet been decided, and conflictive voices still railed at me: the order, my family, my history. It was always cold in the house, food was meager, and work became more and more exhausting.

I sustained myself with a promise that, come the spring, I would be able to do the really big *eremo*, the forty days of private retreat in one of the cottages. Carlo had said this would be permitted, and I was desperate he would not go back on it. I needed time to myself. I needed to recover physically and mentally. I needed to hear the voices, and to decide finally between them; and most of all I did not want to wait until summer for that to happen. The big groups arrived from June onward and my time would not be my own. As Lent drew near I kept up my bothering of Carlo: When would I be able to start the forty days? Finally, somewhat to my surprise, he gave the signal. I would be allowed to do my time alone, coinciding with Lent itself, beginning the evening of Ash Wednesday. I was given the beautiful hermitage of Santa Chiara, a stone cottage nestling on a hillside above an olive orchard and a murmuring stream. It had a bedroom, a kitchen, an undercroft as a chapel, and a vine and fig tree outside the window.

I kept a journal of my "quarantine," my forty days. I wrote down each little thing I did, together with visits and letters I received, letters I sent, and through it all my thoughts, feelings, dreams, moments of inspiration. My intention was to be like Samuel, to "let no word fall to the ground": in this way to examine my life as carefully as possible and reach a clear as possible decision. Rereading the record after almost forty years I am struck by things that had slipped somehow from memory. For example, a series of comments from members of my order, including that I was emotionally immature. One member said he would not personally bless a marriage between me and Linda on the grounds of my "lack of due discretion," a term for legal impediment to marriage because of emotional unfitness. How peculiar that I was judged emotionally unready for marriage, but no less than eleven years prior I had been given the green light for vows to celibate priesthood! Also, that the order "felt unloved and rejected" by me. Even now it comes as news that the religious community wanted my "love." I always felt on the outside of the zesty junior-common-room in-crowd that set the tone and shaped identity. But I suppose the real answer is in the first remark. The brothers should not feel unloved or rejected because, yes, they were right, I had never been emotionally competent to commit to *their* relationship. I was like a bride that never really said yes to a union because she was never in a position to say no. And thus, now, after a hard-traveled journey to personal maturity, they should not stand in my way.

In the last analysis, however, love in religious matters is not a high school popularity event. It is about a body of spiritual teaching and tradition that grips the heart and soul. My whole experience was of all of that being continually marginalized and demolished, beginning in novitiate.

What then was there to love? In contrast, here in Spello, Carlo had not asked for my love but had evoked it almost immediately. Why? Because he was a man of immense passion who was not afraid to let his life hang on a thread from God, and yet—and because of that—he ultimately imposed nothing on anyone. About a dozen years after my time in Spello there was an occasion to meet one of the Claretian community of those years, and at that point he took a little bit more responsibility. It was the lay brother named Dennis, someone who had always belonged to the inner circle of things. He faced me, saying quite unexpectedly and abruptly, "We ruined you!" I didn't feel particularly ruined, and it was a double-edged statement, but it was good to hear the first-person pronoun and its acknowledgment of some kind of agency. If, at this distance, I can answer my good brother Dennis, I might say, "Don't worry, even if you had agency, it was not your final doing. It was decided long ago that you would indeed 'ruin' me, and so free me for another life. In the same spirit I do not exactly know what this other life means and where it will end, but, take it from me, the parting of the ways between us was neither a disaster nor a dead end! History itself will decide. There is still a road on which we will one day meet in fellowship and peace."

Carlo was the true context in which I undertook the forty days. It was he who gave me permission to do it, in every sense, including when finally I made my choice. There is no need to recount the agonizing time I put myself through, the days of depression and doubt, the moments of relief and hope, the point where I thought that perhaps everything had to be surrendered in a kind of personal historical suicide, and the point where I rejected this as impossible because of the very values the gospel taught. Whatever the signs I sought and the things I saw as signs, whatever the tortuous path of discernment I pursued, in the last analysis it was my individual freedom at stake. And it was the closeness of earth, of the fields and hills, and the moonlit heaven above, that proved ultimately the most eloquent advocate on behalf of that freedom. Everything pivoted around the twentieth and twenty-first days. The nerve of a decision came together inside me and from then on truly there was no going back. I felt the pain of those I would have to confront, I felt moments of panic, but, weak at first, and then, progressively, day by day, my choice of life showed its bones. The endless solstice passed, and I felt with a kind of jolt the earth turn both under and within me.

I told Carlo that I would depart Spello directly after Easter. At first, he said I should stay until the middle of May when the rest of the Little

Brothers would arrive for the summer. But then, immediately, he added, "No, you are free, go in peace, God will provide." Carlo let me go, and in more senses than one. Whether he would admit it or not Carlo represented an entirely different kind of church from the formal Catholic organization all around him and which in some measure he depended on. The inspirational founder of his order, Charles de Foucauld, had completely evaporated the public institutional church in his constant search to be close to the hidden Jesus. Carlo had followed the same route, and his classic practice at Spello, displacing the sacramental priest with his powerful commentary "from the side," constantly performed a separate, disruptive "word from below."

On the wall at the hermitage where Carlo lived there was a small icon, an inscription that summarized the thought of Joachim da Fiore, the twelfth-century Calabrian mystic and abbot. It said there were three ages corresponding to the persons of the Trinity: that of the Old Testament belonging to the Father; that of the Son, which was the contemporary epoch of the church; and a coming age of the Spirit, a time of universal love in which the hierarchy would be displaced by a community of genuinely spiritual men and women, and the authentic meaning of God's word would be understood. With this simple piece of wall art, I sensed at once that Carlo and those around him belonged to a deeper fount of European Christian experience, running consistently through and from the Middle Ages, sometimes mainstream, more often named heretical, which sought recognizable social expression of the transformative meaning of the gospel. Joachim also promised a new unity between Christians and "infidels," and certainly the life of Foucauld fulfilled this vision. Many times later, I have thought that my time in Spello represented an embrace of this alternative version of church. Carlo baptized me into it, whether he or I knew it or not, and I have to be thankful for waiting all that time in Hayes and then agreeing to Matt's demand that I spend the year in Italy. In a completely unofficial way Spello birthed me into a form of "heretical" human and religious life.

These days as I am going about my business the thought of Carlo often comes to me unbidden. He is my beloved brother, my constant mentor in faith and spirit. The thing he created at Spello, and into which he welcomed me as a colleague, that thing continues within me as a profound well of strength and encouragement. I even learned sustained physical labor there, really for the first time. How much more then, the discipline of spiritual labor, of showing up when needed, to pray, to teach, to accompany? The paradoxical symmetry of it all—going in as I went out—arriving at authentic, this-worldly spirituality even as I left the priesthood—how can this be construed as anything but grace?

And so, one week after Easter I set out for Rome, having one more task to complete there in the Eternal City. In order to formalize my decision, I judged it better to go to the highest level of government of the religious order than to deal with superiors in England. I made my way to the Claretian general house in Parioli, one of Rome's best neighborhoods, framed by expensive restaurants and the green spaces of the Villa Borghese. With my heart in my throat, I sought an audience with a member of the council. Thank God he was an American. Amid the walls hung with portraits of founders and past superiors, he made the process amazingly painless. I was given the status of "exclaustration," meaning permission to live independently from a community but still obligated to celibacy. I quickly agreed to the deal, reasoning with one part of my brain that Linda and I could yet decide to be together as celibates, and, with another, that this was a transitory state anyway, one that could easily morph into full lay life. Better to get some legal arrangement—for the sake of family and of my Christian community, which was still almost totally Catholic—than to disappear at once into an ecclesial black hole, which would happen were I openly to flout the law. Later I did attempt to get a dispensation, meaning dispensation from the vow of celibacy. There is no possible reversal of the actual sacrament of ordination, but rights to exercise the office of priesthood are permanently suspended when a priest loses the clerical state. The vow of celibacy is really a separate issue, but it is welded together legally to the exercise of priesthood. Only the pope has the power of granting a dispensation from the vow, and at the same time he suspends (laicizes) the individual from the priesthood. You can't get one thing without the other. Absent this permission to marry, a priest and his wife live outside the Catholic communion and are barred from the sacraments. I started the process with a well-disposed priest named Michael Cooley in a parish near London Bridge, but in the end trying to stay inside the law proved fruitless.

Over time (while working later in the mission—next chapter) it became less and less tolerable not to go ahead and marry Linda, and yet at the same moment my attempts at moving forward the process of a canonical dispensation hit an invisible wall. At some point shortly before my wedding Father Cooley spoke to me on the phone, telling me, "Forget it; just get on with your life." I think he found the whole thing stricter and more legally demanding than he anticipated. The process, in fact, is of a unique kind, an official "interrogation" with only one possible favorable decision—that the petitioner was suffering from some deep-seated disabling condition unrecognized by his superiors. In other words, there must be proof that the ordination was a mistake from the very start. This, from one angle, seems to be my story, but the huge downside is that it cuts off entirely from any larger history and the possibility of a spiritual vocation that in any way exceeds the ideology and control of the Roman church. In the end I reckon it much more truthful not to have undergone the canonical process. If Carlo had said it was "impossible" for me to leave the priesthood, how should the Vatican be allowed to contradict him? To this date, apart from a somewhat melodramatic letter from Matt, I have not received any official form of suspension from the priesthood, or, of course, a dispensation from celibacy.

I spent a few more days in Italy visiting with Eloy and Paola, staying at their lovely little house on the coast. On my way back to Rome I traveled with a Turkish sea captain, a Muslim who impressed me deeply. He told me that every morning he stepped outside his front door and thanked God for the new day and for all the people living in the houses near him. I made my way back through France, visiting friends there, finally crossing the English Channel, and arriving at Dover in the early morning of May 8. On the boat train from Paris there was a deranged man wandering up and down the aisle, waving a knife around. I thought it would be horribly ironic if I got stabbed to death just as I was emerging from prison. But, no, I arrived safely, and there on the dock was Linda, a solitary beautiful figure in a wash of sunlight. The day was her twenty-first birthday, and the day effectively we began our life together.

Detaching itself from its exoskeleton is a vulnerable moment for the insect called a cicada; the new skin is not hardened, and the molting creature offers a juicy morsel to any sharp-eyed bird in the vicinity. For the little instars emerging, it takes only a couple of hours to complete the process, but I needed at least a couple more years before I was able to get married and begin a more or less ordinary life with Linda. Then some more years after that before you might say I was fully and completely "hardened." On the other hand, perhaps it's true that the experience of Spello meant that there I formed a skin that represented its own kind of species altogether. Perhaps the "hardening," therefore, is not really that, so much as the passing of the years in which I have gained the confidence and trust to be exactly the kind of different creature God intended.

Maybe this creature has its own kind of identity, affirmed in the noninstitutional, mystical kind of environment around Caretto, the kind, in fact, who becomes a priest by unbecoming one.

eighteen

REENTRY FOR THE FIRST TIME

Returning to London at the age of thirty-seven I began ordinary life as a kind of game, doing all the things that I knew other people did and had known only in my imagination. I "signed on" with the Department of Employment and began receiving unemployment support and housing benefit. I lived in a tiny, wedge-shaped room over a Wimpy's eatery, sleeping in the narrow end, the walls next to me covered in the restaurant chain's trademark grease. I spoke with an employment counselor who told me I was not unqualified, just "misqualified." I asked God what I should do. While I was in the order, I had constantly complained that our lives were not close enough to the poor, but the question was, who were the poor in a welfare-supported society. Traveling on a bus I looked out at one of the parks of London and saw, as if for the first time, a congregation of homeless people slumped around on the grass. I decided this was where my task was and I started volunteering, first at a feeding center, then at a halfway house. Soon I was given a job, and after a year I found myself in charge of a whole project in East London. It's not hard to rise swiftly in agencies working among the homeless; the burnout rate is high and the opportunities for mismanagement and bad practice legion. At a certain moment I was the only person available who could be asked to take on the role.

It was at Tower Hamlets Mission, a throwback Dickensian mission-hall started by a brewing heir. He received a revelation witnessing a pathetic mother and children pleading with a drunken father not to spend their last coins on beer brewed by his own father's company. He then dedicated his life to the relief of the poor who so evidently drowned their sorrows in the family mash. The board of the organization were strongly evangelical and wary about taking on an ex-Catholic priest—they quizzed me as to whether or not I believed in justification by faith—but, really, they were in no position to be picky. I was initially hired as a superintendent-preacher, whose job was to conduct two services a week, seeking the salvation of some of the most abject human beings in London. But within a couple of months, I had to take over the actual running of the day center. We discovered the previous director kept order with two dogs and a baseball bat, plus was skimming the donated food, selling it in the local street markets.

The whole place was in a sad decline from its glory days when it really had supported the poor from the East End's mean streets. There were three wonderful sisters who came to my services and were the only remnant of those founding years. They would sit demurely among the hundreds of semi-psychotic men waiting for the food distribution to begin while I talked haplessly about Jesus. These sisters remembered coming to the mission as children to get handout lumps of coal to keep a modicum of heat in their homes during the winter. This was the class of people that used to attend the "Great Assembly Hall," as the original mission was, but the Germans bombed it to bits along with a good measure of those local streets during the Blitz. After the war, compensation and reconstruction ensured the mission was rebuilt but also that many of those who had lost their houses were moved to spanking-new towns further north. Thus, most of the original community was lost and those who took their place were the rootless and soulless, the military vets, ex-prisoners, orphans, and nobody's children who gravitated to the dead zones of the capital city. It was somehow weirdly appropriate when we emptied out the flat of the dismissed day center manager we found two copies of *Mein Kampf*, one in German Gothic script.

The assembly hall was rebuilt as a ridiculously modern church with sloping floor, cinema seats, and heated baptismal pool, but any ministry there was stillborn. Rather, I was thrust headfirst into managing the day center, the big building behind the church where food was served. The cavernous hall provided daily shelter to a huddled mass of humanity, open sixty-five hours a week, dishing out hundreds of meals, supplying clothing, trying to find accommodation for some, and always stretched to keep order between deeply disturbed individuals. The normal mode of operation was to employ clients as helpers, getting them to prepare and serve meals, and repaying them in kind, with various perks. These helpers were the best of the bunch, basically decent people, but unhesitating in responding to violence with violence. If a fight erupted, they would wade in eagerly, using whatever weapon that lay to hand, beating on anyone involved and throwing them out on the street. Except, of course, if someone truly criminal or dangerous was involved, then they would barricade themselves in the kitchen. My first policy decision was to insist that violence not be used, after which they told me I was on my own if there was trouble. Sure enough, the next time there was a fight they disappeared into the kitchen and locked the doors. A truly crazy guy was throwing billiard balls around and a thickset, threatening man objected when one hit him. It took me over an hour to get hold of the billiard balls, while separating the combatants, and then talk both of them out of the building. I was entirely on my own and at the end totally exhausted.

I was actually hired by the mission through a separate Christian agency, the Kenward Trust, and with the support of the trust's director, Godfrey Featherstone, we began to build up a bigger staff of employees and volunteers, including Godfrey's daughter, Natalie. Linda also came to work at the mission; by this time, she had finished her theology degree. Godfrey knew about our situation and he and his wife, Carol, as good Evangelicals, supported us heartily: they were positively willing us to be married. Godfrey also believed our status as a couple was good for the stability of the project. He designed an apartment for us on-site and we moved in together. With the additional staff, the day center started a door policy, banning alcohol, and trying to keep known offenders out, preventing trouble before it happened. But it all took its toll. Our work included going to Oxford Street in the West End once a week to pick up a load of past-sell-by-date food from Marks & Spencer. We also did a soup run, carrying a huge tureen of hot broth to a spot under Waterloo Bridge. Trains rumbled darkly overhead as we doled the soup from the back of our VW van, the same trains I used to hear passing twenty years before on their way up from Portsmouth.

I became quite ill. Indeed, many of the staff and volunteers seemed to fall ill in that period. Recovering in bed, I decided we could not go on that way. Regardless of established practice and my own lack of experience, I felt there had to be a better approach. There had to be something other than the rote function of charity, without real challenge or opportunity to change. I began to research other agencies and soon discovered the famous twelve-step program from Alcoholics Anonymous. I went on to implement it as the basis for a residential program on-site. From there the mission changed progressively from revolving-door practices to specialized intervention for a pathway out of despair. True, the volume of individuals we supported dropped dramatically, and for a while I was public enemy number one on the Whitechapel Road. I was seen to be denying so many things they considered their right. In AA terms, however, alcoholism and substance abuse are a "family disease" and you have a choice either to become sick by colluding with it, or to find yourself in harsh tension with the addicted persons. There was a man who came to the center called "one-legged Michael." I don't know how he lost his leg, but he was continually filthy, unkempt, emaciated, barely capable of intelligible speech. On one occasion when we ran a bus outing to Brighton, an attempt to get some of the clients away from the city to enjoy some sea air, Michael showed up. I think he just happened to be passing and decided he wanted to come, but he was thoroughly soiled and stank like a dunghill. The other guys bluntly refused to have him on the bus, so I took him into the lobby of our apartment, stripped him naked to his shit-covered stump, and propping him with one arm washed him down from a basin, with several refills and fresh clothes from our store. Michael's drink of choice was methylated spirits, wood alcohol, which is cheaper than standard alcohol but extremely toxic, causing loss of nerve function, including blindness, and frequently death. Meth users could survive, for a while at least, by "boxing," mixing a little meth with water or soda. Michael was one of these, able to stay permanently drunk but somehow alive. One time he brought his poison with him into the center, and someone helpfully passed along the information. I went to his table and attempted to take his cup from him, reminding him of the rules. It was hard to imagine much resistance from this man who could barely stand, but the snarl of murderous fury he turned on me from his toothless mouth was truly frightening. It was a beast from the abyss, and in it was packed all the titanic violence this man had been subject to somehow, somewhere. It was not possible to fight this beast; but neither was it possible to compromise.

Ultimately, the fruits of the policy showed. We undertook a program of rebuilding that ended by replacing the existing barnlike buildings with attractive smaller spaces, involving good-quality accommodation, in either rehabilitative and supported group settings or independent apartments. Fundraising took off (trusts and charities like to see results), and top names were attracted as patrons, including Anthony Hopkins (someone with a great recovery story of his own) and the archbishop of Canterbury. A steady stream of individuals entered our programs for various degrees of successful change, and always with a decisive stress on the unconditional value of each person. Not a few turned their lives around completely, and went on to become staff members responsible for mission programs, or work elsewhere in similar projects.

Not all of this happened on my watch. Little by little a team of committed people had come to work at the mission, and they were there to take over and continue when I left. One of these was Andy Bannell, a Jesuit seminarian whom Linda introduced to us. Andy went on to quit the Jesuits and then become crucial to the whole mission project, taking over as leader and director when eventually I was running on fumes alone. By 1988 I had reached a point of burnout. My nerves were laser thin. I could no longer completely trust myself in the many situations where, without warning, you could find yourself in confrontation with a difficult, dangerous man.

One of the things that increased my vulnerability was the arrival of my first child. By the end of 1985 it had seemed futile to wait for a dispensation from Rome and we decided to get married. I took a trip to Galway, Ireland, to inform my mother and over the space of three days we argued back and forth about God, sex, heaven, hell, vows, family, priesthood, and death. In the end it was a stalemate and she quit talking. When I said goodbye, she was watching the movie *Masada* on TV, about the final suicidal Jewish resistance during the Jewish-Roman war, with her favorite star, Peter O'Toole, as the Roman general. She didn't respond and essentially never spoke to me again. I went to see her one more time, eight years later, just before coming to the US. By that time, she was suffering dementia and rambled on with bits of stories I had often heard before. Then, all at once, she told a new one. It was about her oldest brother, Bartley, when he first emigrated to the US. He was working in an iron foundry in Boston, and had grabbed and threatened to kill a coworker who had upset him. Apparently, Bartley was going to throw him in the furnace, until he was restrained by fellow workers. Afterward, one of these asked him, "You weren't really going to throw him in, were you?" To which he replied, in my mother's relished retelling, "Oh, yes, I was." I could take it no more, and got up to leave. Only then did she suddenly seem to stir herself away from her mind's dark labyrinth. She abruptly declared, "Don't worry, Anthony, Jesus has plenty of experience of dealing with heroes like you." These were her only direct words to me, and the last.

Our wedding ceremony took place in May 1986 at the mission church; a Methodist woman minister from a neighboring project conducted the service and we celebrated the reception in the day center. Scores of the homeless were there, as well as friends of mine from Buckden, mission staff, and Linda's friends and family. It was the homeless who made the occasion, the most relaxed of all the wedding guests. Before the ceremony my brother, Terence, turned up to protest. He was hunched over in pain from a slipped disk, and looked terrible, like a bird of evil omen, a figure of supernatural doom. When the minister saw him through the window, color visibly drained from her face. Some of the mission helpers, the ones well versed in throwing people out, surrounded him and told him he had to leave. He explained that his only intention was to raise his voice at the part where people were asked if there was any legitimate objection to this union. Having stated his purpose, he was glad to go and allowed himself to be ushered out. I forgot about him during the course of the ceremony, but when Linda and I finally exited in the church courtyard to the triumphant strains of the wedding march he was there just outside the railings. He certainly put a damper on things. I went up to him, and he asked, "Is it over?," as if it were a kind of execution. I said, "Yes." He nodded grimly, and stumped off, like some dinosaur unfit to walk in a modern world. I felt sorry for him, for a man who did not really believe in the rules of the church but was doing this because of the rules of the family. It was not my vows that made my marriage illegitimate, but our childhood family system—a structure he still very much needed and believed in for his own private reasons. Later in life he apologized for his performance, but without analyzing it, as I knew he was capable of. Basically, his was the sole representation of my family at my wedding, and nothing that happened since has essentially changed that. And it achieved its purpose: to put a huge family question mark of illegitimacy (in concert with the church's) over the entire symbolic occasion.

I must exclude my father in these remarks, as by this point, he had been dead for four years. I did not tell the story of his passing in its place— during my time as a priest at Hayes—because it was so much a matter of internal family dynamics. But these are certainly relevant here. In 1982, on August 6, my father had a heart attack at Victoria Coach Station and the ambulance had to fight its way through rush hour crowds to get to him. He was returning to Ireland from Portsmouth where he had just lost a court case seeking to claim rent arrears on a property there. When my parents bought a new house on a better street in the mid-'60s, they kept our old house where I had been brought up, operating it for rent. Very quickly—maybe even from the beginning—it was let at low cost to a young woman and child escaping an abusive husband. Of course, the husband eventually showed up again and the wife took him in. From then on, my father had to deal with this man's bullying tactics. I believe my parents had agreed on the arrangement partly because it was offering a woman righteous protection from the classic evil husband—a way, perhaps, for my father to relive his own story but this time on the side of the good guys. But he was doomed to lose again. My mother began to urge him to manage the rent to a reasonable sum, and increasingly so when both my parents retired to Ireland in the mid-'70s. They sold their own home but unwisely kept hold of the renter. Inevitably its physical maintenance was neglected and eventually the abusive husband and his good wife felt entitled to withhold rent altogether. As I said, my father lost the ensuing court case held in Portsmouth, more or less having to surrender the house to the couple. After spending the night with me in Hayes he died in the ambulance on the way from Victoria to the hospital. He was sixty-eight years old.

He was buried in Ireland, and it took another nine days to get his body back there for the interment. The ironies pile up. My father, vilified for being English, ended up being buried in Galway. The locals in the village of Moycullen, who had gotten to know him, turned out in their several hundreds for the funeral, easily eclipsing any crowd he would have had in England. The grave that was dug for him is in the prettiest spot imaginable, under an oak tree, overlooking Loch Corrib, a final resting place far exceeding in beauty the pile of house bricks he lost in Portsmouth. One of my cousins who helped dig the grave rejoiced in the fact that the Englishman was apparently buried right on top of a well-known IRA militant, the latter's purgatory clearly marked out for him. My father was buried surrounded by my mother's family, whereas when she died, after eventually moving back to England, she was buried in an anonymous northern England cemetery.

The reason for mentioning these stark ironies is that if we are heirs of the sins of the fathers, we also inherit their reversals and redemptions. My father perhaps gave me more in his death than he imparted in life. When he died, he was no longer around to be blamed, and a great weight of family anger simply lifted. The harsh circumstances of his death plus the honor accorded him in his funeral all told their own tale. There was a kind of parable there, laying bare who really was the victim and where the fund of violence was maintained. August 6 is the anniversary of Hiroshima (1945), and just before I drove my father to the railway station to take his train to Victoria, he told a story he had never uttered before. I was preparing a commemoration prayer service for the victims, and as he sat there in my office with me, he began to talk—as if his throat and tongue were unsealed by a moment of grace that he knew now was upon him. He recalled how when they dropped the atomic bomb, he was a conscripted British soldier in India and together with his friends he "danced" because the war would be over. Afterward, they went every day down to the docks to check the bulletin board for troops slated for transports home, and his battalion was among the first. But now he was sorry, because he understood what that bomb truly meant. These were among the last words he said to me, and it's as if he opened a way. I was conceived and born the year after my father's return from India (1946), and it was if he were passing on to me a story of my origins. He was letting go of the violence of his life and world, back then, and now, and the whole thing considerably strengthened me and redoubled my inner resolve to break free. So, in 1986 when my brother sought so egregiously to reassert the family system, that ship had already sailed; the mystifying forces of my family were already exposed and essentially disabled. But that does not mean the awful scene he created did not linger in me, especially in its inner sense of tribal curse launched against the truth of my marriage.

After the wedding, and a shoestring honeymoon in Scotland among the lochs, we were back in harness running the day center. Linda started a women's program, essential service to a small, vulnerable group of women, fallen far beyond usual supports, drifting like wraiths among the much more clamorous body of destitute men. Linda's work became well respected, and formed the first steps of a career in care, as she initially went on to become an RN in England, and then, after we settled in the US, qualified as a nurse practitioner and served at-risk populations suffering from HIV. Her time at the mission proved invaluable grounding in accompanying and serving severely marginalized persons. Linda also helped prepare the weekly community meals and led the singing afterwards when we prayed and studied the Bible, giving spiritual support to the group of staff and helpers.

In the following year, our son, Christopher, was born, and living as a young family on-site did not feel quite so tolerable. One time I had to fire someone for drinking in the mission. He came to our front door, demanding his job back, and crashing into the door until the hinges popped in their sockets. He swore and said he hoped my son died. It was hard to bear. We took a vacation in Italy and while we were there decided to hand in our notice. Italy was always able to put things in perspective. When we returned we announced the decision to quit. Even then it was difficult to leave; we actually gave twelve months' notice so people would get used to the idea, and for the sake of a smooth transition. Really, it was far too long, and in the end made everyone uncomfortable. Eventually in August of 1989 we made our farewells. Linda was nearly at term with our second child, and we went to live briefly at her parents' house until Susannah was born.

A home of our own was a major issue. After having earned a minimum wage over the past five years we had nothing sufficient for a mortgage. We inquired with scores of housing associations and with public housing but there was absolutely nothing available. We decided that we would move to Italy where my friend Franco (from Spello) said he had use of a farmhouse where we could live, while I looked for work teaching English. But then something completely unexpected, in fact plainly miraculous, occurred. During the early summer of '89 Linda had been attending evening classes in Italian in preparation for the move. Her brother, Keith, found out and said he also wanted to learn Italian and began attending with her. One evening returning from the class he inquired why she was learning the language and she told the story. At once he offered, "Don't worry, I'll buy you a house!"

Keith was a computer nerd back when the term had not been invented, and Linda and I were oblivious to the fact that he had recently been extremely successful in a small software and systems startup. So much so, he could buy his sister a house outright for cash! It was like manna out of heaven, and yet it still seemed to fit into our day-to-day world where we trusted the Lord would and could supply all our needs. Only in hindsight is it clear how massive this was. People spend their whole working lives paying for a mortgage and we have never had to worry about anything like that. Because of this, we were able to buy a house in England and then in a few years sell it and quickly buy a home in the US when we moved there. We were able to make the giant step of emigrating, with two small children already in tow, and place a solid foot down in the new continent without ever a backward glance. All the things that developed afterward in the US—a PhD, books published, children brought up (including our third, Liam, born in the US), and funded throughout the Gradgrind American college system—none of this would have been possible without Keith's cloudburst of generosity.

I don't know what this will count for to the reader, but it seems like the hand of an elegant and faithful providence to me. I have to remind myself of its amazing symmetry and kindness when I am tempted to feel bad about my various cultural and spiritual exiles. That gift from Keith is a pledge of God's faithfulness.

We moved to Norfolk and bought a house in a quiet little market town called Aylsham about a dozen miles north of Norwich. Once, in the Middle Ages, Norfolk was the sheep-raising hub of English wealth and culture, but now it was a whimsical out-of-time kind of place. It was ideal for repairing the frazzled nerve ends of the last twenty years. At last, I could truly say I was emerging from my ecclesiastical and societal cocoon. I had brief employment as a social worker and a nursing aide, and then Linda began nursing training while I stayed at home to care for the children. I changed diapers, cooked, cleaned, took the kids to playschool and elementary school, got to know the mothers of other children, and piece by piece began to construct a selfhood outside of institutional Christianity. I began to write short articles for the *Guardian* newspaper, the first of which was accepted at the end of 1989, celebrating the year of miracles when the Berlin Wall came down. I managed to mark out some quiet times when I began to read and study again. It's not necessary to recount many details, because those years were essentially a fallow season restoring a depleted emotional and spiritual soil. But once the soil is ready, new seeds can grow, and indeed this happened. In 1993 I applied for and was accepted to the doctoral program at Syracuse University, New York. Doors seemed to fly open, beginning with contact with the author, René Girard, whose work had impressed me deeply. I had written to him, asking his suggestions as to where I could further study his thought. His reply led to a professor in Syracuse, James Williams, who then worked hard to guide my admission to the college as a doctoral student. From then on life was radically changed in a practical sense. I summoned my energies one more time to take a new step, and once more Linda endured nine months of separation. After that, the whole family transferred to the USA, in the summer of '94, selling our house in England and buying one in Syracuse in the space of a month. This was yet another leap because we had no guarantee of staying in America.

But America is now my home; America with its vast open landscape where no one symbol of transcendence can claim ownership, if not perhaps the dollar. I can breathe here. Although I don't believe in the dollar, such is its callous confidence it does not care. The landscape still accepts me. I studied at what is known as a postmodern Department of Religion, in the university setting. I read Girard, and I also read Nietzsche, Heidegger, and contemporary French deconstructive philosophy. I delved back into Augustine, into the Middle Ages, into human prehistory, and then nineteenth-century anthropologists, Freud, feminism, the Holocaust, Dostoevsky, and Kierkegaard, along with many contemporary North American authors. The education was eclectic and systematically non-systematic. It suited me fine. My mind learned to range over the whole table of human expression and thought, to drop off the edge and come back again. Jim Williams gave me constant encouragement and friendship, and the department gave me the possibility of thinking well and professionally. I received my doctorate in 1999, and a revised version of my dissertation was published as a book in 2001. I started to teach as an instructor, and since graduating have been employed as an adjunct and assistant professor, first of religion, and then of theology in an Episcopalian seminary. Nowadays I am officially retired, but over twenty years ago Linda and I started a local prayer and study community, and have continued to teach there every week. Since COVID, as for many groups, this has expanded online, reaching people across geography, denominations, and age groups. My life has changed almost completely, and yet it hasn't. I still carry this story with me and am glad for the opportunity to let it unfold in the light of day.

CONCLUDING ANARCHISTIC POSTSCRIPT

ONE TIME TOWARD THE end of my time with the Claretians, Phil—my companion since novitiate days—said to me, in a matter-of-fact kind of way, "You are an anarchist." He had known me for nigh on twenty years so probably he more than anyone was in a position to say something like that. And from a certain perspective he was surely right. When I went on peace demonstrations and the political anarchists would join the march at Hyde Park, I was always pleased to see their black flags fluttering so bold and free. They seemed so much more real and radical than any other flag or design.

But what Phil meant was not political; it had to do with my ministry as a priest. He could see that I did not want to pursue any kind of activity that owed continuity to structures that came before. Everything for me had to be new, coming from the ground up. His remark was prescient, because it obviously implied an incompatibility with the Roman Catholic Church, which is the definition of continuity.

The literal meaning of anarchism is an-*archon*, the absence of central government, and, by extension, the absence of *arche*, of established metaphysical principle or sacred authority. Politically it intends a completely different order of things, a beginning over arising out of the dark space of human suffering, through cooperation and community. Phil was using the term in an extended but insightful way regarding my approach to the priesthood.

Phil could not know about the details of my upbringing—I paid hardly any attention to them myself. But really, I had grown up entirely without any social or institutional *archon*. There was no social authority in my life, except for a rarified, out-of-time, Irish-famine-inspired, heavenly-escape-from-earth concept of church. Along the trajectory from novitiate in 1964 to Rome in 1973, I found progressively and painfully that this otherworldly church did not exist. During the years of '60s disorder (a more conventional sense of anarchy) I was promising myself again and again I would find my heavenly church, but I was just putting off a genuine encounter with reality. When I finally discovered the actual church, I had no remaining desire to be part of it and turned instead to create my own spontaneous versions of community. Out of the ministerial options available to me, I selected models that allowed me to begin almost everything afresh, from the ground up. This also responded automatically to my childhood absence of world. Once my unreal *archon*, the church, was gone, a visceral human need to mold my own personal human space took its place. No wonder someone like Dan was so badly scandalized. Almost by definition he loved the institutional church just the way it was.

So, let's for a moment think about Jesus.

Before I was fully irradiated by my family story, and surely before I was overtaken by the heavenly ideology of the Catholic Church, I had those amazing encounters with Jesus. Jesus entered my life in a fully "anarchic" way—immediately, from the ground up, out of the dreamscape of human passion and suffering. Those visions and dreams stand with a freshness and vivacity that bely any sense of mediation let alone any dues to be paid to a hierarchic church. You could say I was "turned" by the anarchism of Jesus from the beginning! It was this that called me, and to this I have been true.

Is not Jesus, in fact, the original and only true anarchist?

Another story, therefore. Again, in the latter years of my time in the Claretians, there was a provincial retreat. That means almost everyone was there. The man who led the retreat was a Mexican of a gentle yet effusive disposition. He certainly had a healthy feminine side. At one point he told the story of how watching the movie *Jesus Christ Superstar*, he had been very moved at the portrayal of the scourging. He said he had felt pity and tenderness toward Jesus there in the cinema. He invited the priests and brothers present there to share their own moments of personal feeling for Jesus. I thought to myself, "Wow, this is it! At last, I will find out about these men's primary relationships with Jesus on which our whole mutual enterprise must depend."

There was a strained silence. At last, one of the more senior men broke the ice-jam. He said, "You have to forgive us. That's just not how we were trained. We just don't think in those ways."

In a flash I realized something I had been almost willfully ignorant of before. These men had joined a huge organization, each for their personal reasons. Now, since joining, they were all in a place they more or less liked, but it had very little to do with the dramatic figure of Jesus that was at the source of the whole thing. For me, it was entirely the other way around. No matter my locked-in existential need for the organization, my original inspiration was about a Jesus I knew and whom I had spent my ministry talking about. If anything could or should convince me that I was in the wrong place, this was it. All during my time in seminary, and even after when I was working as a priest, I cherished the assumption that ultimately the organization I was in mediated the Jesus I knew from childhood and in the Spirit. All you had to do was dig away the surface and finally you would get down to this man. My colleague who spoke up at the retreat disabused me in one sentence.

For sure, there were individuals who connected vitally with Jesus. There was the retreat leader for one. And my time at Spello would teach me the stellar example of Charles de Foucauld. But these were outliers, and my long, fraught journey had revealed in me a chronic lack of human grounding that would give me an actual human space in which and from which to relate to Jesus. The classic story of the saint—including that of Francis, Ignatius, and indeed de Foucauld—tells of someone who had a very worldly experience before turning their whole life around for the sake of Jesus.

But everything was upside down and back to front for me. I am set apart, sealed for the church from the get-go. My early experiences of Jesus could have only one possible outcome—the priesthood. As my violent family system came online, more or less in parallel, there was absolutely no turning back. Priesthood equaled the escape valve for my mother's psychosis. Period. So, the anarchy of Jesus was swallowed up in ecclesial fate, only very slowly to separate itself once more as my church identity crumbled. But it did separate itself, and I am forced to conclude that, for me at least, the anarchic Jesus precedes the church and stands as judgment over it.

And coming to the end of the story here it cannot escape attention that the one consistent thread is Jesus. Without him my narrative would have no center, no heart, no authentic, self-affirming life. Without him I would have broken down, broken out, in so many different ways, at so many times. The times that I did break down or out he has been there consistently to see me through. I have no explanation for this enormous presence in my life, outdistancing and outclassing any other motif. My wife, Linda, says ultimately this is his story and, although I have not told it plainly as such, in the end this is what becomes apparent. In which case, all the circumstantial details, family, school, country, church, are all exactly that. This story is an homage to Jesus and an acknowledgment that he is Lord, not in any distant theological sense, but exactly in the sense here, of someone who justly claims authorship of my life.

I know, I know. People will say, your Jesus is mediated too, and they will find some language to show why that is so (ego heroics, immune response to my mother's sacrificial projection). I would not argue. I would likely find truth in everything they say. But there can be no doubt that studying the Gospels shows a bold, uncompromising, semiotically incomparable, and utterly radical figure. The Gospels tend to demonstrate a Jesus that is closer to mine than that of the church, and you have to look there for at least some of the inspiration of what I experienced. Jesus has entered the collective imagination of our culture, and although we don't like to acknowledge it too much—like a family secret we don't talk about—there can be little doubt that Jesus has profoundly infected our Western world. I would take so many of my experiences as firsthand symptoms of that infection.

As I have continued also to meditate on and think through those symptoms it has become more and more inescapable to see them belonging to a definitive revelation of the victim-making character of human violence and its revolutionary alternative in forgiveness and nonviolence. These days my work as a theologian is entirely caught up in demonstrating the truth of this.

I do understand the Catholic Church's position. It has weathered numerous historical storms and oppositions, and it is implicitly founded on what it sees as its greatest victory, the "conversion" of imperial Rome in the fourth century. But it is now late in the day, and I tend to think that the reach of Jesus has overtaken the reach of the church, considerably. If the church wants to "win" the twenty-first century it has to pay much closer attention to the anarchist Jesus.

The earth with its human rulers is poised on the edge of extinction. What kind of gospel will it be if there is no one left to preach to? To say they "all went to heaven" is as biblically meaningless as it is cynical. For sure, this is a conversation that goes beyond the scope of the memoir. The memoir is about "me," and at this point I officially stand outside the church. But coming to the end of the story here I am obliged to claim a different root dynamic to that famous conversion of imperial Rome. Making sense of my unbecoming priesthood can be only by means of a wider and deeper concept of the work of Jesus, one that offers a genuine peace, not a collusion. I did not want the lord mayor at my ordination, not because I was making any judgment on his personal virtue. I was simply claiming, even then, that to be a priest is something other than that old imperial function that has brought us all to the point of crisis.

And so, to my final, final story.

It is the Holy Saturday night, the night of the resurrection, very near the end of my time in Spello, 1984. I had been the officiating priest at the late-hour Easter Vigil at the main community house, Girolamo. It was the last official mass I would ever celebrate. I remember Carlo's glance at me during it, kind, peaceful, loving, devout. After it finished, a few of us attended another liturgy. It was with a group who followed their own intensive pathway of faith and practice of the sacraments. We had been going to some of their classes and now they were doing their own version of the Easter liturgy after everyone else had concluded. We walked into town and found the place where they were meeting. They started the ceremony, and I was fighting to stay awake. At a certain moment all the symmetry and depth of the words and actions dissolved into empty meaningless rote. The poignancy of the first liturgy became a mere pointless chatter in the second. It was four in the morning and my soul was dead and ashes to the taste, denuded outside and in of all its priestly role and meaning. We walked outside onto the deserted piazza, and though it was still dark the fronts of the grocery shop and the fine art shop glowed with their unmistakable Mediterranean warmth in the soft light of the streetlamps. Something about the scene said the dawn was close. Then over on the left there was movement. A solitary man came into view, working his way up from the narrow street leading onto the square, sweeping in a rhythmic movement as he went. A solitary man who did this same job just before dawn, every day the same, whether it was Good Friday, Easter Sunday, or the Fourth of July. It was all the same to him, he swept the street.

Or did he? I don't know. For something in me said, I know that man. It's Jesus, appearing with the first glimmer of the dawn. And, yes, I know I was thinking symbolically, but it was real and vivid, fresh and clear.

And my soul rejoiced. It said there, there is Jesus, and always will be. The dirt of the street, the taut bristles of his broom, the muscles on his back, the worn workman pants on his legs, all of this and this alone is the matter of redemption. That man was the same man I saw in my house as a little boy in Gloucester. Back then he was in the robes of a king, or a priest, but that was a disguise made up by my childish mind. Now he was here in his real regalia, and he was leading me onward, like he had never stopped. And never will.

Printed in Great Britain
by Amazon